BYRON'S TRAVELS

BYRON'S TRAVELS

Allan Massie

Sidgwick & Jackson
London

For Mary and Gordon

First published in Great Britain in 1988 by
Sidgwick and Jackson Limited

Copyright © 1988 by Allan Massie

Designed by Michael Head
Picture Research by Deborah Pownall
ISBN 0-283-99408-8

Photoset by Rowland Phototypesetting Limited
Bury St Edmunds, Suffolk
Printed in Great Britain by
Butler and Tanner Limited
Frome, Somerset
for Sidgwick and Jackson Limited
1 Tavistock Chambers, Bloomsbury Way
London WC1A 2SG

CONTENTS

INTRODUCTION BY ELIZABETH LONGFORD

Byron has been written about by poets, travellers, academics, novelists, professional biographers, devoted amateurs, *et al*. Indeed the books on this extraordinary man come tumbling out with such zest and regularity that a phrase has grown up, 'the Byron business'. The phrase may be critical in intent, suggesting a rich literary seam that continues to be assiduously worked because it is unfailingly successful. Yet the opposite is true.

Byron's life and poetry are subjects so fertile, so productive of thought and ideas, that every writer at one time or another has been genuinely tempted to present to the reading world 'his' or 'her' Byron. I succumbed myself. How delighted I am that Allan Massie has yielded most gracefully and imaginatively to the temptation, bringing his fine skill with words to bear on this perenially enthralling story.

He rightly entitles his striking study *Byron's Travels*. The poet, however, spent nearly one third of his short life travelling outside England. His poetry was influenced far more by Greece and Rome than by London and Cambridge. (Allan Massie, a Scot himself, thinks Byron more Scottish than English, and quotes effectively from Burns and Boswell.) In a way, therefore, this book is nothing less than a new biography of a complex and compelling character. And it is a biography that will provide an engaging portrait for those who do not already know Byron. As for the generation older than Allan Massie who *think* they know their Byron, this book will stir and stimulate in just the way that is good for all of us.

Of course the story of Byron's life abroad, rather than in Britain, will have its own range of ogresses, villains and heroines. The unforgiving Lady Byron is left by Allan Massie to rest in peace, while an intriguing analysis is made of the sinister Count Guiccioli. At the same time Teresa Guiccioli, the Count's young wife and Byron's mistress, takes the centre of the stage in place of Byron's half-sister Augusta, whom incidentally Massie has no doubt was Byron's lover.

I particularly like the way Allan Massie's book is divided into three parts – *not* like Caesar's Gaul, for all the parts are emotionally and atmospherically different, developing from each other. First, 'The

Adventurer', in which Lord Byron sets off through Portugal, Spain and Malta for Greece and Turkey, 'frolicsome as a kitten'. Here we have the wilful charmer with the soft clustering curls and sweet rhetorical voice. Despite his baron's title, this young pedigree animal lacks 'assured social position'. One life-long trait is emerging: hatred of cruelty; among Turks now, among terrorists – even Italian and Greek terrorists – later. Byron's homosexuality is seen as part of adolescence, his 'sentimental' last attachment (unrequited) to the Greek boy Loukas being dealt with in a powerful passage towards the end of the book.

Second, 'The Exile.' After journeying with Byron over the battle-field of Waterloo, up the Rhine and into Switzerland, I feel that Allan Massie is as happy as Byron was to be in Venice and Rome. Massie knows Italy well and describes it vividly. He sees Byron's mature poetry as no longer dressing up his own personality in rhetoric. Byron now approached the events of his revolutionary era both rationally and as emotive forces. 'He thought as a Classicist,' writes Massie; 'he felt as a Romantic. It was this division which supplied his poetry with so much of its nervous energy.' I find this specially true of his great *Don Juan*.

When we come to the third part, 'The Hero', Massie is lucid and revealing over Byron's central dilemma: the conflict of his duty to Teresa and to Greece. The subsequent problems of Byron and all outsiders who support nationalist causes are perceptively dealt with. As an example of Massie's sensitive appreciation, I will end by quoting his moving view of Byron's heroism. Massie says that when he was young he felt disappointed by Byron's frustrated and apparently unheroic role in Greece. 'Now it is precisely his willingness to accept the limitation of what was possible, and his acceptance of necessity that proves him a hero.'

That is the kind of tribute that Byron, the realist, would have liked and which makes this book so rewarding to read.

DECEMBER 1987

PART I

THE ADVENTURER

I

Johnson observed that the grand object of all travel was to see the shores of the Mediterranean. (He never saw them himself, and travelled little.) Despoiled and vulgarized as great stretches of its coasts now are, there remains substantial truth in what he said. No one can fully understand the riches of antiquity or of Christian Europe who has not exposed himself to the clear light and harsh outlines of the Mediterranean world. Norman Douglas, the author of *Old Calabria* and *Siren Land* and a profound lover of the Mediterranean, once remarked that the luxuriant flora of California held no charms for him; they lacked associations. By contrast every plant, every flower, every spot in Mediterranean Europe summoned up memories. One of Douglas's enthusiasms was for the Scots Presbyterian minister Crawfurd Tait Ramage who, armed with a sun-hat and parasol, set himself to visit every site in Southern Italy mentioned in classical literature, the result being a work of curious and entrancing erudition *Nooks and By-ways of Southern Italy*.

Byron was no antiquary like Ramage, or indeed Douglas himself. He was too impatient, too slapdash. Yet he felt the charms of antiquity also: a ruin delighted him – he carved his name on the column at Cape Sounion. The pleasure he took in landscape was enhanced by its associations. Though well aware of the deformities inflicted on the Greeks and Italians of his time by centuries of misgovernment, he yet hoped that they could aspire to equal the heroes of the Ancient world. His poetry is saturated with the sense of that world. It was also confoundedly modern; he expressed the sensibility and fought the political battles of his own time.

Byron is such an interesting and compelling figure that it is possible to delight in his life almost without reference to his poetry. Certainly the man presented to us in his letters and journals would be memorable and significant if he had never written a line of verse. There are few poets of whom this can be said. Yet, of course, his contemporary importance rested on his poetry; it was a revelation and a call to action at the same time. Mazzini, the apostle of Italian liberty, found that Byron 'combated aristocratic prejudices, and developed in men's minds the sentiments of equality'.

His literary influence was great. He is the only English poet to have had a profound effect on the European literature of his own day and the succeeding generation: Pushkin in Russia, Leopardi in Italy, Hugo and Lamartine in France, would all have written differently if they had not read Byron. He represented, as much as any writer can do, the spirit of his age.

Mazzini again: 'Poet that he was, he preferred activity for good, to all his art could do. Surrounded by slaves and their oppressors; a traveller in countries where even remembrance seemed extinct; never did he desert the cause of the peoples; never was he false to human sympathies. A witness of the progress of the Restoration, and the triumph of the principles of the Holy Alliance, he never swerved from his courageous opposition; he preserved and publicly proclaimed his faith in the rights of the peoples and in the final triumph of liberty.'

And, in a footnote, Mazzini quoted these lines, so well-worn that it is hard now to recapture the sensation with which they broke on the ear:

> Yet, Freedom! yet thy banner torn, but flying,
> Streams, like the thunder-storm, *against* the wind;
> Thy trumpet-voice, though broken now and dying,
> The loudest still the tempest leaves behind;
> The tree hath lost its blossoms, and the rind,
> Chopp'd by the axe, looks rough and little worth,
> But the sap lasts – and still the seed we find
> Sown deep, even in the bosom of the North;
> So shall a better spring less bitter fruit bring forth.

He quoted, too, a passage from the journals, which is less well known, but even more significant, if only because Byron strikes no attitudes in his journalizing:

'Onwards! it is now the time to act; and what signifies self, if a single spark of that which would be worthy of the past can be bequeathed unquenchably to the future? It is not one man, nor a million, but the *spirit* of liberty which must be spread. The waves which dash on the shore are, one by one, broken; but yet the ocean conquers nevertheless. It overwhelms the Armada; it wears the rock; and if the Neptunians are to be believed, it has not only destroyed, but made a world.'

'So,' writes Mazzini, 'at Naples, in the Romagna, wherever he saw a spark of noble life stirring, he was ready for any exertion; or danger, to blow it into a flame. He stigmatized baseness, hypocrisy, and injustice, whensoever they sprang.'

For Mazzini, 'never did "the eternal spirit of the chainless mind" make a brighter apparition amongst us.' He seemed to him 'at times a transformation of that noble Prometheus. . . . While the Christian powers were protocolising or worse – while the Christian nations were doling forth the alms of a few piles of ball in aid of the Cross struggling with the Crescent; he, the poet and pretended sceptic, hastened to throw his fortune, his genius and his life at the feet of the first people that had arisen in the name of the nationality and liberty he loved.'

No doubt there is a degree of wild verbiage in this – Mazzini had, almost to excess, the Latin love for grand abstractions; that is immaterial, for this eulogy represents the effect Byron made. 'The day will come,' Mazzini wrote, 'when Democracy will remember all that it owes to Byron.' That was what Byron meant to the Europe of his own day. He was an object of fear and suspicion to the established powers; a beacon of hope to Liberals and Nationalists, the two being generally coincidental.

What did Europe mean to him? Between leaving Cambridge in 1809, aged twenty-one, and his death in 1824, he spent eleven years out of Britain, principally in Greece and Italy.

II

For centuries English and Scottish travellers had gravitated to Italy, 'the mother of arts'. Great noblemen returned laden with paintings, statues, and even ideas. For painters a season or two in Italy was an essential part of education. Poets also found inspiration there, from Chaucer onwards; Milton's Italian years were among the happiest of his life, and his discovery of Salandra's epic poem *Adama caduto* contributed to his *Paradise Lost*. Throughout the eighteenth century, while Italy was sunk in political decadence, most of the peninsula languishing under a dull, incompetent, restrictive and frequently foreign rule, the flood of visitors continued to swell. In 1786 the British ambassador at Naples, Sir William Hamilton, expressed his concern at 'the enormous sum of money spent abroad by subjects of Great Britain. I had the curiosity to enquire of the two principal bankers here what was the amount of money they had furnished the English travellers with at Naples this year, and they can assure you it was nearly fifty thousand pounds.' The great English houses of that period drew inspiration from the villas which Palladio had built for the Venetian aristocracy on the banks of the Brenta, while their gardens imitated the classical landscapes of Poussin and Claude Lorraine. No one who had failed to visit Italy could avoid a feeling of inferiority, for though the country itself produced little of the first quality then, it remained the fountain head and repository of culture.

In 1809, however, Italy was out of bounds. The Revolution had struck there in 1796 when the young General Bonaparte had swept the Austrians out of the north, reduced the papal states of central Italy to a French dependency (or, if you preferred, liberated them from a dank conservative stupefaction and superstition). A couple of years later Naples too was liberated by the French. After his coronation as Emperor in 1804, Napoleon made his brother-in-law, the innkeeper's son and glittering cavalry officer Joachim Murat, King of Naples, while Italy north of the old *regno* was transformed into a kingdom. Napoleon, who had crowned himself with the old iron crown of Lombardy, retained it for himself – in time his little son would be called King of Rome – and appointed his stepson, Eugène de Beauharnais, as viceroy. Only Sicily escaped his liberation. Protected by the Royal Navy, its Bourbon king Ferdinand still held court there, but it was a long time – some six hundred years – since Sicily had flourished or counted for much; it had attracted few English travellers except for those merchants who had secured the trade in Marsala wines for themselves.

So Napoleon deprived the young Byron of the Italian experience he would otherwise have enjoyed. He did not repine. For one thing, he admired the Emperor – he would call him 'my poor little pagod' when news of his fall came in 1814. He was aware of the tyranny and miseries which the Emperor had inflicted on France and Europe, so that his attitude was somewhat ambivalent. Nevertheless, when he measured Napoleon against his enemies – the Holy Alliance of obscurantism and privilege, represented by Russia, Austria and the restored Bourbons, and the steely hypocrisy of the English oligarchy – there could be no doubt where his sympathies lay. For Byron was a Liberal – a new foreign term just coming into vogue – and belonged to that section of the old Whig party which had followed its hero, Charles James Fox, in welcoming the fall of the Bastille and the outbreak of revolution in France. The principles of the Revolution, its promise of liberty, equality and fraternity, might have been submerged in the two decades of subsequent war, but they were still preferable to those of the *ancien régime*. So the Whigs continued to admire Napoleon as the embodiment of the Revolution even when he set himself to the suppression of its democratic tendencies, though retaining its faith in Reason, a faith to which the structure of French society and the French state bears enduring testimony. Why, the great Whig hostess Lady Holland, at whose table Byron would be welcomed in his years of London glory, used to refer to Napoleon during his exile on St Helena as 'the poor dear man'.

Besides, there was a deeper reason for Byron's admiration of

Napoleon. They had much in common. The young Napoleon, as depicted by David, astride a rearing steed before a backcloth of Alpine scenery, might be taken as a representation of one aspect of Romanticism: he was a man apart, a solitary hero, a Titan, who had formed the world to suit himself. Inasmuch as Romanticism was first of all an assertion of individuality, it found in Napoleon its supreme self-expression. His defeat served only to reinforce the myth; he then became the broken hero destroyed by dull men and dull custom; the pinioned eagle; but also – this was important – a being brought low by his own unchained and untameable passions. He was in short very like Childe Harold.

Yet at the same time the real Napoleon was a man of the eighteenth century, given to sentiment certainly – he never travelled without a copy of Macpherson's Ossian in an Italian translation; but also possessed of a lucid and critical intellect, contemptuous of cant, distrustful of sentimentality. Here too he resembled Byron, for the Byron who wrote poems full of wild and intoxicating passion, poems in which self-expression surged like an angry and unprecedented ocean, was also the man who admired Pope above all poets of his own day, who, standing on a balcony overlooking a moonlit Venetian canal, was quick to tell his friend Tom Moore, the Irish bard, not to be 'poetical', and whose masterpiece *Don Juan* mocked all manifestations of emotional and intellectual insincerity.

How could he fail to recognize Napoleon as his fellow? He and I, he would say (after the death of his father-in-law had enabled him to add the name 'Noel' to his) 'are the only two who can sign ourselves NB.'

III

The young man who boarded the Lisbon packet at Falmouth on 2 July 1809 had reason enough to think of himself as different from the common run of mankind. In the first place he was a lord – the sixth Baron Byron – at a time when to be a peer of the United Kingdom was to receive as of right an absurd degree of adulation and servility. Henri Beyle (Stendhal), who knew Byron in Milan in 1816 (if hardly as well as he later pretended), considered that 'in his ordinary everyday moments Lord Byron would think of himself as a mighty aristocrat; this was the breastplate by which his delicate and susceptible nature was protected against the infinite grossness of the vulgar.' Then he was remarkably handsome, even beautiful; Sir Walter Scott, by no means given to exaggerated or vapourish judgments, considered that 'his countenance was like an angel's'. Finally he was conscious of his genius, though this had hardly yet manifested itself, and his pride would always render him shy of asserting it.

Yet these blessings were mixed. The coin of race and beauty showed a very different figure on its obverse.

He might be a peer of the realm, but his family background was made embarrassing and oppressive by scandal and misfortune. The Byrons could trace their descent back to the Norman Conquest, and had obtained the abbey and lands of Newstead in Nottinghamshire at the time of the Dissolution of the Monasteries. The barony had been created during the Civil War for Sir John Byron who served as a royalist commander. (His second wife Eleanor subsequently served as Charles II's seventeenth identifiable mistress, according to the diarist Samuel Pepys.) The fifth Baron, the poet's great-uncle, was known as 'the Wicked Lord'. He had killed a neighbour, William Chaworth, after a drunken quarrel about the best way to preserve game, but had been acquitted of murder by his fellow peers, and then retired to his estates, where he was reputed to engage in orgies in a Gothick castle he had built on an island in a lake. He had stripped the estate of its timber, run up debts and, with dubious legality, mortgaged his Rochdale estates in Lancashire.

His brother, the poet's grandfather, was an admiral known as 'Fou-weather Jack' on account of his propensity to attract storms at

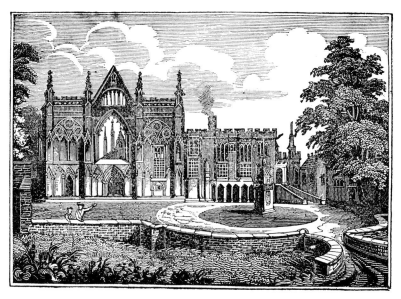

Newstead Abbey, Nottinghamshire, seat of the Byron family

sea. His son, 'Mad Jack', was known for extravagance, wildness and drunkenness. In 1778, having left the Army with the rank of captain, he had eloped with the wife of the Marquis of Carmarthen, whose charms were improved by her independent fortune of £4,000 a year. She died in 1784 leaving him one daughter, Augusta. The next year, considerably in debt, he arrived in Bath seeking a new heiress, and found one in Catherine Gordon of Gight. Her fortune was not in fact large, though it would have been sufficient to allow a gentleman to live quietly. That was not, however, to the Captain's taste. He soon ran through all he could get his hands on, and then retired again to the Continent where he died in 1791. Mrs Byron, it is fair to say, mourned him: 'notwithstanding all his foibles, for they deserve no worse a name, I sincerely loved him'. Her son, however, had – Byron is said to have told Thomas Medwin, an English acquaintance, met in Pisa, who published an account of his conversation with the poet, more than thirty years later – acquired 'very early a horror of matrimony, from the sight of domestic broils'. Since Byron was born in January 1788, and the Captain made the last of his fleeting visits to his wife in September 1790, this memory may probably be discounted, and be thought to owe more to Byron's own experience of marriage than to that of his parents.

From the Byrons then he got his title, his pride of race and a taste for dissipation; he also got a rather adolescent sense of the glamour of wickedness. What he didn't get was the assured social position suggested by his title. The Byrons were neither rich nor grand enough to flout convention with impunity. A Duke of Norfolk could, like the 11th Duke, dress and talk like a coachman, and consort with jockeys and ostlers; he could smoke a foul pipe, swill gin and beer, and be thought no more than eccentric; a Byron was more easily *déclassé*. Certainly the Byrons were not respectable. Stendhal, not for the only time, misunderstood the English; he didn't realize that Byron's insistence that he was an English milord in fact indicated his social uncertainty. A more acute observer was Lady Blessington – whose own social position was decidedly rocky – who declared that she 'had never met anyone with so decided a taste for aristocracy as Lord Byron,' and added that 'this vanity . . . resembles more the pride of a parvenu than the calm dignity of an ancient aristocrat.'

His mother's family was more remarkable than the Byrons. The Gordons were the greatest house of the north-east of Scotland. Catherine Gordon could boast of royal descent from James I of Scots, by way of his daughter Annabella. The head of the family, the Marquess of Huntly, was known as 'the cock of the north'. Their history was turbulent and chequered. One branch of the family, the

Byron: 'But I was born half a Scot and bred a whole one'

Gordons of Haddo, had been rising fast in the eighteenth century and had been created Earls of Aberdeen. They would continue to flourish in the nineteenth, producing a prime minister, the fourth earl, whom Byron in *English Bards and Scotch Reviewers*, hailed as 'the travell'd thane, Athenian Aberdeen'; and also a Viceroy of Ireland, the first marquess. But even the Gordons of Haddo had their oddities; the fourth earl married a cook whom he discovered in a Yorkshire inn.

Catherine Gordon belonged to a collateral branch, the Gordons of Gight, notorious for their wildness. The seventh laird, at the time of the Civil Wars, had buried a treasure in the river Ythan to protect it from the Covenanters. Having received a pardon for his royalist activities in 1647, he sent a diver down to recover it. The diver found the devil himself sitting at table with the laird's silver before him waiting for dead babies to be cooked for his supper. He returned, not surprisingly, to the surface, and refused to go back for the treasure until the laird persuaded him by pulling out his fingernails and sticking him with pins. 'Better the devil than the laird of Gight,' he cried and plunged into the water. This time his quartered body surfaced with a knife impaled in his still quivering heart. The seventh laird was clearly an ancestor of whom any boy might be proud.

There was nothing to boast of, however, in the circumstances of Byron's early childhood. It is hard not to feel pity and respect for Catherine Gordon. She was left in an unenviable position. The Captain had run through her money, and the Wicked Lord offered her no support – Byron didn't become his heir until his cousin William was killed in Corsica in 1794, but even subsequently the boy was ignored. He had been born in poor lodgings in London, and his childhood was spent in poor lodgings in Aberdeen. His mother inculcated a pride of race; it was as well that the boy should be made aware of his difference from the sons of lawyers, merchants and tradesmen with whom he consorted at the Grammar School in the city.

His aristocracy was tarnished then. So was his beauty. He had been born with a deformed foot. Despite much argument the evidence seems to be that it was a true club foot, with the heel turned up and the sole turned inward. He was noticeably lame as a child, though he developed a light tripping gait which disguised it. One of his earliest memories was of a scene in the street in Aberdeen, when a passer-by said to his nurse: 'What a pretty boy . . . what a pity he has such a leg,' and the child struck her with a little whip he was carrying, calling out 'Dinna speak of it!' He could never escape consciousness of his deformity, and though at school he flung himself into sports on equal terms – even playing cricket for Harrow in the first match against Eton

– in adult life he was happier on horseback or especially in the water.

He was very much the centre of his mother's life. She was a woman of strong emotions who, like many mothers of gifted only children, alternately bullied and spoiled him. She had a quick temper which often led her to behave foolishly, and she lacked social grace, but she was by no means a fool. Byron resembled her rather than his incompetent flibbertigibbet father. Their politics were similar; she too was an aristocratic Liberal. Byron described her as 'haughty as Lucifer with her descent from the Stuarts' and she was 'always reminding me how superior her Gordons were to the Southron Byrons'. Yet she approved of the French Revolution, writing in 1792 to her sister-in-law that 'I am quite a Democrat and I do not think the King [Louis XVI] after his treachery and perjury, deserves to be restored.'

Byron's mother

The early years in Scotland left a lasting impression on Byron. 'I was born half a Scot, and bred a whole one,' he wrote. His nursemaid instructed him in the theology of a narrow and perverted Calvinism, and all his life he indulged the temptation of believing that he had been damned from birth; she also, when he was eight or nine, formed the habit of coming to his bed at night, and engaging him in sex-play, which gave him a lively and premature sense of sin. More happily, a holiday on Deeside opened his eyes to the splendour of wild landscape; a love of mountain scenery, that sure mark of the Romantic temperament, never left him.

In character Byron seems to me more Scottish than English. Identification of national traits is always a tricky business, and often a foolish one. It must be haphazard and tentative. Exceptions are always to be found. Byron lacked the robust complacency of the English; he was easily able to lay himself alongside foreigners and see the world from their point of view. He had an impatience with the Englishman's consciousness of his own virtue and his own superiority. Professor Gregory Smith in *Scottish Literature: Character and Influence* coined the phrase 'the Caledonian antizyzygy', which is as beloved of Scots writers as it is tiresome and now inescapable. Smith used it to describe 'the zigzag of contradictions' which he found in Scottish literature. It offered 'a reflection of the contrasts which the Scot shows at every turn, in his political and ecclesiastical history, in his polemical restlessness, in his adaptability, which is another way of saying that he has made allowances for new conditions, in his practical judgment, which is the admission that two sides of the matter have been considered.' Byron himself, writing of Burns, said: 'What an antithetical mind! – tenderness, roughness – delicacy, coarseness – sentiment, sensuality – soaring and grovelling, dirt and deity – all mixed up in one compound of inspired clay.' It is a fair judgment on Burns; it is a still more exact one applied to Byron himself.

IV

The death of 'the Wicked Lord' in 1799 rescued Byron from a life of provincial indigence. They moved to Nottinghamshire, but the estate of Newstead was so embarrassed that it was impossible to take up residence there, and indeed Newstead had to be let. Byron might now be a lord, but he was still a poor boy, and could hardly be a confident one. Their friendly neighbours in Nottinghamshire, the Pigots, thought him 'a fat bashful boy'.

He had little acquaintance with the great world. His family lawyer,

Cricket at Harrow: Byron played in the first Eton match

an estimable man called Hanson, who was kind and hospitable to him and whose household he enjoyed visiting, persuaded Lord Carlisle, a first cousin of the Captain, to act as his guardian. Unfortunately Carlisle took a dislike to Mrs Byron on their only meeting, and was thereafter cold and distant in his duty. Lord Grey of Ruthin, who had rented Newstead, was friendly, but then, it seems, he was more than friendly. He made advances to Byron which frightened or disgusted the boy, and for the last years of his lease, Byron refused to visit Newstead. At Harrow Byron at last acquired friends of his own rank, especially Lord Clare, to whom he was to remain devoted all his life in an idealized friendship, but most of his Harrow friendships – 'passions' he called them – were with younger boys; the inequality of age redressed the inequality of social assurance that Byron experienced with those of his own age and class.

He blossomed at Cambridge, as many have done who feel themselves different from others and are consequently insecure in their relationships. He cultivated eccentricity, keeping a bear in his rooms in Trinity. Throughout his life Byron was devoted to animals and birds; his homes were always stocked with an assortment of pets. At Cambridge, too, he discovered that he was a poet. His first volume,

Hours of Idleness was on the whole weak, conventional and sentimental, but it meant much to him, and he was distressed when it was savaged by the critics. He replied with *English Bards and Scotch Reviewers*, a robust satire in the mode, though without the skill, of his admired Pope. This excess of sensitivity – the quickness to take offence of the poor lame boy uncertain of his place in the world – remained with him. His aristocracy was a defence against criticism and the assumption of equality.

Yet among friends few revelled more in repartee, reckless candour and easy relations than Byron. He was the merriest of companions whenever he felt himself free of disapproval; Scott once compared him to a kitten. It is this side of his nature which makes him such a splendid letter writer. None of his Cambridge friends touched his heart as Lord Clare had done – that was reserved for a choir-boy at Trinity called John Edleston, whom he christened 'the Cornelian' – but they appealed to the lively, social, and unsentimental side of his divided nature. Since one can learn much of a man from a study of his friends, it is worth glancing at them.

Trinity College, Cambridge: Nevile's Court

John Cam Hobhouse was two years older than Byron. A taste for satire and nonsense drew them together. They remained friends throughout Byron's life because Hobhouse, though often tiresome and sometimes boring, was utterly reliable and devoted. He was to be best man at Byron's wedding; he accompanied him to Dover in 1816 when Byron went into exile; he visited him in Italy and hoped to join him on his Greek expedition. Byron often laughed at him, but never cruelly. Hobhouse was the son of a Whig member of Parliament, and in 1820 himself entered the House of Commons; he belonged to the radical wing of the party. Both enjoyed travel, literature and ribaldry; their political opinions were similar, though Byron did not care for Hobhouse's more extreme views, while being at the same time irritated by his outbursts of cautious prudery. The worst that can be said of Hobhouse is that in his concern for Byron's posthumous reputation he persuaded Tom Moore to burn the memoirs which Byron had entrusted to him. He survived his friend by more than thirty years, and was created Baron Broughton de Gyfford in 1851.

Charles Skinner Matthews played a much smaller part in Byron's life than Hobhouse. He was at first Hobhouse's friend rather than Byron's, though he and Byron were closer in the extravagance of their humour. Byron respected in Matthews a scholarship of which he knew himself to be incapable. Matthews was also the son of an MP – a country squire from Herefordshire. In 1808 he had been elected a Fellow of Downing College. Byron was first attracted by his 'droll sardonic humour'. During the year of Byron's absence from Trinity, Matthews (who did not yet know him) lodged in his rooms. His tutor, by name of Jones, warned him: 'Mr Matthews, I recommend to you, sir, not to damage any of the moveables, for Lord Byron, sir, is a young man of tumultuous passions.' This delighted Matthews, and Byron too, when the story was retailed. It seems likely that Matthews and Byron shared another, and more dangerous, taste: for boys. The tone of Byron's letters to him suggests this; on the other hand, he wrote in the same vein to his clergyman friend Francis Hodgson and his Harrow tutor Henry Drury. Matthews was drowned in the Cam in August 1811; both Byron and Hobhouse were deeply affected by his death, and Byron added a note to the first canto of *Childe Harold* commemorating him. Throughout his life he never wrote of Matthews without affection and admiration.

A third friend was Scrope Davies, who was five years older than Byron, a fellow of King's and very much a man of the world. Byron found him 'one of the cleverest fellows I ever knew, in conversation', and he lent him large sums of money, an act of generosity which their friendship survived. Byron once found him drunk in bed, after an evening of drinking and gaming, with the chamberpot below the bed overflowing with banknotes. Davies was the genuine Regency rake, eventually, like so many, ruined by his addiction to gambling. He ended his days in exile in France, though, more fortunate than some, he had his Fellowship, in those happier days a freehold for life, to sustain him and provide an income.

John Cam Hobhouse,
Byron's lifelong friend

These three friends indicate the range of Byron's interests: literature, politics, travel (Hobhouse was an assiduous writer of travel books and sketches), boxing (Matthews and Byron both frequented the boxing saloon kept by the retired heavyweight champion 'Gentleman' John Jackson), drinking, gambling, dandyism, women and boys, jokes. All were addicted to nonsense and exuberant flights of fancy, but there was little fundamental nonsense about them. They all had gusto, that great Regency word, and they lived life to the full. They were free of domestic ties; and, though there was a cosy domestic side to Byron, shown in his relations with his half-sister Augusta and later with Teresa Guiccioli, he delighted in the tough masculine society of Regency London, with its gin parlours, boxing saloons and gaming clubs. There was nothing stuffy about them – though Hobhouse would develop a stuffy side in time – and not much damned sentimentality. Byron came of age in their company, and these friends of his youth remained warm in his affections, even when Matthews was dead and he no longer saw Davies.

V

Byron resolved to go abroad as soon as he came of age. Hobhouse would accompany him. They hoped Matthews would come too, but this proved impossible. The idea of such a journey had long been with him. It is natural enough for young men to wish to travel, and Byron had good reasons. A journey is always perhaps as much away from one place as towards another. If it is an expression of a desire to see new places and new ways of life, it is also an expression of dissatisfaction with the place where you are and the life you are leading. Byron's dissatisfaction was strong.

His finances were horribly embarrassed, partly as a result of his own extravagance, more fundamentally because Hanson had not yet, over the course of some ten years, been able to resolve the complications of his inheritance. Byron had considerable property and a constant shortage of ready cash. He was determined not to sell Newstead; the place appealed equally to his imagination and his sense of himself as a landed proprietor. But matters of business he left Hanson to arrange.

None of the great houses of London – none of the people of his 'own rank' as he put it – showed any willingness to open their doors to him. The Byrons, as I have said, had no standing, and Lord Carlisle had shown no eagerness to take the boy under his wing. Consequently, Byron felt himself to be disregarded and unvalued; he was an outsider. He could not shine at home. Very well then, he would travel abroad and so hope to acquire a reputation.

He sought freedom from his mother's solicitude which he felt as interference; and he was still at a sensitive stage when young men may unfairly feel embarrassed by their parents. At Harrow a friend had unkindly but unequivocally informed him that his mother was a fool, and Byron had shamefully felt constrained to agree. Yet too much can be made of this. He was to write regularly to her throughout his travels, which is more than many mothers can expect even from sons who are not particularly rebellious. A good deal of nonsense has been written about poor Mrs Byron, though her own letters show her to have had plenty of good sense. Byron's letters to her are often extremely long, going well beyond what a sense of duty might demand. They are informative and not short of jokes, a good measure of intimacy. Relations between mother and son could be easy enough, at least at a distance: 'So Ld Grey is married to a rustic, well done! If I wed I will bring home a sultana with half a score of cities for a dowry, and reconcile you to an Ottoman daughter-in-law with a bushel of pearls not larger than ostrich eggs or smaller than Walnuts.' This is not the language of a son who finds his mother excessively difficult, or who detests her.

His first stated intention was to visit the Greek archipelago. Then in October 1808, writing to his mother, he announced Persia as his destination. Perhaps even India might be possible? He wrote to the Prime Minister, the Duke of Portland, asking him 'to procure me the permission of the East India Company to pass through their settlements'. This wasn't quite an idle whim, as he explained to Hanson: he wished to study India and Asiatic policy and manners, a reasonable ambition since he had political ambitions, and in fact postponed his departure till he was able to take his seat in the House of Lords. So he told Hanson that he was determined 'to take a wider view than is customary with travellers'. When he returned his judgment would be more 'mature' and he 'would still be young enough for politics'. Byron was aware of his position as an hereditary legislator at a time when most Cabinet offices were still held by peers; at the age of twenty-one a political career was as alluring as poetry; he had been praised for his skill in debate at Harrow.

Aware that Hanson doubted whether the journey was wise in view of his financial position, he assured him that 'travelling in the east is rather inconvenient than expensive'. Why, he would even save money: 'A voyage to India will take me six months and if I had a dozen attendants cannot cost me five hundred pounds; and you will agree that a like term of months would lead me in England into four times that expense.' Looking over his account books Hanson could not dispute that statement. Byron told him that he had written to the government for permission: 'So you see I am serious.' Portland however, a dull man, was unhelpful, despite owing the Byron estate a thousand pounds, and the Indian project was shelved.

Byron mystified Hanson by telling him there were circumstances which rendered it 'absolutely indispensable' that he should leave England, a statement which he would repeat in a letter from Albania in November of the same year: 'I never will live in England if I can avoid it, *why* must remain a secret.' It still does, and it is quite likely that there was nothing more to these dark suggestions than Byron's love of self-dramatization. However, he may have feared the consequences of his homosexual affairs; the Cornelian had expressed a wish to live with him in London. There was danger in such a proposal – Byron and his friends were very conscious of the disgrace suffered by William Beckford, 'the great apostle of Pederasty', as Byron called him – and indeed, during their tour, a 'messenger arrived from England', as Hobhouse noted in his diary, 'bringing letters from Hodgson to B – tales spread – the Edleston accused of indecency'.

[27]

Yet if Byron had any such worries, they no more impaired his spirits as the hour for departure approached than his financial straits did. Both could be accommodated in sufficiently light-hearted manner. He wrote to his mother from Falmouth to announce his immediate departure: 'As to money matters I am ruined, at least till Rochdale is sold & if that does not turn out well I shall enter the Austrian or Russian service,' – he probably knew that a Gordon connection had served the Tsar Peter the Great as an admiral – 'perhaps the Turkish, if I like their manners, the world is all before me, and I leave England without any regrets, and without a wish to revisit anything it contains except *yourself*, and your present residence.' This was facetious and high-spirited, and the compliment to Mrs Byron probably a truer expression of his feeling for her than his more frequent complaints of her temper and possessiveness.

So, despite last-minute worries about the availability of money and despite being 'sadly fleabitten' at Falmouth, his mood was buoyant. Hobhouse, he told Henry Drury, hoped 'to indemnify himself in Turkey for a life of exemplary chastity at home by letting out his "fair bodye" to the whole Divan,' while he himself had promised to contribute a chapter on the state of morals in Turkey and 'a further treatise on . . . Sodomy simplified or Pederasty proved to be praise-worthy from ancient authors and modern practice'.

> 'Huzza, Hodgson, we are going . . .' he carolled,
> 'Our embargo's off at last. . . .
>
> Now at length we're off for Turkey,
>   Lord knows when we shall come back!
> Breezes foul & tempests murky,
>   May unship us in a crack.
> But, since life at most a jest is
>   As philosophers allow,
> Still to laugh by far the best is,
>   Then laugh on – as I do now.
>   Laugh at all things,
>   Great & small things,
> Sick or well, at sea or shore;
>   While we're quaffing,
>   Let's have laughing –
> Who the devil cares for more? –
>   Save good wine! and who would lack it?
> Ev'n on board the Lisbon Packet.

This was the Byron his friends loved, whom the world, eager to be deceived by his pose, refused to recognize; the young man who could be frolicsome as a kitten.

[28]

VI

Their route to the East would take them by Lisbon and through Spain to Gibraltar. The peninsula was ravaged as a result of the French invasion of 1807, the Spanish resistance and the establishment of a British Expeditionary Force, but the armies had for the time being moved east from Portugal. They would return there when Masséna, one of the most skilful of Napoleon's marshals, took over command of the French, and forced Wellington (still at the time of Byron's visit only Sir Arthur Wellesley) to retreat behind the defence-works of Torres Vedras; but for now the fighting was in Spain. The great battle of Talavera was indeed fought while Byron was in Portugal, on 27 and 28 July. Like most of us, Byron was apt to let his judgment be coloured by his political opinions, and he was scornful of Wellesley's success: 'In England they will call it a victory, a pretty victory! Two hundred officers and 5,000 men killed all English, and the French in as great force as ever.' When not dazzled by the glamour of Napoleon's career, Byron had little time for military glory; he was ever more alive to the miseries than the splendours of war. For the moment, however, this battle was a mere aside, and there was more interesting matter to relate and discuss, as there were more interesting things to do.

They reached Lisbon after a voyage lasting only four-and-a-half days – good sailing. The city had been rebuilt since the earthquake of 1757 – the disaster which had shocked Voltaire into writing *Candide*. Byron dismissed it: 'It has often been described without being worthy of description' – a fine Johnsonian phrase that – 'for, except for the view from the Tagus which is beautiful, and some fine churches & convents, it contains little but filthy streets & more filthy inhabitants.' Cintra, fifteen miles distant, aroused very different feelings. After a week out of England, he was ready to pronounce it, 'the most beautiful, perhaps in the world'. Hobhouse was impressed by a visit to the 'very room' in the palace there in which General Sir Hew Dalrymple had the previous year signed a Convention with the French general Junot (to the great displeasure incidentally of Napoleon), but Byron found this merely 'a secondary consideration', and raved about its beauties: 'palace and gardens rising in the midst of rocks, cataracts & precipices, convents on stupendous heights, a distant view of the sea and the Tagus'.

Childe Harold, who would make his first appearance within a few months – for Byron began the poem on 31 October in that year – would dwell on Cintra's beauties more poetically:

The horrid crags, by toppling convent crown'd,
The cork-trees hoar that clothe the shaggy steep,
The mountain-moss by scorching skies imbrowned,
The sunken glen, whose sunless shrubs must weep,
The tender azure of the unruffled deep,
The orange tints that gild the greenest bough,
The torrents that from cliff to valley leap,
The vine on high, the willow branch below,
Mixed in one mighty scene, with varied beauty glow.

More poetically, but perhaps with less effect. It is interesting to see how Byron's first impressions of places, thrown any old how on to the pages of his letters and journals, are dressed up later in verse. It was to be some time before he managed to bring the two together, and so allow his poetry to express his full personality. *Childe Harold* is full of fine things, surging rhetoric, striking phrases and slashes of colour; one can still take great pleasure from it, and even now catch something of the excitement with which these first two cantos, which were the fruit of this journey, fell on the ears of his contemporaries, striking them with the sense that a new thing had come into the world and with the awareness that they were hearing a new music. It is indeed a

Cintra, Portugal: 'the most beautiful [place], perhaps in the world'

remarkable work coming from such a young writer – remarkable for for its assurance and for the mastery of the rhetorical tone which it exhibits – but it is still Byron dressed up for show. He told his mother that he had acquired 'a most superb uniform as a court dress, indispensable for travelling', and it is as if he wore that uniform to write *Childe Harold*. For all the pleasure one can still take in the poem, Coleridge's dismissal sticks in the mind: 'A man accustomed to cast his words in metre and familiar with descriptive Poets and Tourists, himself a Picturesque Tourist, must be troubled with a mental Strangury, if he could not lift up his leg six times at six different Corners, and each time piss a Canto.'

What doesn't get into the poem is the young Byron's zest and bubbling happiness: 'I am very happy here, because I loves oranges, and talks bad Latin to the monks, who understand it, as it is like their own – and I goes into society (with my pocket-pistols), and I swims in the Tagus all across at once, and I rides on an ass or a mule, and swears Portuguese and have got a diarrhoea and bites from the mosquitoes. But what of that? Comfort must not be expected by folks that go a-pleasuring.'

Seville delighted him even more than Cintra – and indeed displaced it from its position as 'the first spot in creation'. And then there were its women: 'long black hair, dark languishing eyes, clear olive complexions and forms more graceful in motion than can be conceived by an Englishman used to the drowsy listless air of his countrywomen, added to the most becoming dress & at the same time the most decent in the world, render a Spanish beauty irresistible,' he told his mother. The lady with whom he lodged, Donna Josepha, was open in her admiration for him – at her suggestion they would exchange locks of hair on parting. Then a girl whom he met at Cadiz (which itself immediately supplanted Seville as 'the most delightful town I ever beheld') 'dispossessed an old woman (an aunt or a duenna) of her seat' in a theatre box, 'and commanded me to be seated next to herself, at a tolerable distance from her mamma.' He was impressed and delighted by their freedom of manners and conversation, observing with approval how married women were accustomed to throw off all conventional restraint. 'If you make a proposal which in England would bring you a box on the ear from the meekest of virgins to a Spanish girl she thanks you for the honour you intend her, and replies "wait till I am married, & I shall be too happy."'

In short, he could have stayed in Spain where there was so much to delight him; but he must get on. He never returned there. Yet the memory remained warm, and when he came to write his masterpiece, *Don Juan*, he cast his imagination back thither:

In Seville was he born, a pleasant city,
   Famous for oranges and women – he
Who has not seen it will be much to pity,
   So says the proverb – and I quite agree;
Of all the Spanish towns is none more pretty,
   Cadiz perhaps – but that you soon may see –
Don Juan's parents lived beside the river,
   A noble stream, and call'd the Guadalquivir.

Gibraltar however was a different kettle of fish. He wrote from there to Hanson as well as to his mother, and described it as 'the dirtiest most detestable spot in existence'. From Gibraltar he delivered to his lawyer his judgment on the war and conditions in Spain: 'Spain is all in arms, and the French have everything to do again, the barbarities on both sides are shocking. I passed some French prisoners on the road from Badajoz to Seville, and saw a spy who was condemned to be shot, you will be surprised to hear that the Spanish roads are far superior to the English turnpikes, and the horses excellent, eggs & wine always to be had, no meat or milk, but everything else very fair.'

At Gibraltar he decided to send his boy-servant Robert Rushton home. He was the son of one of his tenant-farmers at Newstead, and Byron had an affection for him. But, he wrote to Mrs Byron, 'You know boys are not safe among the Turks.' He was anxious, however, lest Robert's father should assume that he had been sent home in disgrace, and so wrote assuring him how well he had behaved. He told him to spend twenty-five pounds a year on his education: 'deduct the expense of his education from your rent'. Byron's care for his dependents is one of the attractive features of his character; Fletcher, his much-complaining and very English valet, remained in his service all his life, despite the hardships of foreign travel, the pain of separation from his wife, and the lack of English beer and beef.

They left Gibraltar for Malta on 16 August, sailing on the Townsend Packet. The voyage took a fortnight, being broken at Sardinia, and so they did not reach Malta till the last day of the month; both Sardinia and Malta, like most of the other islands of the Mediterranean, avoided incorporation in Napoleon's empire thanks to the dominance of the Royal Navy, which had been absolute in the Mediterranean since Nelson destroyed Napoleon's fleet in Aboukir Bay in 1798 and confirmed that supremacy at Trafalgar.

One of their fellow passengers was the Scots novelist John Galt who was exploring the possibilities of setting up a trading company able to break the embargo Napoleon had imposed in 1807 on the import of British goods anywhere in Europe. This embargo – known as the

Continental System – was less than effective; when the Grande Armée invaded Russia in 1812, most of the soldiers marched in English boots. Galt, some ten years older than Byron and more than ten years older in experience of the world, in which he had had to make his own way, would later write a biography of Byron. He was at once impressed by him, and also irritated. He saw the young poet seeking 'poetical sympathy from the gloomy rock', and observed him 'sitting amidst the shrouds and ratlings, in the tranquillity of the moonlight. . . . He seemed almost apparitional, suggesting reminiscences of him who shot the albatross. He was as a mystery in a winding-sheet, crowned with a halo.' If the young Byron did in fact make such an impression on Galt at the time, he would doubtless have been delighted, but one can hardly avoid the suspicion that Galt was actually dressing up his first impressions of the poet in order to present them in a manner acceptable to the public's image of him.

When they were all invited to dine at the British Embassy in Cagliari, Galt was more critical: 'Byron and his Pylades [Hobhouse] dressed themselves as aides-de-camp' – doubtless in the uniform of which Byron had written so enthusiastically to his mother – 'a circumstance which did not tend to improve my estimation of the solidity of character of either.' Byron's sensitivity was excessive, and such a judgment coming from a social inferior would have distressed him. Yet at the same time it showed that the costume had achieved its purpose: it had attracted attention and distinguished him from the common run.

They paused at Malta where the 'inhabitants were civil and pleasant', and he took the opportunity to write to Hanson in some-what peremptory fashion: 'It is rather singular that you have not addressed any letter to this place since my departure from England.' He had hoped for news of money matters, and reminded Hanson, who was in fact doing his best to bring some order to the Byron estates, that though he was in no immediate need of funds, yet he should remember that remittances might take as much as six months to reach Constantinople. On all his travels Byron was periodically assailed by the suspicion that those who were administering his affairs in England, and on whom he was of course dependent for supplies, had forgotten his existence and were neglecting his business.

Malta, however, held a more pleasant diversion. This took the form of a young lady called Mrs Constance Spencer Smith. She was four or five years older than Byron, and very much more experienced. 'She was born at Constantinople, where her father Baron Herbert was Austrian Ambassador, married unhappily [to an Englishman] yet has never been impeached in point of character, excited the vengeance of

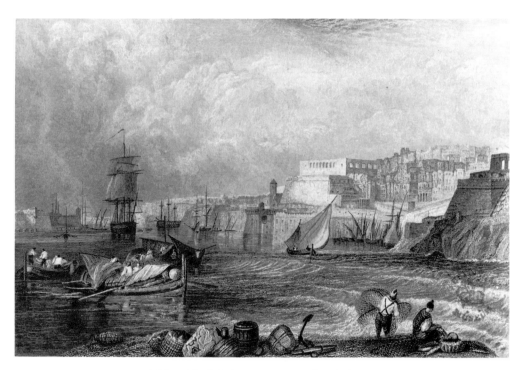

Malta: 'the inhabitants were civil and pleasant'

Bonaparte by a part in some conspiracy, several times risked her life, and is not yet twenty-five.' Her escape from Napoleon had been dramatically effected by an Italian nobleman called the Marchese de Salvo, who had published an account of his exploit, which had rendered her a figure of some celebrity. All in all she was a suitable lady – 'very pretty, very accomplished, and extremely eccentric' – to arouse the passions of both Byron and Childe Harold. Byron soon challenged an officer of the garrison of Malta to fight a duel over her, and he himself, as he told Lady Melbourne three years later, was quite ready to accompany her to Friuli, where she was supposed to rejoin her husband. That plan was thwarted by the treaty concluded after the battle of Wagram, which saw Friuli ceded to the French.

Byron's heart might be touched; the Childe was made of sterner stuff, and his proud and tortured spirit was proof against her charms:

> . . . on that lady's eye,
> He look'd, and met its beam without a thought,
> Save admiration glancing harmless by:
> Love kept aloof, albeit not far remote.

[34]

'She is now,' he told Lady Melbourne in 1812, 'I am told writing her memoirs in Vienna, in which I shall cut a very indifferent figure.'

The tourists left Malta on 19 September. The island's Governor, Sir Alexander Ball, had obligingly obtained them a passage in a brig-of-war, *The Spider*, which, despite the approach of the autumn equinox when the Mediterranean is traditionally disturbed, was convoying a fleet of fifty merchant ships to Patras in the Morea (the Peloponnese) and Preveza in Albania. At Patras they found the Greeks 'polite and hospitable' and walked in what Hobhouse called the 'currant-grounds'. Byron's spirits soared with the voyage and arrival in Greece:

> Morn dawns: and with it stern Albania's hills,
> Dark Suli's rocks, and Pindus' inland peak,
> Robed half in mist, bedew'd with snowy rills,
> Array'd in many a dun and purple streak,
> Arise; and, as the clouds along them break,
> Disclose the dwellings of the mountaineer;
> Here roams the wolf, the eagle whets his beak,
> Birds, beasts of prey, and wilder men appear,
> And gathering storms around convulse the closing year.
>
> Now Harold felt himself at length alone . . .

(Not counting Hobhouse, of course, who was excised from the poem, though himself journalizing with a view to publication.)

> And bade to Christian tongues a long adieu . . .

(A strange, inaccurate judgment, since Greek was spoken by most of the inhabitants, but, of course, a dramatic one.)

> Now he adventured on a shore unknown,
> Which all admire, but many dread to view:
> His breast was armed 'gainst fate, his wants were few;
> Peril he sought not, but ne'er shrank to meet:

So, girding up his rhetoric, the Childe disembarked:

> The scene was savage, but the scene was new;
> This made the ceaseless toil of travel sweet.

Some twenty-five years later, Alexander Kinglake, who had had the advantage of poring over *Childe Harold's Pilgrimage*, would write in more ironic, yet still enthusiastic, vein in the first chapter of *Eothen*:

[35]

The first night of your campaign (though you be but a mere peaceful campaigner) is a glorious time in your life. It is so sweet to find oneself free from the stale civilization of Europe. Oh my dear ally: when first you spread your carpet in the midst of these eastern scenes, do think for a moment of these your fellow creatures, that dwell in squares, and streets, and even (for such is the fate of many) in actual country houses; think of the people 'that are presenting their compliments' and 'requesting the honour' and 'much regretting' – of those that are pinioned at dinner-tables, or stuck up in ball-rooms, or cruelly planted in pews – ay, think of these, and so remembering how many poor devils are living in a state of utter respectability, you will glory the more in your own delightful escape.

Though Byron would on his journey endure his full share of 'presenting his compliments', which, as Kinglake himself found, was indeed an inescapable part of travel in the Orient, every bit as exigent in Greece and Turkey as in England, these were nevertheless Byron's sentiments exactly. He had entered on a season of delightful irresponsibility; a period when he could indulge his genius, as the mood took him.

The mountains of Epirus, Northern Greece

VII

The Ottoman Empire which Byron was entering and which was to determine the course of his life, was unlike any state in Europe. Indeed it is almost misleading to call it a state, for it lacked almost everything that we might regard as properly pertaining to such an institution. Since the Turks believed that they were engaged in permanent religious war with the infidel world, with all those who did not belong to the Muslim faith, the Empire could have no settled frontier, and its masters had no care for civil administration. The Empire existed for the sole purpose of making war on the Infidel, and therefore the principal, even the only, functions of the administration in the provinces were the maintenance of the military establishment and the collection of taxes.

Greece and the Balkans had been almost completely under the rule of the Turks for three centuries now, though Venice had held parts of the Morea in the seventeenth century. The Empire was incapable of organic development, for it could only contract or expand as the frontier shifted. Its Christian population was rarely subject to persecution, and no attempt was made to convert it to Islam. To have done so would indeed have undermined the fiscal basis of the Empire which was supported principally by a poll tax levied on all the Sultan's non-Muslim subjects. At the same time the Turks entertained a sublime contempt for their Christian subjects who were referred to indifferently as 'cattle'. As long as they paid their taxes, which included a tribute of children instituted in the fourteenth century as a means of recruiting a regular infantry force – the famous Janissaries – they were left largely to their own devices. Certain things were forbidden: only a Muslim, for instance, was permitted to possess or ride a horse – though this prohibition did not extend to visiting foreigners, and was anyway by Byron's time scarcely observed.

He and Hobhouse travelled, as befitted English milords, in some style. They carried four leather trunks, each weighing about 80lb when full, and three smaller trunks. They had a canteen – 'quite indispensable' in Hobhouse's opinion; three beds with bedding and two light wooden bedsteads; 'the latter article some travellers do not carry with them, but it contributes so much to comfort and health as to be very recommendable' – for all that, Byron later noted that 'when we were wayfaring men, Hobhouse used to complain grievously of hard beds and sharp insects, while I slept like a top.' They had brought English saddles – the Turks being accustomed to use wooden pack saddles – and bridles, and they had large sacks, each capable of holding a bed, a large trunk and smaller articles, slung over pack-horses. 'Some travellers', Hobhouse observed, 'prefer to take only a large pair of saddle-bags, and to send the rest of their baggage ahead of them by sea, but this is a bad plan.'

It was a strange discordant world he had entered. Its structure was fragmentary and hard to comprehend. The Christian subjects of the Empire were still governed by their own traditional laws, partly because the Turks provided no services of any kind for their subject populations, partly because, there being no distinction in Islam between religious and secular law, it was impossible to apply the legal system of the Empire to the inferior nations. Consequently, each religious community was regarded by the Turks as an autonomous nation (*millet*) to be governed by its own religious leaders. Thus the Patriarch of Constantinople enjoyed, by a strange irony, more power under the Ottoman Empire than he had done in the days of Christian Byzantium, and, since the Turks found it convenient to regard him as the head of the whole Orthodox community, his supremacy caused the Greeks to be resented by the other Christian peoples of the Empire.

In the seventeenth century other Greeks had also begun to acquire great influence: these were the Phanariotes, merchant families living in the vicinity of the Pharos (lighthouse) of Constantinople. They had commercial connections throughout the Mediterranean and even beyond – there were colonies of Greek merchants in both London and Moscow. These Phanariotes came to dominate the administration of the lethargic Empire; they controlled the elections to the Greek patriarchate, and being better educated and far more skilled in the complexities of the non-Muslim world than their Turkish masters, they soon came to control the Empire's diplomatic service as well. As the Ottoman Empire declined – the unsuccessful siege of Vienna in 1685 may be taken as its high watermark – the possibility presented itself that the Phanariotes might even manage to take over the whole Empire.

However, the animosity which the supremacy of the Greeks in the administration and the Church aroused among the other Christian peoples such as the Bulgars, Rumanians, Slavs and Albanians, checked their ambitions. A rift also developed between those few Greek families who benefited from the Empire and flourished accordingly, and the very much larger number who felt only the oppression of high taxation and the denial of freedom. Sporadic rebellion broke out. Many Greeks took to the mountains where they maintained themselves in brigand bands known as *klephtes*, who were more or less self-governing. In 1770 a rising in the Morea received some help from Russia, though far less than had been promised. The Tsarina

Catherine the Great, aware of Moscow's claims to be the 'third Rome', even formed plans for a restored Greek Empire at Constantinople, and was ready to supply an emperor in the person of her grandson who had been conveniently or far-sightedly named Constantine. This came to nothing, and the Tsarina's attentions were diverted, and her ambitions satisfied, by the opportunity offered to share in the partition of Poland. Nevertheless, this expression of Russia's willingness to play the role of the protector of all Orthodox Christians was to be a recurrent theme of the nineteenth century, and the territorial ambitions it revealed accounted for the often ambivalent view which British governments would take of Greek independence and the Turkish Empire.

Meanwhile the outbreak of the Revolution in France stirred even the Greeks and the other subject nations. A *klephte* chief, Theodore Kolokotronis, wrote later that 'the French Revolution and the doings of Napoleon opened the eyes of the world'; a significant, and true, observation. But even before the Revolution, the French Foreign Office had drawn up a paper setting out the case for the annexation of the Morea. In 1797 Bonaparte (as he still was) acquired French sovereignty over the Ionian islands, but two years later, after the failure of his direct assault on the Egyptian and Palestinian provinces of the Empire, these were reconquered by a Russo–Turkish fleet, operating in temporary and uneasy alliance. Under a treaty signed at Constantinople, they were then formed into a self-governing state, though still under the nominal suzerainty of the Sultan, this limited liberty being guaranteed by the Tsar. The inhabitants of this Septinsular Republic were thus the first Greeks for three-and-a-half centuries to be self-governing, at least in name. Their Republic did not last long, for in 1807 the Russians ceded their right to protect it to Napoleon in the Treaty of Tilsit, and a French occupation soon followed. Nevertheless, this little Republic was the first sign that 'Greece might yet be free', though in 1807 almost nobody contemplated a Greek state.

When Byron arrived in Greece in 1809 it was therefore premature to talk either of a Greek struggle for independence or even of the dissolution of the Ottoman Empire. Yet in truth that Empire had already reached such a condition of decadence that provincial governors could act as if they were independent princes. One such was Ali Pasha who in 1788 had become the Veli (Governor) of Epirus, and who had subsequently, by ability, cunning and unscrupulousness, established what was in all but name an independent state for himself. He was an Albanian by birth, a member of one of the strangest and most persistent national groups in Europe.

Byron responded enthusiastically to the Albanians, and no wonder.

[39]

Byron in Albanian dress

They indeed claim that they are 'the oldest people on earth' and that their language is 'the divine Pelasgic mother-tongue'. They despise the Greeks, even those of the Age of Pericles, as upstarts; the Albanian Mazzini, Girolomo da Rada, who spent all his long life in Italy, dying only in 1903, was wont to assert that Achilles, Philip of Macedon and his son Alexander, Pyrrhus, Aristotle, and the Roman Emperors Diocletian and Julian the Apostate, were one and all Albanians. Riven by internal disputes and blood-feuds – and incidentally unable even after three thousand years to decide which of five alphabets, one containing fifty letters, they should adopt – they had nevertheless offered a long resistance to the Turks under the leadership of their national hero Skanderberg. When he died in 1467 – fourteen years after the Fall of Constantinople – many fled to Italy, where Albanian villages are still to be found in Calabria, though these may date from a later migration in the eighteenth century; there is an Albanian College in Calabria at San Demetrio Albanese, and at the beginning of this century there were said to be 200,000 Albanians in Italy. There is a Via Skanderberg under the Quirinale Palace in Rome, and the Bourbon kings of the Two Sicilies had their own Albanian regiments, for these mountaineers were as great warriors as the Highlanders of Byron's own Scotland, and indeed wore a garment rather like the kilt.

Many of the Albanians who remained within the Ottoman Empire had been converted to Islam, probably on account of a natural dislike for paying taxes rather than from any religious conviction. The Grand Vizier – a title loosely translated as Prime Minister – Mohammed Kiuprili, the ablest of the Sultan's ministers in the seventeenth century, was an Albanian; he passed on his post to his son, so that, despite frequent Albanian revolts, there was a considerable and enduring Albanian presence in the central authority of the Empire.

Ali Pasha was born in 1744. He was therefore well over sixty when Byron met him. He had achieved much. He had crushed the Greek Suliotes, and consistently ignored the Sultan, on occasion putting his emissaries to death. He had intrigued with Greeks, French, Russians and British with a blithe and indiscriminate indifference. It was his aim to control the Ionian islands and their dependencies on the mainland as well as Epirus, and in 1809 he was well on his way to doing so. He was certainly a man to arouse Byron's interest, and indeed Byron would use him as the model for Haidée's irate father in *Don Juan*:

> . . . the mildest manner'd man
> That ever scuttled ship or cut a throat,
> With such true breeding of a gentleman,
> You never could divine his real thought.

VIII

Byron and Hobhouse landed at Preveza, where Hobhouse found the streets 'like dirty lanes'. A less intrepid traveller than Byron, he confessed that he would have been happy to set off home straight away: 'Properly speaking, the word comfort could not be applied to anything I ever saw out of England.' They visited the ruins of Nicepolis, the city built by the Emperor Augustus to celebrate his victory over Antony and Cleopatra in the Bay of Actium below. 'A solitary shepherd', Hobhouse wrote, 'was the tenant of Nicepolis, and the bleating of the sheep, the tinkling of the bells, and the croaking of the frogs, were the only sounds to be heard within the circuit of a city whose population had exhausted whole provinces of their inhabitants.' With this reminder – of a kind very pleasing to Byron – of the

View of Ioannina, capital of Ali Pasha, Governor of Epirus

vanity of human greatness, they proceeded over the mountains to Ioannina, the Pasha's capital.

At Ioannina they discovered that the Pasha was away with his army in Illyricum. He had, however, left orders that Byron, as an Englishman of rank, should be supplied with everything he required free of charge. They crossed the mountains in pursuit of him to Zitza (Zita) where the monastery and its setting delighted Byron:

> Monastic Zitza! from thy shady brow,
> Thou small but favour'd spot of holy ground!
> Where'er we gaze, around, above, below,
> What rainbow tints, what magic charms are found!
> Rock, river, forest, mountain, all abound
> And bluest skies that harmonize the whole:
> Beneath, the distant torrent's rushing sound
> Tells where the volumed cataract doth roll
> Between these hanging rocks, that shock, yet please, the soul.

This was precisely the sensation he had hoped to experience. The monastery is now abandoned, but a plaque on the wall records his visit, and quotes the first two lines of this stanza.

After nine days' journey, in which they were frequently delayed by 'torrents that had fallen from the mountains & intersected the roads', they reached Tepalene where the Pasha was to be found. The scene recalled to Byron Scott's description of Branksome Castle in *The Lay of the Last Minstrel*, and the feudal system. It was the first time he had seen an armed camp, and he was delighted to find it came up to expectations: 'The Albanians in their dresses (the most magnificent in the world, consisting of a long white kilt, gold-worked cloak, crimson velvet gold-laced jacket & waistcoat, silver mounted pistols & daggers), the Tartars with their high caps, the Turks in their vast pelises and turbans, the soldiers and black slaves with the horses, the former stretched in groups in an immense open gallery in front of the palace, the latter in a kind of cloister below it, two hundred steeds ready caparisoned to move in a moment, couriers entering or passing

Drawing of Albanian soldier, made by Hobhouse

[43]

out with dispatches, the kettle drums beating, boys calling the hour from the minaret of the mosque . . .' To the modern reader all this may suggest nothing so much as the script directions for a Hollywood epic, but Byron found that it 'formed a new and delightful spectacle to a stranger'. He was so enthralled by the scene that the poetical word 'steed', which he would normally have reserved for *Childe Harold*, found its way into his letter to his mother. But he could hardly be blamed. Just as Scott's poetry had led readers into unfamiliar realms of the imagination, so now Byron revelled in finding the same world spread around him. The rhetorical note so frequently struck in *Childe Harold* does not mean that the poet is insincere.

Ali Pasha, having dispensed judgment

Yet though Byron was so delighted by what he saw, his critical faculties were not annulled. He was introduced to Ali Pasha himself. His reception was more than cordial. The Pasha received him standing, which – Byron told his mother – 'was a great compliment from a Mussulman'. He then asked him to sit at his right hand, assured him that he had learned from the English minister, Captain Leake, that he was from a great family, and desired him to present his compliments to his mother. He told him that he could see he was well born 'because I had small ears, curling hair and little white hands', and expressed his approval, even his admiration, of his appearance and dress. He assured him that he would look on him as a son, and begged Byron to regard him as a father. Indeed, Byron told his mother, 'he treated me like a child, sending me almonds and sugared sherbet, fruit and sweetmeats 20 times a day'.

All this was very gratifying, especially perhaps to a young man who had encountered no such cordiality from 'people of my own rank' at home. All the same, though Byron found the Pasha very kind and possessed of 'that dignity which I find universal among the Turks', he wasn't deceived by him. He understood the nature of the attentions the Pasha paid him, and though he enjoyed the fuss, he did not allow it to cloud his judgment. He knew Ali Pasha to be 'a remorseless tyrant, as barbarous as he is successful, roasting rebels &c &c'. Flattery and affection were all very well, but Byron didn't allow himself to be fooled – evidence surely of his innate good sense. It would have been easy to let himself be overcome by the Pasha's attention, and consequently to discount what he had learned of his history and character. He was, after all, still very young, and when one thinks of the literary men of our own times who have been seduced by the charm of dictators, Byron's robust judgment is the more worthy of admiration. He was not insensible to the glamour of power, but he knew that power encouraged men to be cruel. Perhaps because he was aware of an impulse to cruelty in himself – manifest later during his marriage and in his satirical writings – he was always alert to cruelty, and quick to identify and deplore it.

Hobhouse was eager to leave in order to reach the antiquities of the Morea and Attica, but Byron found a wild and peculiar charm in the Albanians. They recalled his boyhood: 'The Albanese struck me forcibly by their resemblance to the Highlanders of Scotland. . . . Their very mountains seemed Caledonian, with a kinder climate. The kilt, though white, the spare active form; their dialect, Celtic in its sound, and their hardy habits, all carried me back to Morven' – a hill that overlooks the Dee between Ballater and Aboyne. He would have lingered, for Albania was a season out of life, but Hobhouse was impatient, and Fletcher, too, was anxious to move, being 'like all Englishmen very much dissatisfied . . . though he has suffered nothing but from cold, heat, & vermin which those who lie in cottages and cross mountains in a wild country must undergo, & of which I have equally partaken with himself, but he is not valiant, & is afraid of robbers and tempests. . . .'

They accordingly left Tepalene on 23 October, travelling back to Ioannina. They remained there for a week during which Byron began to write *Childe Harold*. He also purchased some 'very "magnifique" Albanian dresses the only expensive articles in this country they cost 50 guineas each & have so much gold they would cost in England two hundred' – one of these may now be seen in the Museum of Costume in Bath. At Ioannina Byron was introduced to the Pasha's grandsons who were 'totally unlike our lads, have painted complexions like rouged dowagers, large black eyes & features perfectly regular'. They greatly amused Byron who told his mother that the younger of them hoped to see him again: 'We are friends without understanding each other, like many other folks, though from a different cause.'

After a week they were ready to leave for the Morea. Their party had received the addition of an Albanian soldier, Vassily, given to

House at Ioannina where Byron lodged

Byron by the Pasha. He was a Christian 'with a great veneration for the church, mixed with the highest contempt for churchmen, whom he cuffed upon occasion in a most heterodox manner. Yet he never passed a Church without crossing himself:' 'Our church is holy, our priests are thieves,' he explained.

Their first start was a failure. The ship they took ran into a storm in which its captain and crew showed themselves thoroughly incapable. Fletcher despaired, seeing 'a watery grave' open before him, but Byron, being more fatalistic, wrapped himself in his Albanian cloak and lay down on the deck, an action which suggests that the storm cannot in fact have been too severe. However, it was sufficient to deter them, and instead of trusting to the sea and Greek seamanship again, they acquired a guard of fifty soldiers and took the overland route through the passes of Acarnania and Aetolia to Missolonghi. The guard was necessary for the country was infested with brigands, a role indeed which most of their soldiers had played themselves, and were quite ready, should circumstances suit, to play again.

It was a journey that fired his imagination. No wonder. He was traversing some of the wildest and most dangerous country in Europe, where every crag, every glen, had a story to tell. 'It was a world,' Patrick Leigh Fermor, who of all modern English writers has most magically evoked the spirit of Greece, and whose exploits in Crete during World War II gave him himself a Byronic aura, has written in *Roumeli*, 'of strife, ambush, revenge, burning villages, massacre, impaling and severed heads.' They had passed the precipice of Zalongo where Suliote women fleeing Ali Pasha's Muslim Albanians, who had already burned their villages, threw themselves over the cliffs rather than be taken; now, after their shipwreck on 'Suli's shaggy shore', he faced a journey through a mountain-land where:

> Combined marauders half-way barred egress,
> And wasted far and near with glaive and brand.

Nothing could be more satisfactory, He had achieved what any young Romantic must desire; he had contrived to make the picturesque stride out of its frame and come to life.

'This part of Greece', Patrick Leigh Fermor tells us in *Roumeli*, 'was the scene of some of the most dramatic events in history and myth; names and reminders of the great days of ancient Greece were everywhere; above all, the Greeks still lived here. He was able to discern, among the ruins, in the seeming docility of the plainsmen and in the fierceness of the mountaineers, compelling messages of magnificence and servitude and the hint of future resurrection; a resurrec-

[47]

View of the Vikos Gorge, Pindus Mountains

tion which was to happen sooner and affect him more than he can ever have thought.'

It is not too much to say that this journey from Ioannina to the Morea committed Byron to Greece. The seed of his last adventure, the most noble act of his life, was sown.

The first hint of the resurrection was offered almost as soon as he had crossed the mountains. They stayed for a few days with Andreas Londos, Governor under Ali's son, Veli Pasha, of the district lying along the south side of the Gulf of Corinth. Londos was a Greek, and seemed at first only an agreeably lively and even frivolous host. Then, one evening, the name of Constantine Rhiga was mentioned. He had been one of the first to whom the name of Greek Nationalist might be applied; he had founded a society called the Philike Hetairia, written a Greek version of the 'Marseillaise' and been executed by the Turks in 1798. Now, at the sound of his name, Hobhouse recounts, Londos leapt to his feet and 'repeated the name of the patriot with a thousand passionate exclamations, the tears streaming down his cheeks'. A dozen years later Londos would be a leader in the Greek War of Independence. Over the next weeks Byron would muse on the matter. The thought of the Greeks' servitude occupied him, and found expression in four stanzas of *Childe Harold*.

In all save form alone how changed! and who
That marks the fire still sparkling in each eye,
Who would but deem their bosoms burned anew
With thy unquenched beam, lost Liberty!
And many dream withal the hour is nigh
That gives them back their fathers' heritage:
For foreign arms and aid they fondly sigh,
Nor solely dare encounter hostile rage,
Or tear their name defiled from Slavery's mournful page.

But, he reflected,

Hereditary bondsmen! know ye not
Who would be free themselves must strike the blow?

It was a lesson the Greeks had not yet learned, as some looked to France, others to Russia, and others still to Britain, for assistance. Liberty, therefore, it seemed to Byron, remained no more than an empty aspiration, an airy abstraction. Nevertheless, in Londos's response to the name of the patriot Rhiga, he had seen the possibility of Greek resistance. The idea that he might help would remain at the back of his mind till the Greeks themselves took the first decisive steps.

They remained at Patras for two weeks, and then set off for Athens. In order to visit Delphi they crossed the Gulf of Corinth again on 14 December and arrived there the following day. Few modern tourists omit Delphi; it is the best-known and most-visited of classical sites. Even today, overrun as it is by camera-clicking foreigners, the narrow street of the modern town thronged with buses and cars, it can make an astonishing and profound impression. In Byron's time there was both less to see, and more. The theatre and most of the temples had not been excavated, and the scene was probably closer to that described by the medieval geographer Pausanias almost a thousand years before than to that which confronts the twentieth-century visitor. But if there was less to see, there was also less to disturb the mood. They were able to walk in empty olive groves, to drink from the Castalian Spring, to watch eagles soaring above Mount Parnassus, and to scratch their names on a column that stood at the entrance to a monastery on the site of the old Gymnasium. 'Wandering slow by Delphi's sacred side', he brooded on 'the remnants of thy Splendour past.' Byron was being educated in feeling, and Delphi, though in some ways disappointing, was part of the lesson:

And yet how lovely in thine age of woe,
Land of lost Gods and godlike men, art thou.

[49]

Delphi, as Byron saw it, before the excavations

General view of Athens, no more than an overgrown village, drawn by Hobhouse

They reached Athens, by way of Thebes, on Christmas Day. Byron was delighted by his first view of the city from a pine-covered hill: 'the plain of Athens, Pentelicus, Hymettus, the Aegean and the Acropolis, burst upon the eye at once; in my opinion, a more glorious prospect even than Cintra'.

The Athens which Byron knew bore almost no resemblance to the modern city. The population, a mixture of Greeks, Turks and Albanians, amounted to no more than 10,000 folk. It was an over-grown village, some 1200 houses huddled around the north and west sides of the Acropolis, surrounded by a medieval wall, beyond which a few farmhouses and villas straggled over the plain. Its atmosphere was one of decay, for the visitor could not fail to be oppressed by the contrast between its great past and its ignoble present. The city of free men, which had defied the mighty Persian Empire, was now subject to a dull despotism; its moral decay was as evident as its physical deterioration. Yet at the same time, the very contrast between past and present – and the small scale of the modern town, brought the splendour of antiquity into sharper and more immediate life than the twentieth-century tourist can hope to experience. The reality of the ancient world was inescapable, and it had not yet become a museum.

They lodged under the shadow of the Acropolis in a house owned by the widow of the British Vice-Consul. She was called Tarsia Macri, and she had three beautiful daughters, Mariana, Katinka and Teresa, all below the age of fifteen. Byron flirted with all three, especially Teresa who, though she was only twelve, was in Hobhouse's view, 'quite *nubila*'. They would remain in the house three months, and when they left Byron wrote one of his tenderest lyrics:

Maid of Athens, ere we part,
Give, oh give me back my heart!
Or, since that has left my breast,
Keep it now, and take the rest!

The Parthenon, 1826, in use as a Turkish arsenal

It was a Romantic, but chaste, attachment; the presence of Teresa's mother ensured that, at this stage anyway.

It was some time before they could visit the Acropolis itself, for it was used as an arsenal and munitions store by the Turks – much damage was to be done to the Parthenon by an explosion in 1827 – and the permission of the city's governor was required. Till this could be obtained, they would ride out every morning, either towards Eleusis, from where they could gaze to Salamis, where the Athenians had destroyed the Persian fleet, and to Aegina; or up Hymettus to the monastery of Katerina; or north to Pentelicus, where they could view the abandoned quarries which had supplied the marble for the Parthenon. Everywhere they went, Hobhouse was busy with map, compass and notebook, for he took his intention of writing an account of their travels very seriously; Byron, on the other hand, was happier mooning around: his impressions would be distilled in verse.

On 8 January they were at last permitted to visit the Acropolis. They were accompanied by a Neapolitan painter Giovanni Batista Lusieri; he was employed by Lord Elgin, who had, some seven years earlier while British Ambassador at Constantinople, received permission first to copy, then to remove, some of the marbles from the Parthenon. Byron's first reaction to the Parthenon – 'very like the Mansion House' he said – shocked Hobhouse, who sometimes failed to see his friend's jokes; but his true feelings were different. Byron, whose interest in the visual arts was not great, had thought little of the marbles when they had been put on display in a museum in Park Lane. Now, however, seeing the companion pieces in their proper place, he changed his mind. His new impulse could only loosely be termed aesthetic; it was the associations of the frieze and statues which moved him, and convinced him that Elgin had been guilty of deplorable vandalism:

> Cold as the crags upon his native coast,
> His mind as barren and his heart as hard,
> Is he whose head conceived, whose hand prepared,
> Aught to displace Athena's poor remains . . .

So much for Lord Elgin, 'the last, the worst, dull spoiler'. When Hobhouse objected that the removal of the marbles to London would benefit 'an infinitely greater number of rising architects and sculptors', Byron would have none of his sophistical argument: he mocked and deplored 'the robbery of ruins from Athens, to instruct the English in sculpture (who are as capable of sculpture as the Egyptians are of skating)'.

The Temple of Poseidon at Cape Sounion, where Byron carved his name on a column

There were numerous excursions in the following weeks. They rode to Cape Sounion on 23 January, the day after Byron's twenty-second birthday, and to Marathon, the scene of the great battle in which the Persians had been defeated by Miltiades in 490 BC. As usual Hobhouse busied himself with the details, Byron imbibed the mood. His memories would not find their way into *Childe Harold*, but, years later into a heroic song for Greece embedded in *Don Juan*:

> The mountains look on Marathon –
>   And Marathon looks on the sea;
> And musing there an hour alone,
>   I dream'd that Greece might still be free;
> For standing on the Persians' grave,
> I could not deem myself a slave . . .
>
> Place me on Sunium's marbled steep,
>   Where nothing, save the waves and I,
> May hear our mutual murmurs sweep;
>   There, swan-like, let me sing and die:
> A land of slaves shall ne'er be mine –
> Dash down yon cup of Samian wine!

Greece now has three summer visitors for every one of its inhabitants. It is impossible in summer for anyone to find himself alone at Sounion or Marathon. Athens is a brisk and ugly commercial city; anywhere in its vicinity it is hard to recapture how it seemed to Byron. The freshness has gone, and the melancholy too. Yet, in reading *Childe Harold* and his letters, it is possible to understand how it came on him as a revelation. And even now the light, the sea, the harsh outlines of the landscape remain the same, reminding one of primal realities, which serve to cut through our northern sentimentality and cant. Greece for Byron was first of all a liberating and elucidatory experience. It taught him to feel an impatience with the hypocritical conventions of English society. 'I like the Greeks', he told Henry Drury, 'who are plausible rascals, with all the Turkish vices without their courage – However some are brave and all are beautiful, very much resembling the busts of Alcibiades, the women not quite so handsome.'

IX

It had never been their intention to remain in Greece, and with the spring they were ready to move again. All his life Byron was distinguished equally by the ease with which he settled himself into an unaccustomed way of life, and the boredom and impatience with it which subsequently overtook him. So, on 5 March 1810, they sailed on the British sloop-of-war *Pylades*, and reached Smyrna in Asia Minor three days later. Smyrna (modern Izmir) was the main point of commercial contact between Europe and Asia. Kinglake thought it could be called 'the chief town and capital of the Grecian race, against which you will be cautioned so carefully as soon as you touch the Levant'. It remained so till the Greco–Turkish War of 1920–22 when it was sacked and looted, and all the Greeks who were unable to escape were massacred. But Byron regarded the town as a staging-post. They rode out to Ephesus to view the ruins, Hobhouse enthusiastic, but Byron merely muttering that 'St Paul need not trouble himself to epistolize the present brood of Ephesians', and was more impressed by the 'mixed and mournful sound' of jackals in the deserted city.

More satisfying however, were visits to the plains of Troy. The Troad was 'a fine field for conjecture and Snipe-shooting, and a good sportsman and an ingenious scholar may exercise their feet and faculties to great advantage on the spot, or if they prefer riding lose their way (as I did) in a cursed quagmire of the Scamander who wriggles about as if the Dardan maidens still offered their wonted tribute. The only vestige of Troy, or her destroyers, are the barrows supposed to contain the carcases of Achilles, Antilochous, Ajax &c but Mt Ida is still in high feather, though the Shepherds now are not much like Ganymede.'

This was frivolous enough – rather in Kinglake's later mode – but the scene had affected him more deeply than he was ready to confess to Drury. Years later, brooding in a Ravenna January, in weather 'so humid and impracticable, that London, in its most oppressive fogs, were a summer-bower to this mist and sirocco,' his mind was drawn back to Troy by an expression of the poet Thomas Campbell's which he had 'chanced upon': 'Speaking of Collins, he says that "no reader cares any more about the *characteristic manners* of his Eclogues than about the authenticity of the Tale of Troy." 'Tis false – we *do* care about "the authenticity of the tale of Troy". I have stood upon that plain *daily*, for more than a month, in 1810; and, if any thing diminished by pleasure, it was that the blackguard Bryant had impugned its veracity.' (In a *Dissertation concerning the war of Troy, and the expedition of the Grecians as described by Homer; showing that no such expedition was ever undertaken, and that no such city as Phrygia existed*, published in 1796.) 'It is true that I had read *Homer Travestied* (the first twelve books) because Hobhouse and others bored me with their learned localities, and I love quizzing. But I still venerated the grand original as the truth of *history* (in the material *facts*) and of *place*. Otherwise, it would have given me no delight. Who will persuade me, when I reclined upon a mighty tomb, that it did not contain a hero? – its very magnitude proved this. Men do not labour over the ignoble and petty dead – and why should not the *dead* be Homer's *dead*.' The warmth of feeling is evident.

At Smyrna he continued to work on *Childe Harold*, and indeed finished the second canto, though he protested in a letter to his mother that 'the further I go the more my laziness increases,' and to Francis Hodgson, his poetical cousin, muttered that 'Hobhouse rhymes and journalizes; I stare and do nothing.' It wasn't true, but, for all his veneration for the facts of antiquity, Byron preferred to absorb impressions, rather than scurry around like his friend noting and comparing details.

On 11 April they sailed in the brig *Salsette* for Constantinople. They were delayed by contrary winds at the mouth of the Dardanelles – the ancient Hellespont; and Byron, with one of the ship's lieutenants, by name Ekenhead, resolved to emulate the famous Leander who had nightly swum the straits to meet his mistress Hero. Their first attempt was a failure but on 3 May they tried again, and Hobhouse noted in his diary, 'Byron and Ekenhead . . . now swimming across the Hellespont – Ovid's *Hero and Leander* open before me.' 'The total distance E

Istanbul (Constantinople) from the sea

and I swam,' Byron wrote, 'was more than 4 miles the current very strong and cold . . . we were not fatigued, but a little chilled; did it with little difficulty.' General Wolfe, having recited Gray's 'Elegy in a country churchyard' as he sailed up the St Lawrence river to attack Quebec, reputedly said that he would rather have written that poem than take the city; Byron by contrast was probably prouder of having swum the Hellespont than of the writing of *Childe Harold*. He referred to it constantly. All his correspondents were told of the feat. To Henry Drury, he said that 'the current renders it hazardous, so much so, that I doubt whether Leander's conjugal powers must not have been exhausted in his passage to Paradise'. He told his mother that he had swum from Sestos to Abydos 'in imitation of Monsieur Leander whose story you no doubt know too well for me to add anything on the subject except that I crossed the Hellespont without so good a motive for the undertaking'. He recalled the swim again in *Don Juan*: than whom:

> A better swimmer you could scarce see ever,
>   He could, perhaps, have pass'd the Hellespont,
> As once (a feat on which ourselves we prided)
> Leander, Mr Ekenhead, and I did.

The next stop was Constantinople. They anchored between the Seven Towers and the Seraglio on 13 May, and landed the next day.

[57]

Two dogs were gnawing a dead body under the walls of the Sultan's palace; a nice image of the moribund and deplorable empire. Byron was already disillusioned by the Turks, who lacked the vivacity of the Greeks, but he wished to see the Sultan, 'the last of the Ottoman race'. As for Constantinople itself, he couldn't be bothered to describe it: 'You have Gibbon's description, very correct as far as I have seen,' he told Hodgson; 'I refer you for descriptions to the various travellers who have scribbled on the subject' was Hanson's portion; 'Of Constantinople you have of course read fifty descriptions by sundry travellers, which are in general so correct that I have nothing to add on the subject,' he informed his mother.

The truth was he was bored. He had had enough for the moment of Hobhouse. He had lost the sense of adventure and freedom which he had found in Albania and Greece. He disliked the evidence of Turkish cruelty and indifference to human life. He was dismayed to find himself regarded as of no particular consequence, and gave a foolish display of pique, when, having been invited by the British Minister Robert Adair to join an official procession, he found he would have to march behind Stratford Canning, the Secretary to the Embassy.

Istanbul from the land: Byron loved riding by the triple walls

There were compensations. He enjoyed riding out of the city, and found 'the ride by the walls of the city on the land side . . . beautiful, imagine, four miles of immense triple battlements covered with Ivy, surmounted with 218 towers, and on the other side of the road Turkish burying grounds (the loveliest spots on earth)'. That was fine enough, and he had 'never beheld a work of Nature or Art, which yielded an impression like the prospect on each side, from the Seven Towers to the End of the Golden Horn'. Yet, not even Romantic poets can live on beautiful views, and Byron was bored.

The Turks were 'sensible people' but no better than the English:'I see not much difference between ourselves & the Turks, save that we have foreskins and they none, that they have long dresses and we short, and that we talk much and they little – In England the vices in fashion are whoring and drinking, in Turkey, Sodomy and smoking, we prefer a girl and a bottle, they a pipe and pathic.' And what was the point of travelling if you came to that sort of conclusion? Perhaps the cause of his boredom was simply that he was not in love with anyone. At any rate, he was happy enough to quit Constantinople, though pleased to have been there.

X

He parted from Hobhouse on 17 July. 'Took leave,' Hobhouse noted, *'non sine lacrymis*, of this singular young person, on a little stone terrace at the end of the bay, dividing with him a little nosegay of flowers.' There was sentiment in their parting, but Byron was glad to be rid of his friend, even though it was not long before he was writing 'you cannot conceive what a delightful companion you are now you are gone'. In fact, both Byron and Hobhouse had managed well enough. There are few tests of friendship greater than a long journey together, and, considering Byron's moodiness and Hobhouse's capacity to be solidly boring, the survival of their friendship does them both credit. Hobhouse had moments when he was jealous of both Matthews and Scrope Davies; but he had established memories in common with Byron of which nothing could rob him, and, in doing so, he had stolen a march on them.

Without Hobhouse's tiresome enthusiasm for the detailed examination of sites of antiquarian interest, Byron would have been content to be by himself, and indolent. However, he was at once seized on by the Marquess of Sligo – another Old Harrovian – who was touring the Aegean in 'a brig with 50 men that wont work, 12 guns that refuse to go off, and sails that have cut every wind except a contrary one', and who at once pressed him to be his companion on a tour of the Morea. Byron had intended returning there anyway, and was too good-natured to decline the invitation, even though he was, as he told Hobhouse, 'heartily disgusted with travelling in company'.

The tour was comic. It was very hot (Byron's thermometer registered 125°), and two of the cavalcade, which consisted of twenty-nine in all, were confined in leather breeches. Poor Fletcher, too, 'with his usual acuteness contrived at Megara to ram his damned clumsy foot into a boiling teakettle', and they had to halt every half hour to permit the painter in the Marquess's employ to produce 'what he himself termed a "bellissimo sketche"'. However, they soon separated, Byron going on to Patras to collect mail awaiting him at the address of the British Vice-Consul Strané.

Stopping on the way at Vostitzia, where he and Hobhouse had stayed the previous December with the Governor Andreas Londos, he took a pretty Greek boy, Eustathios Georgiou, into his suite, and, one supposes, his bed. They had met in December and Byron had suggested that the boy join him in Athens. He had been ill, however, and unable to do so. Absence had made his heart grow fonder and he now greeted Byron with protestations of undying love. If Byron had been looking forward to the reunion, he was soon disillusioned: the boy was absurdly jealous and absurdly affected. The affectations could amuse Byron: 'I found the dear soul upon horseback, clothed very sparsely in Greek Garments, with those ambrosial curls hanging down his amiable back, and to my utter astonishment, and the great abomination of Fletcher, a parasol in his hand to save himself from the heat.' On the other hand, 'I think I never took so much pains to please anyone, or succeeded so ill.' Eustathios made the great error of fussing Byron – the one thing that was sure to bring any affair to an abrupt end. He soon threatened to send the boy back home. The prospect of parting induced 'as many kisses as would have sufficed for a boarding school, and embraces enough to have ruined the character of any county in England, besides tears (not on my part) and expressions of "Tenerezza" to a vast amount'.

The return to his father was therefore postponed, but not for long. Meanwhile Byron took him to Tripolitza where Veli Pasha, Ali's son, was to be found. Veli greeted Byron with even less restraint than his father had done – perhaps the presence of Eustathios in Byron's suite encouraged him to display his tastes openly. He told Byron he wished all the old men to go to his father and the young men to come to him: 'Vecchio con Vecchio, Giovane con Giovane'; and that he was 'a brave young man and a beautiful boy'. His 'awkward manner of throwing his arm around one's waist, and squeezing one's hand in public' was embarrassing, all the more so because the amorous Pasha had a beard down to his middle. He was – fortunately perhaps – off to campaign, but pressed Byron to join him at Larissa; Byron returned an equivocal answer. He had had enough of these amiable tyrants, and though amused by their attentions, also found his position disagreeably ridiculous.

He was soon back in Athens. He had moved from the Macri house, because the widow seemed to have become 'mad enough to suppose imagine I was going to marry the girl; but I have better amusements'. Eustathios had been one of these. There was soon another. This was a boy called Nicolo Giraud. He was fifteen; his sister was married to the painter Lusieri; and he was half-Greek, half-French; more important he was devoted to Byron. They had met before Byron left for Constantinople and he had accompanied him on several expeditions. Now Byron took him into his service, and with him he was able to recapture the mood which he had shared with his Harrow favourites and with Edleston. It was a cooler mood perhaps, for Byron was on the point of outgrowing his adolescence. Moreover, if Nicolo pleased him, and if love for a boy seemed as natural in Plato's city as it had done at Harrow, Byron could not escape a nagging Calvinist sense of sin and an awareness of how his affair would be viewed by all but a few

Franciscan monastery in Athens where Byron lodged on his second visit to the city

[61]

friends in England. His letters to Hobhouse drop innumerable hints; they play with naughtiness, and yet they always strike a light-hearted note, making it clear that he is not taking the affair too seriously and that Nicolo is more enamoured than he is. It was Nicolo who 'concluded that it was proper for us not only to live but "morire insieme" [to die together]'; Byron hoped to avoid the latter, 'as much of the former as he pleases'. Nevertheless, his classical hints – quoting Horace, he wrote of 'Lycum nigris oculis, nigroque crine decorum' [Lycus beautiful with black eyes and black hair] – were intended to leave Hobhouse in no doubt. So when, years later, Moore wrote that it was Byron's fondness for solitude which caused him at last to grow weary of Hobhouse's company, Hobhouse scribbled the note: 'On what authority does Tom say this? He has not the remotest grasp of the real reason which induced Lord Byron to prefer having no Englishman immediately and constantly near him.' It was typical of Hobhouse's brand of aristocratic radicalism that he should have forgotten, or have chosen to ignore, the presence of Fletcher.

Nicolo was a pupil at a school for the sons of Franks, as Western Europeans were known, which was situated in a Capuchin monastery at the foot of the Acropolis. Since it also served as a hotel for travellers, Byron was able to take up residence there too. He enjoyed a season of delightful irresponsibility. There were half a dozen boys living in the monastery and they competed for his favour – it was rather like his last year at Harrow all over again, with the addition of the delicious freedom that came from being out of England. He fell easily – as he always did – into an habitual way of life. He often said that if he stopped in one place for six days, he would stay six months. This was by no means true; yet for a person of wandering and often apparently disordered life, Byron was remarkable for the ease with which he formed habits. In the morning he studied Italian and Modern Greek, joked with the Abbot and the boys, encouraged the laundresses to tease Fletcher, and was merry in a romping schoolboyish way. In the afternoon he would ride to the Piraeus and swim, observing that 'it is a curious thing that the Turks when they bathe wear their lower garments as your humble servant always doth, but the Greeks not . . .'; however, he added, 'questo Giovane [Nicolo] è vergogno [is ashamed]', which presumably means that he followed Byron's example.

Returning from this excursion one day, he had an adventure which was to find its way into one of his most successful poems, *The Giaour*. They encountered a troop of soldiers sent by the Voivode (Governor) of Athens to execute a girl who had been guilty of illicit love. She had been sewn into a sack and was to be cast into the sea. She was a Turkish girl whom Byron knew, though it is impossible to say how well, and he was horrified by her sentence. Already understanding how things were arranged in the East, he persuaded the soldiers to delay execution till he had seen their master. He then bribed the Voivode to surrender the girl to him and sent her secretly to Thebes. This is the story as related by Lord Sligo, though he was not in Athens at the time, and therefore was only reporting what he had been told; one part of the adventure, Byron later said, was 'more singular than any of the Giaour's'. In his diary, of 5 December 1813, when the poem was published, he wrote: 'to describe the *feelings* of that situation were *impossible* – it is *icy* even to recollect them.' The horror the incident inspired may have been no more than a natural response to what by any standards was an appalling thing to happen upon. It doesn't require much imagination to realize how coming upon such a scene would affect a young man of Byron's nervous sensibility. It was a story that would prey on his mind. Years later, when he was in Switzerland with the Shelleys and Claire Clairmont, and they spent the evenings frightening each other with ghost stories – one of which was the first version of *Frankenstein* – he thrilled and horrified his audience by relating how, while living at Constantinople, he had had an unfaithful concubine sewn up in a sack and thrown into the Bosphorus. It was characteristic of Byron that he should transform a story in which he had played a humane and honourable part into one in which he was a dark and guilty figure. It is tempting to find a psychological explanation for this in the surmise that the Turkish girl whom he saved in Athens had indeed been his mistress, and that it was on account of her affair with the infidel nobleman that she was sentenced to this ghastly death. There is however no evidence to support such a speculation, and the wretched girl's experience was horrible enough to have made an indelible impression on Byron's mind. As for his eagerness to cast himself in the role of villain for the Shelleys and Claire, that was in keeping with his occasional readiness to play the hero of his verse; it was, after all, just the sort of crime with which he might have saddled the poor Childe.

For the most part these months that were left to him in Greece were happy. Besides the charm of the boys' company at the monastery and the loving companionship of Nicolo, 'I had a number of Greek and Turkish women, and I believe the rest of the English were equally lucky, for we were all *clapped*.' There might be too many English, as he complained, but most were agreeable enough. The foreign community in Athens was small, and, as usual when he became well acquainted with people, Byron dropped his affectations and enjoyed company. There was always a gap between the Byron his friends knew and the chilly, withdrawn and superior being who presented himself to strangers; but he had been long enough in Athens to feel no need to be on his guard. He had friendly acquaintances among the Greek and Turkish officials too: 'the Voivode and the Mufti of Thebes [a sort of Mussulman Bishop] supped here and made themselves beastly with raw rum, and the Padre of the Convent being drunk as we, my *Attic* feast went off with great *éclat*'.

A less agreeable acquaintance was Lady Hester Stanhope. Lady Hester, herself eccentric to the point of absurdity, and, in the opinion of many, a good way beyond, was the niece of William Pitt – not a relationship to commend her to Byron. She had acted as her uncle's housekeeper in Downing Street, and, feeling her status diminished by

Lady Hester Stanhope

his death, had set herself up as a traveller, and would soon pose as the great authority on the Orient. At the time of their meeting she was, however, just beginning her Eastern travels, which by her own account, as given thirty years later to Kinglake, would result in her 'exercising something like sovereignty among the wandering tribes' of Bedouin. She would in time become mistress of astrology and all occult arts, and would settle in a splendid but half-ruined convent in the Lebanon, guarded by her private corps of Albanians. She was perfectly ridiculous, as the wholly self-obsessed usually are.

She did not take to Byron. 'One time he was mopish and nobody must speak to him; another, he was for being jocular with everyone. Then he was a sort of Don Quixote, fighting with the police for a woman of the town; and then he wanted to make himself something great. . . .' She told Kinglake that she had been 'vastly amused at his little affectations; he had picked up a few sentences of the Romaic, with which he affected to give orders to his Greek servant'. Kinglake couldn't 'tell whether Lady Hester's imitation of the bard was at all close, but it was amusing; she attributed to him a curiously cox-combical lisp' – unrecorded by others. Since Byron had been in Greece for almost a year when they met, had had Greek or Albanian servants throughout that time, and had studied the Romaic formally too, it is probable that his mastery of the tongue was rather greater than the lady's, who had just arrived there. His own judgment of her was equally dismissive: he found 'nothing different from other she things, except a great disregard of received notions in her conversation as well as conduct. I don't know', he added, 'whether this will recommend her to our sex, but I'm sure it won't to her own.'

He was more interested in the increasing confusion of the Empire: 'Ali Pasha is in a scrape, Ibrahim Pasha and the Pasha of Scutari have come down upon him with 20,000 Gegdes and Albanians, retaken Berat and threaten Tepaleen, Adam Bey [Ali Pasha's nephew] is dead, Veli Pasha was on his way to the Danube, but has gone off suddenly to Ioannina, and all Albania is in an uproar – The Mountains we crossed last year –' he told Hobhouse, 'are the scene of warfare, and there is nothing but carnage and cutting of throats.' He would have accepted Veli Pasha's invitation to join him at Larissa and see his army, but for this 'rupture with Ibrahim'. 'Sultan Mahmout is in a phrenzy because Veli has not joined his army, we have a report here that the Russians have beaten the Turks and taken Muchtar Pasha [Ali Pasha's eldest son] prisoner, but it is a Greek Bazar rumour, and not to be believed.'

With his mind full of these matters, which were indeed an indication of the weakness of the Empire which would so slowly, painfully, disintegrate over the next century, he made some notes for *Childe*

Harold in which he offered an analysis of the state of Greece and the prospects for Greek independence. 'It seems to me,' he wrote, 'rather hard to declare so positively and pertinaciously, as almost everybody has declared, that the Greeks, because they are very bad, will never be better.' Their vices were the consequence of centuries of misgovernment, so that at present, 'like the Catholics in Ireland and the Jews everywhere' they were victims of history, who 'suffered all the moral and physical ills that can afflict humanity'. This was a mature perception for a young man of twenty-three. His recognition that nations which have suffered under alien, tyrannous and incompetent rule for generations cannot be expected to exhibit the qualities possessed by a free people did credit to his understanding. It would be echoed later by Lord Palmerston, the Liberal guide of Britain's foreign policy over thirty years, when he answered the objection that the Greeks were not yet fit for a Constitution with the argument that the only way to make them so fit was to give them one.

Yet Byron was already aware of the enormous difficulties a Greek renaissance faced. This was why he concluded that 'the interposition of foreigners alone can emancipate Greece'. The Greeks themselves were divided – naturally enough, for the Ottoman system of rule gave power to selected members of the subject races. The attitude of the Church for instance to the independence movement was ambiguous; under the Empire the Patriarch of Constantinople was responsible for all Orthodox Christians, not merely Greeks. A Greek national state would therefore deprive him of power. In 1789 a work had been published in Constantinople which was known as the *Paternal teaching* and which was probably written by the Future Patriarch Grigorius V. It praised the Sultan as the protector of Christianity and attacked ideas of revolution. (Despite this Grigorius would himself be put to death by the Turks in 1821 after the first outbreak of revolt.) Many of the Greek intellectuals, too, who were mostly living abroad, deprecated the use of force. They saw education as the means of Greek development, though it was hard to see how this could be effective in practice against a despotism that had no conception of representative government. Then the Phanariote families in Constantinople itself had no time for the idea of an independent Greece; like the Patriarch they already enjoyed real power within the Empire, and their ambitions were directed rather to the extension of that power and influence in the existing multi-national state rather than to the creation of a national one. There were exceptions, of course, as also among the ecclesiastics; Prince Alexander Mavrocordatos, who later became a friend of Byron in Italy was one; so was Bishop Ignatios of Arta, but he, too, had to flee to Italy. Moreover, the exceptions merely underlined the way in

Byron in dressing gown

which divided purposes would render the achievement of a Greek national unity difficult.

Finally, many landowners and village headmen – the *cogia bashis* – who had been granted administrative authority and personal privileges under the regime, were naturally disinclined to favour any movement which threatened their position. The fact was that the Turkish Empire over the Greeks had lasted a long time, and as a natural consequence, many groups and individuals had a vested interest in its survival. Those who were opposed to the Empire were the *klephtes* – semi-independent brigand chiefs, the merchants who had wider economic interests and who were anyway often also privateers, and the idealistic members of the *Philiki Hetairia*, or 'Friendly Society', most of whom lived in exile. Clearly co-operation between these diverse groups would be difficult.

Byron appreciated this even then – he would come to do so still more when he returned, committed to the cause of Greek independence. He appreciated, and understood, why the Greeks might seem – might even be – morally degenerate: 'Their life is a struggle against truth; they are vicious in their own defence.' They had lived for generations under a regime which regarded them as 'cattle'. They had no civil code, no concept of civic virtue, and it was impossible that they should have.

Byron's analysis of the state of Greece and the Greeks is not only interesting in itself; it is important evidence in any attempt to understand him and the course of his life. He was wayward, passionate, easily bored and diverted, but in fundamentals consistent. And Greece and his Greek experience were fundamentals. His return there in 1823 has too often and too facilely been accounted for in terms of his personal dissatisfaction, as an act of self-therapy. Action would resolve the doubts and disillusion into which he had sunk; it might help to restore his reputation in England; and so forth. These elements were certainly present. Men and women rarely act from any single impulse. Byron's was a complicated nature, and one which puzzled him himself. Yet it is equally clear that he returned to Greece for other reasons. A sense of duty was one. He had committed himself, in his imagination, to the Greek cause, and that committal was absolute. Idealism was present, too. Greece represented for him the best he had known. It was, of course, corrupted and deformed by history and circumstance, but it was still something good. It was not simply that he had been happier in Greece than anywhere else, not simply that it stood in his memory for the delightful freedom of youth, for that freedom was not peculiarly personal. Greece had made him what Mazzini saw he was: an apostle of liberty:

[68]

> The mountains look on Marathon –
>> And Marathon looks on the sea;
> And musing there an hour alone,
>> I dream'd that Greece might still be free;
> For standing on the Persians' grave,
> I could not deem myself a slave . . .

These lines, among the most famous he ever wrote, were penned not in Greece, but in Venice, at a time when he seemed, even to friendly observers, to be sunk in the utmost self-indulgence. (He was actually working at the height of his powers, and the verses, attributed to an imaginary poet of modern Greece, are in the third canto of *Don Juan*, perhaps in all that marvellous poem the one which most surely shows him at the zenith of his genius.)

XI

In the winter of 1811–12 he contemplated further travels, and went so far as to obtain permission to visit Syria and Egypt. Money, however, was short, Hanson being apparently unable to send any, and coming up instead with proposals that Newstead should be sold. Byron would have none of it. Newstead, he told his mother, was his 'only tie to England'. If it had to be sold, then he would live abroad. 'Competence in your country is ample Wealth in the East such is the difference in the value of money & the abundance of the necessaries of life, & I feel myself so much a citizen of the world, that the spot where I can enjoy a delicious climate, & every luxury at a less expense than a common college life in England, will always be a country to me, and such are in fact the shores of the Archipelago. – This then is the alternative, if I preserve Newstead, I return, if I sell it, I stay away.'

It was an ultimatum of sorts, but a whimsical half-hearted one. There was anyway no immediate prospect of selling Newstead, and Hanson was in fact busy trying to raise a purchaser for the embarrassed Lancashire estate, Rochdale. Equally, however, no remittances arrived, and Byron's enthusiasm for further travel evaporated. He was writing again, a satire called *Hints from Horace* of which he was inordinately and unjustly proud, and a further attack on Lord Elgin, *The Curse of Minerva*, which was at least vigorous. This activity prompted or revived his wider literary ambitions, and he suggested to Hobhouse that they should found a review or magazine – 'some respectable novelty, which I recommend & leave to your brilliant considerations'. This notion, first mooted in March, stayed with him at least till July, when he was suggesting that Hobhouse should be editor, 'as you have more taste and diligence than either Matthews or myself'. It withered in the unhappy turmoil of his return to England when first his mother and then Matthews died within a few days of each other. Nevertheless, like many literary men, Byron continued to hanker, from time to time at least, for a magazine in which he could propagate his own views.

Meanwhile, the last weeks in Athens passed pleasantly, feeding upon woodcock and red mullet every day, riding out on one of his three horses to the Piraeus, Phalerum, or Turcolimano, taking Turkish baths – 'an immense luxury to me' – dining with the Athenian Franks, and consorting with Greek and Turkish women. Life was good and even his embarrassments – and the clap he got from the women – seemed tolerable. After all, his mother told him that his property was 'estimated at above a hundred thousand pounds, even after all my debts etc are paid off – And yet I am embarrassed and do not know where to raise a Shilling.' It was a rum world, but despite his immediate impecuniosity, he reassured Hobhouse that neither he nor his father need trouble themselves to repay the money which Byron had lent his friend to finance his share of their travels 'till you are in a state to pay it as easily as so many shillings'. This was generous for Hobhouse owed him more than £800.

At last the day of departure arrived. His Albanian servants wept, he was tempted to bring Teresa Macri with him, but, he told Hobhouse, desisted when her mother fixed the price at £600. Nicolo Giraud, however, would accompany him as far as Malta where Byron intended to establish him in school. He was at the time probably fonder of Nicolo than of anyone else, besides owing him 'some knowledge of the Italian & Romaic languages', but, if he was tempted to bring him to England, he must have seen that it wouldn't do. Perhaps his affection had cooled; perhaps the boy's parents were unwilling that he should travel further. Nicolo remained devoted to him, and was still writing letters protesting his fidelity for at least three years. And Byron's feeling may be measured by the fact that when he came to draw up his will in August 1811, after his mother's death, he left Nicolo £7,000 'to be paid from the sale of such parts of Rochdale, Newstead or elsewhere, as may enable the said Nicolo Giraud to receive the above sum on his attaining the age of twenty-one years.' Incidentally, in the same will he left his Albanian servant Demetrios Zograffo £50 a year for life. Byron's faults did not include indifference to the condition of his dependents, and as Fletcher's loyalty showed, he contrived to be a hero to his valet.

He sailed from Athens in April, on the *Hydra*; his luggage included four skulls abstracted from 'Attic sarcophagi' and four tortoises. By a happy irony, another passenger on the ship was Lusieri, Nicolo's brother-in-law, Lord Elgin's agent, and, despite this, Byron's friend; and he brought with him the last consignment of the marbles which Elgin had removed from the Parthenon.

In Malta he suffered from fever, met Mrs Constance Smith again – but the fever damped his ardour – and parted from Nicolo. His spirits were low; 'At twenty-three', he noted, 'the best of life is over and its bitters double.' He was 'sick at heart' – 'neither maid nor youth delights me now,' he quoted from Horace, getting the quotation, as was his habit, a little wrong. 'I have outlived all my appetites and most of my vanities aye even the vanity of authorship.'

But his mood was, in fact, volatile. The letters which he wrote in the course of the voyage veer from melancholy to hilarity. For all his protestations that he was 'so out of Spirits, & hopes, & humour, & pocket & health, that you must bear with my merriment, my only resource against a Calenture', he was proud of his travels – 'very few have penetrated so high' into Albania, 'as Hobhouse and myself,' and eager, though nervous, to discover how the poetry he had written in the last two years would be received. Then there were friends with whom he would delight to renew acquaintance, and this might offset the imminent meetings with 'a lawyer, the next a creditor, then Colliers, farmers, surveyors, & all the agreeable attachments to Estates out of repair, & Contested Coalpits'.

His moods were transient, as ever; the effect of his tour enduring. There are those for whom the first journey abroad, however long it lasts, is merely an incident in life, which becomes an agreeable memory but one that does nothing to alter their way of looking at the world. Such was the Grand Tour for most of Byron's equals; they returned to immerse themselves in the life of the countryside and the duties of their station. It was quite different with Byron. Henceforth he lived, emotionally and intellectually, in what he called 'the clime of the East'. He had discovered habits of thinking and feeling which seemed to him truer and more admirable than those he found in England. His subsequent experiences of English hypocrisy and spleen would confirm him in this belief. 'If I am a poet', he said near the end of his life, 'the air of Greece made me one.' He could never after his experiences in the East subscribe to the Englishman's sense of complacent superiority. 'I have seen mankind in various Countries and find them equally despicable,' he had noted at Malta, 'if anything the Balance is rather in favour of the Turks' – even though he hated their cruelty and the oppression they dealt out to the Greeks. Byron was never consistent in detail, but he was not to waver for long from the convictions he formed in Greece.

Norman Douglas wrote in *Old Calabria* that we northerners do well to 'mediterraneanize' ourselves for a season: 'A landscape so luminous, so resolutely scornful of accessories, hints at brave and simple forms of expression; it brings us to the ground, where we belong; it medicines to the disease of introspection and stimulates a capacity which we are in danger of unlearning amid our morbid hyperborean gloom – the capacity for honest contempt. . . . From these brown stones that seam the tranquil Ionian, from this gracious solitude,' the wise man, he considered, could 'carve out and bear away into the cheerful din of cities, the rudiments of something clean and veracious and wholly terrestrial – some tonic philosophy that shall foster sunny mischiefs and farewell regret.'

These words might have been written with Byron in mind. They express exactly the effect of Greece on his mind. It dissolved mists and scattered cobwebs. It remained with him as a talisman of whatever was good and true; it cleared his mind of cant.

PART II

THE EXILE

I

Byron sailed from Dover to Ostend on 25 April 1816. His mood could hardly have been more different from that in which he had boarded the Falmouth Packet in his hot youth. Then all had been jollity, jokes and expectation; now he could look back on the wreck of his life. Then he had been obscure, and his departure had gone unremarked by all but his few friends and exiguous family; now he was – after Wellington and the Prince Regent – the best-known man in England, and he was fleeing the outraged British public in the throes of one of its unlovely fits of morality. 'The obloquy', Macaulay wrote in 1831, 'which Byron had to endure was such as might have shaken a more constant mind. The newspapers were filled with lampoons. The theatres shook with execrations. He was excluded from circles where he had lately been the observed of all observers. All those creeping things that riot in the decay of nobler natures hastened to their repast. . . . It is not every day that the savage envy of aspiring dunces is gratified by the agonies of such a spirit, and the degradation of such a name. The unhappy man left the country for ever.' And all this happened only because he could not get on with his wife – for that was all that was certainly known, though the bare fact was licked into a diversity of hideous shapes by the forked tongue of rumour.

He had been hurled from a pinnacle of fame. He had been painfully and publicly spurned by the society which had delighted to fawn on him. The evening at Lady Jersey's reception when the company turned their backs on him would have lacerated a far less sensitive nature. He was, moreover, embroiled in debt; bailiffs had entered his house in Piccadilly and made free with his possessions; he was reduced to asking Hanson to try to rescue 'one trunk of wood – with papers etc – also some shoes', and – a characteristic touch – to endeavour to see that his servants should have their things, which had also been seized, returned to them.

The shipwreck of his marriage had shocked him. Whatever his feelings for his wife, no matter how confused and uncertain they had always been, he had been sure that she loved him; indeed the possessive nature of her love had alarmed him. On 3 April, he sent her a note which she had written before their marriage. It read: 'I shall be too happy – there will be no reverse; whilst you love me there cannot.' He underlined the word 'there will be no reverse', and added 'Prediction fulfilled, February 1816.' The rights and wrongs of the Byron marriage have been exhaustively rehearsed, and it is absurd now to set up as a judge of the case. Two things are certain, however. First, in the words of their great-grand-daughter Lady Wentworth, 'Lady Byron had rotten bad luck with him.' Second, Byron was astonished and wounded by her abrupt hostility, and remained so for the rest of his life.

Two other points may be made. First, we know far more of Lady Byron's side of the case than of his. While she spent much of her later life composing 'narratives' of their marriage, and, as his supreme biographer Leslie A. Marchand puts it, imparting '"confidences", which she shared with a surprising number of people, while giving the impression to the world that she bore her wrongs in silence', he was far more reticent. There may have been a full account of his side of the story in his Memoirs, which he entrusted to Tom Moore, but which were burnt in John Murray's office at the instigation of his friends.

Lady Byron

Second, it is quite possible that Byron never realized just how appallingly he had spoken to his wife – and that he had done so cannot be doubted. His state of mind was such during the months of their marriage that Lady Byron questioned his sanity, and had him surreptitiously examined by doctors. They pronounced him sane, and this determined her to leave him; but if sane, he may very rarely have been sober. He swam through the marriage, fortified by draughts of brandy; and it is quite likely that he passed many hours in a condition of alcoholic amnesia. In such a state, doubts, fears, confessions, which would normally be suppressed, are often articulated; the speaker retains no memory of his words, and would frequently be horrified to know what he has revealed. Things normally locked in the sub-conscious are uttered; tendencies which in a sober state would be repressed are made manifest; self-disgust is directed outwards; self-doubt is transformed into cruel acts and words. This seems to have been Byron's condition, and it is no wonder that Lady Byron was horrified and uncomprehending.

In leaving England, he was also leaving his baby daughter Ada, whose image came to be so important to him, and his half-sister Augusta, 'almost the last being', he rashly told his wife, 'you have left me to part with – & the only unshattered tie of my existence'. All Byron's deepest attachments, save that to Lady Byron, and his only happy ones, were to women who made him comfortable: Lady Oxford, Lady Melbourne and Teresa Guiccioli: and no one made him more comfortable than Augusta. They had been lovers, briefly – there can be no doubt of this now; and their affair, as Augusta realized with dread, and Byron with a tremor of adolescent excitement, was incestuous. Of course they were only half-brother and half-sister, sharing a father whom neither had known, and brought up apart, and it was only in Byron's blackest moments that the idea of incest was part of Augusta's charm; far more important was her nature. It was Byron's misfortune – indeed, it was at the root of all his misfortunes – that, though he could feel passion, and was far more capable than most of arousing passion in others, he was nevertheless made uneasy by passion, and then bored by its expression. He liked warmth and jokes, and being made to feel valued and welcome, he required affection, and uncritical affection at that; but he was alarmed, and always had been alarmed, when demands were made of him. No doubt this owed something to this turbulent relationship with his mother; perhaps it was what had promoted his recoil from Lord Grey of Ruthin; it was surely based on the insecurity of the poor lame boy. This fear, and the capacity for boredom that went with it, lay at the heart of his character.

Augusta Leigh, Byron's beloved half-sister

But he was also resilient, and his resilience is part of his attraction. He might howl, but he did not mope. The day after arriving in Ostend he wrote to Hobhouse, and his mood was cheerful. The crossing had been rough, which pleased him. 'As a veteran I stomached the sea pretty well, till "a damned merchant of Bruges" capsized his breakfast close by me, & made me sick by contagion.' But he soon recovered, and reached the inn and 'a flagon of Rhenish' which, thanks to the absence of Scrope Davies 'was not indulged in to the extent of the "light wine" of our parting potations'. As for Ostend, it seemed 'a very tolerable town', and he couldn't understand why Hobhouse 'had vituperated it'. Moreover, the customs officers had been very polite.

Ostend, of course, was only a staging-post. The dandies, exiled by debt, might stop off in the Channel ports, as Brummell and Scrope Davies himself would do, but Byron was for travel, and he had fixed with Hobhouse to meet him at Geneva. He had ordered a huge travelling-coach, in the same style as Napoleon's, before leaving England. It cost £500, which bill was not yet settled, a consideration that did not prevent Byron from abusing its faults and deficiencies.

The wheels and springs required attention, and he told Hobhouse to abuse Baxter the coachmaker 'like a pickpocket [that is – he – the said Baxter being the pickpocket]' and to tell him to knock the cost of repairs off the price.

So the journey across the Low Countries was slow and interrupted. At Ghent he stared at pictures and climbed the 450 steps of the cathedral steeple. At Antwerp there were more paintings, this time by Rubens, whom he dismissed as 'the most glaring – flaring – staring harlotry imposter that ever passed a trick on the senses of mankind – it is not nature – it is not art'. He made an exception only for 'some linen (which hangs over the cross in one of his pictures) which to do it justice looked like a very handsome tablecloth'. There was frequently a refreshing philistinism to Byron's opinions of painting and sculpture, but then, as he disarmingly admitted to Augusta, 'I know nothing about the matter.' Still, heresy or not, Rubens was 'a very great dauber', and he much preferred Van Dyke.

He was impatient with the Netherlands – they were only a route after all, and 'a molehill would make the inhabitants think that the Alps' – which he hadn't yet seen – 'had come here on a visit'. They suffered, of course, from not being Greece or Albania. Yet they had their good points: 'comfort and a singular, though tame, beauty'; and he even felt that on another occasion he would have liked to survey them in less cursory fashion.

There was however one scene worth visiting, and this was the field of Waterloo. It was only ten months since the battle, and he was able to gallop over the field on a Cossack horse, and purchase a quantity of souvenirs – helmets, sabres and such like – which he sent to his publisher John Murray for safe keeping. He had been taken to Waterloo by Pryce Lockhart Gordon, a connection of his mother's who noted that the poet seemed 'in a musing mood' as he surveyed the battlefield. That evening at the Gordons, he was asked to write some verses in Mrs Gordon's album, to which Walter Scott had also contributed, and the next day he returned with two stanzas:

Stop! – for thy tread is on an Empire's dust!
An Earthquake's spoil is sepulchred below!
Is the spot mark'd with no colossal bust?
Nor column trophied for triumphal show?
None; but *the moral's truth* tells simpler so.
As the ground was before, thus let it be; –
How that red rain hath made the harvest grow!
And is this all the world has gained by thee,
Thou first and last of fields! king-making Victory?

And Harold stands upon this place of skulls,
The grave of France, the deadly Waterloo!
How in an hour the power which gave annuls
Its gifts, transferring fame as fleeting too!
In 'pride of place' here last the eagle flew,
Then tore with bloody talon the rent plain,
Pierced by the shaft of banded nations through;
Ambition's life and labours all were vain;
He wears the shattered links of the world's broken chain.

Waterloo could not delight him as it had Scott, who, on his last
meeting with Byron the previous September, had been full of his visit
to the battlefield. There was an element of travel snobbery as well as
political prejudice in his judgment: 'The plain at Waterloo is a fine
one,' he told Hobhouse, 'but not much after Marathon and Troy –
Chaeronea and Plataea.' He was ready to admit to the prejudice, but
not to the snobbery, though Hobhouse probably shared both sentiments. 'I detest the cause & the victors – & the victory – including

The field of Waterloo

Blücher and the Bourbons.' Waterloo represented for Byron and his Whig friends a defeat, which had restored a narrow and reactionary tyranny in France. On this journey he would avoid French territory, as when Scrope Davies had to flee England on account of his debts, he too declined to live in France under the Bourbons and took up his residence in the Netherlands. In the same way, in our century, there were those who refused to return to Spain while Franco lived.

These two stanzas would be incorporated in the third canto of *Childe Harold*, for – another mark of his resilience – Byron was already working again, even as he travelled. The Childe, whose pilgrimage had been laid aside in Byron's London years, was dusted down again, and the third canto was begun during his week in Brussels. It had always been a journal in verse, among other things, though only his more elevated sentiments were allowed into the poem. He believed – it was a firm article of his often unstable creed – in the violence of first impressions and in the value of their expression. His poetry poured forth 'like lava' (though he would later declare Europe's most famous volcano Vesuvius to be 'hackneyed'), and in Stanzas XXI–XXVIII the darker emotions which Waterloo aroused found a form, and sounded a note, quite different from the raciness of his letters:

> And Ardennes waves above them her green leaves,
> Dewy with nature's tear-drops, as they pass,
> Grieving, if aught inanimate e'er grieves,
> Over the unreturning brave, – alas!
> Ere evening to be trodden like the grass
> Which now beneath them, but above shall grow
> In its next verdure, when this fiery mass
> Of living valour, rolling on the foe
> And burning with high hope, shall moulder cold and low.

His sympathies might be with the losing side, but he could not fail to respond to the splendour, courage and misery of the battle. Friends had been killed there, and his last letter to Augusta before leaving England had given comforting news about the fate of Lord Carlisle's youngest son which he had gleaned from an old Harrow acquaintance Thomas Wildman (the future purchaser of Newstead), whom he had met by chance in the hotel at Dover.

The third canto of the poem would be ready to be copied by early July, written in a blaze of energy during weeks when he scarcely settled for more than a few days in the same place. Though the third and fourth cantos could not, especially in the circumstances of his departure from England, have the same shattering effect as their predecessors, they are nevertheless greatly their superior. They sound a new note of sincerity, now savage and scornful, now melancholy. The nominal hero, the dreary and self-regarding Childe, almost disappears from view, and in his place we have a splendid brooding on history and place, interspersed with Byron's own reflections on his relation to the past and the scenes he contemplates. A note of peculiar and sombre passion is struck time and again. It is the poem of a man using the experience of travel and the ideas summoned into being by what he sees to help him to come to terms with his own experience. The first two cantos were the work of a richly gifted boy; whenever they moved away from description, they revealed the actor's pose. Now the poem remains a rhetorical performance; but the gap between the poet and his rhetoric has narrowed.

Passing from Waterloo he travelled up the Rhine. The river, neither yet polluted and disfigured by industry, nor swarming as it soon would be with English tourists, delighted him beyond his expectations. It offered exactly the combination of superb natural beauty and historical associations which appealed to his imagination. He was quick, and pleased, to find resemblances 'with part of Cintra & the valley which leads from Delvinachi', and amused to find that this comparison struck even 'the learned Fletcher'. Byron, like many artists and egoists, was in love with his own past. Everything which had happened to him had its own significance; there were few pleasures like that of memory, and a view had only to recall another to be cherished.

He was also amused to find Fletcher, whose complaints had echoed through Greece, now behaving like a seasoned traveller; and at Cologne he enjoyed a jolly adventure straight out of a stage farce. 'The red cheeks and white teeth' of the hotel chambermaid encouraged him 'to venture on her carnally', and he was surprised in the act by the innkeeper who mistook the girl for his own wife – 'till the mystery was developed by his wife walking out of her own room and the girl out of mine.' The ludicrous nature of the encounter allowed him to forget that he was travelling precisely because his own wife had rejected him; but the oblivion was brief.

They crossed the Rhine at Mannheim to keep out of French territory. France was still occupied by the Allied armies, and they would have required passports. Besides, Byron said, he 'had no wish to view a degraded country – & oppressed people'. Most of his compatriots might think that the French had got no more than they deserved, after their own rampages across Europe, but Byron's own recent experiences did not dispose him to agree with anything they might think. So instead, he told Hobhouse, he 'solaced himself with some flagons of Rhenish' though 'without our Yorick [Scrope Davies]

Hôtel d'Angleterre at Sécheron, where Byron first met Shelley

they are nothing.' It is one of the charms of Byron's letters that everything goes spontaneously in. We see the whole man; politics higgledy-piggledy with the beauties of nature, and broodings on his own past mixed with a lively interest in the history of the scenes he visits. Everything is immediate. When a few weeks later, in an Alpine valley, he came upon 'whole woods of withered pines – all withered – trunks stripped and barkless – branches lifeless – done by a single winter', then – what next and what else? – 'their appearance reminded me of me and my family'.

By 20 May he was at Basle, and on the 25th at Sécheron outside Geneva, where he was to put up a fortnight at the Hôtel d'Angleterre, and, two days after his arrival, to meet the poet Shelley for the first time.

II

Modern Switzerland often seems a dull country – 'I suppose it's all right for operations', Sir Harold Acton once said – but in 1816 it was neither hackneyed nor overlaid with the approval of those Victorians who associated mountain scenery with moral rectitude; and there was much to appeal to Byron. The landscape was dramatic – 'clouds foaming up from the valleys below us – like the spray from the ocean of Hell'. Swiss history also pleased him; it was after all the story of liberty. The Swiss had fought for their freedom against Austria and

Burgundy, as the Scots had against England, and maintained it. From the fifteenth-century battlefield of Morat, he happily carried off 'the leg and the wing of a Burgundian', and he told Hobhouse, with a schoolboyish relish, that other bones of the slain had been made into knife-handles by the Swiss. It pleased him, too, to find that the people 'looked free & happy & rich (which last implies neither of the former)', he added, tilting at England, and to be in a district 'famous for cheese – liberty – property – and no taxes.' Byron's politics were never coherent, but it is too easy to say – and his praise for Switzerland disproves the claim – that he was only interested in aristocratic liberty. His speech in support of the Luddites had revealed his respect for the liberty of the poor. His ideal was the early American republic – Jeffersonianism – but without negro slavery. Switzerland approached it as nearly as anywhere in Europe.

Early in June, he moved into the Villa Diodati. Situated in the village of Cologny, two miles from Geneva on the south shore of the lake, it was a handsome four-storeyed building with a balcony running at first-floor level round three sides of the house. It belonged

Byron on the terrace of the Villa Diodati, Lake Geneva

[83]

Shelley in 1819

Mary Shelley

to one Edouard Diodati, whose ancestor Charles had been a friend of Milton, and its chief attraction was the view stretching across the blue water to the Jura mountains. Meanwhile the Shelleys settled a few hundred yards away at Montalègre. Byron had achieved the combination of solitude and companionship which suited him.

Shelley and Byron were not only both poets, but fellow outcasts, Shelley being notorious as an atheist and bigamist. Yet there was one difference between them: Shelley, who had never been in society, was quite happy to be rejected by it. He was a genuine radical outsider, an intellectual who sought to make life fit his theories. Byron's attitude was more complicated. He had once belonged to society, had indeed been regarded as its chief adornment, and he could never relinquish that memory. 'I liked the Dandies,' he noted in 1821; 'they were always very civil to me, though in general they disliked literary people.' In a subsequent passage he listed the clubs to which he had belonged; one cannot imagine Shelley doing likewise. Even Byron's debauchery was, in an odd way, an expression of his respect for convention and morality; he was never able to throw off the memory of his marriage. Shelley, by contrast, was a priggish immoralist; he could dismiss the memory of his first wife, the unfortunate Harriet, with apparent equanimity; the poor girl had been unable to live up to his high standards.

Now Byron found himself joined with Shelley in the public eye, to the consternation of Hobhouse, who knew that the association would make his friend's rehabilitation more difficult. It was soon alleged that the two wicked poets had formed 'a league of incest', for the Shelleys were accompanied by Mary's step-sister Claire Clairmont, who had forced herself on Byron in London the previous year, having made up her mind to have an affair with Genius. Now she resumed her enthusiastic advances, and Byron, though he found her silly, tiresome and affected – in which judgments he was absolutely correct – was too good-natured or weak-willed to deny her: 'I could not exactly play the Stoic with a woman who had scrambled eight hundred miles to unphilosophize me,' he excused himself to Augusta; but it was not long before he was finding poor Claire an intolerable bore.

Meanwhile, however, it was agreeable to discover that Shelley, for all his eccentricities, remained a gentleman. (Moore thought that he was an aristocrat not only by birth, but in manner and appearance; a judgment which prompted Hobhouse to scribble in the margin of his copy of the *Life* of Byron, 'not in the least, unless to be lean and feeble be aristocratical'.) It was not only that Byron felt more comfortable with one of his own rank; he also realized how deeply his London friends, especially Hobhouse, would disapprove of this association, and was glad to think, however erroneously, that on one count at least his new friend couldn't be faulted. Shelley, for his part, was not slow to find out Byron's defects. He told the novelist, Thomas Love Peacock, that Byron was 'a slave to the vilest and most vulgar prejudices, and as mad as the winds'. Despite this, and despite his recurrent disapproval of Byron's conduct, his respect for his genius overwhelmed him; while each succumbed to the other's very real charm. They were always to be very much better friends together than apart.

The summer passed with a superficial agreeableness in expeditions, picnics, sails on the lake in a boat he had purchased, ghost stories, chat, poetry and lovemaking. They visited Meillerie, where Rousseau (whom Mrs Byron had thought to resemble her son) had set his novel *La Nouvelle Héloïse*. Byron had had the forethought to bring a copy of the book with him:

> 'Twas not for fiction chose Rousseau this spot,
> Peopling it with affections; but he found
> It was the scene which Passion must allot
> To the Mind's purified beings; 'twas the ground
> Where early Love his Psyche's zone unbound,
> And hallow'd it with loveliness; 'tis lone
> And wonderful, and deep, and hath a sound.
> And sense, and sight of sweetness; here the Rhone
> Hath spread himself a couch, the Alps have rear'd a throne.

He told Murray he was 'struck to a degree with the force and accuracy of his [Rousseau's] descriptions'. He was moved by the novel itself, that landmark in the history of European sensibility, and seeing the setting intensified his feeling.

The surroundings of the lake had many other literary associations; Voltaire had lived at Ferney, Gibbon at Lausanne. The first

> Breathed most in ridicule, – which, as the wind,
> Blew where it listed, laying all things prone, –
> Now to o'erthrow a fool, and now to shake a throne.

The other

> . . . shaped his weapon with an edge severe
> Sapping a solemn creed with solemn sneer.

Both tributes reveal the Augustan side of Byron's temperament.

He visited Gibbon's villa and was touched to find that the historian was still remembered, though 'the garden – and summer-house where

The prisoner of Chillon, an illustration to Byron's poem by Cruikshank

he composed – are neglected – & the last utterly decayed'. In sentimental reverence he picked a sprig of acacia and some rose leaves from his garden, and sent them to Murray with a reminder that he would find 'honourable mention in his life made of the Acacia when he walked out on the night of concluding his History'.

Such visits and such memorials appealed to Byron's piety and his sense of what was fitting. There were, however, grander things to be seen. There was the prison-castle of Chillon, where the Swiss–Genevan patriot Bonivard had been incarcerated by the Duke of Savoy. Byron visited it twice, first with Shelley, and then later in the summer with Hobhouse, when he at last arrived. It occasioned his most famous sonnet, and a longer, but less successful, poem; but equally memorable, though excluded from the verse, was the old corporal who showed them round the castle and was as 'drunk as Blücher – and (to my mind) as great a man'.

There were Mont Blanc and Chamonix, where he collected agates and crystals and other stones to send to Augusta's children and his own little daughter Ada. At Chillon he had encountered an English lady asleep in her carriage 'in the most anti-narcotic spot in the world', and at Chamonix he was amused to hear another exclaim 'Did you ever see

The castle of Chillon

anything more rural?'; 'as if it was Highgate or Hampstead or Brompton – or Hayes. – Rural quotha! – Rocks – pines – torrents – Glaciers – Clouds – and Summits of an eternal snow far above them, and Rural!'. All the same the offender was 'a very good kind of woman', and it may even have crossed his mind that his beloved Augusta might have responded to the scene in just these very words.

Then in another mood there was the monument to General Ludlow, the old Cromwellian, to brood on in the church at Vevey. He had been an exile 'two and thirty years', he reflected. A bitter thought; yet it was something to observe that Ludlow's wife had recorded her 'long – her true – and unshaken affection'.

So the summer passed in sightseeing and pleasant society. If he could have forgotten England and Lady Byron he might have been happy. But he could not. The memory of her bitter and incomprehensible behaviour never left him, though he did not yet realize how she was working on Augusta and extending her domination over her. He still hoped for reconciliation. He went to Coppet, the home of Madame de Staël, the great bluestocking, copious writer, opponent of

Napoleon, and daughter of the millionaire banker Neckar, whom Louis XVI had belatedly appointed Minister of Finance to attempt reform and avert revolution. This remarkable woman had not been greatly impressed by Byron's affectations when she met him in London society; now, in his misfortunes, she displayed a motherly affection for him. She even dared to lecture him on his treatment of Lady Byron and offered to act as intermediary. 'The separation may have been my fault,' he admitted, 'but it was her choice – I tried all means to prevent it – and would do as much & more to end it – a word must do so – but it does not rest with me to pronounce it.'

He was sensible of her kindness and touched by it. On the other hand he found the visits to Coppet something of a strain. The conversation was too unremittingly intellectual for his taste, and it was a relief when his old friend 'Monk' Lewis – the Jamaican grandee who had written one of the most famous of Gothick horror-romances, the title of which had indeed usurped his Christian name, Matthew – arrived at the Villa Diodati on 14 August. Two days later he took Lewis to Ferney to visit Voltaire's house. Lewis might be 'a damned bore', but he was an undemanding one, and, moreover, an old friend who brought back to Byron memories of nights in London, and so gave him the feeling that he was not quite cut off. A couple of weeks later Hobhouse and Scrope Davies at last arrived, and the Shelleys returned to England, taking Claire, who was pregnant, though Byron

Claire Clairmont, Byron's most tiresome mistress, mother of Allegra and Mary Shelley's half-sister

Switzerland: the wild landscape of Manfred

did not yet know of this, with them. It was with Hobhouse and Davies that he visited Chamonix and Mont Blanc, and, all things considered, the Shelleys' departure was a relief in more ways than one. They wouldn't have done for Hobhouse, and Claire's presence had become intolerable, though she had proved useful for copying out *Childe Harold*. Then, after Davies left, Byron and Hobhouse made a tour of the Bernese Oberland, and he wrote a journal, intended for Augusta, which supplied him with much of the imagery for the dramatic poem *Manfred*.

This journal reveals Byron as living in a welter of sensation. Everything in him responded to the grandeur of Alpine scenery, while its dramatic intensity and swift changes of mood from sun to tempest seemed to reflect his own state of mind. He later declared that he had been 'half-mad' at this time, 'between metaphysics, mountains, lakes, love inextinguishable, thoughts unutterable, and the night mare of my own delinquencies, I should, many a good day, have blown out my brains, but for the recollection that it would have given pleasure to my mother-in-law'. His journals and letters prove his distraction. Before setting out on the tour he wrote to Augusta that he had 'recently broken through my resolution of not speaking to you of Lady B – but do not on that account mention her to me. . . . I do not think a human being could endure more mental torture than that woman has directly & indirectly inflicted upon me.'

Yet, however wild Byron's mood, there was always for him the interest of observing it. Childe Harold took refuge from sincerity in rhetoric, and Byron cut his with humour. A man deterred from suicide by the thought of the pleasure it would give his mother-in-law is a man who has not come close to it.

Switzerland had pleased him – so much indeed that he suggested to Augusta that perhaps she, and one or two of the children, might take a little tour with him there the following year: 'You have no idea how very beautiful great part of this country is – and women and children traverse it with ease and expedition.' But he had no thought of settling there; he had no thought of settling anywhere, for he had not accepted that his exile from England would last. Besides, there was Hobhouse to be thought of and he was eager to see Italy, and Byron no less, stimulated by the news that the road was infested with bandits; for Hobhouse, at least, it would be the Grand Tour of which war had deprived him. Before leaving, Byron consigned his boat to his Genevan banker, and also the bones which he had collected at Morat, which were, he told him, to be conveyed to England by an English friend Mr St Aubyn.

<h1 style="text-align:center">III</h1>

Byron, like most Englishmen, was quite ignorant of contemporary Italy. The country existed for them as a repository of culture. The Ancient world was more real than the modern one, and so was the Italy of the Renaissance. Byron had little taste for opera, which was the one art in which Italy still excelled. He had, of course, a sympathy for the Italian liberals, and was perfectly ready to deplore the Austrian occupation of the north which had been established after the defeat of Napoleon. But at this stage he still didn't understand the depth of the attachment of these same Italian liberals to the principles of the Revolution. The war against Napoleon had been in Germany a war of liberation, but in Italy it meant the replacement of a regime which offered some hope by one which offered none. The novelist Alessandro Mazzoni heard the news of Waterloo while he was browsing in a bookshop and promptly fainted; 'he had,' according to Nathalia Ginzburg, the Italian novelist and author of a study of *The Mazzoni Family* 'placed his hope in Napoleon again during the Hundred Days, and all hope crumbled with this defeat; from then on his nervous troubles grew worse.' The Austrian regime was indeed oppressive:

when Mazzoni tried to go to Paris later in 1815, he was refused a passport. He presented a medical certificate which said that the journey was essential for his health; but a police decree promptly banned journeys undertaken for health reasons.

Byron knew little of this. On his arrival, and for several years afterwards, he was essentially a tourist. He enjoyed the foreigner's sense of irresponsibility, which is, of course, one of the attractions of living abroad. Italy would provide a backcloth for his life, but it did not matter to him as London and England did. His thoughts remained there. On 1 November, only two weeks after his arrival in Milan, he wrote to his wife, and the tone of the letter conveys an urgency which nothing in his accounts of his travels approaches: 'You will not believe me – but I loved you and love you most entirely; – things which you know – and things which you did not know – made me what I was – or rather appeared to you – and amongst others – a want of confidence – had I trusted you – as I had almost resolved soon after our marriage – all would have been better – perhaps well – However I am paying the penalty of my evils – and eating my heart.' It was true, but it was not the sort of stuff to move or appease Lady Byron.

He was still lacerated by memory. He visited the Ambrosian Library in Milan and was entranced by the collection of letters and verses of Lucrezia Borgia and Cardinal Bembo; 'and a lock of hair,' he told Augusta, 'so long – and fair & beautiful – and the letters so pretty & so loving that it makes one wretched not to have been born sooner to have at least seen her. And pray what do you think is one of her *signatures*? – why this + a Cross – which she says "is to stand for her name". Is not this amusing?' he asked, for the same sign had been employed by Augusta and himself in their correspondence, and this coincidence of a doomed love stretching across the centuries and Alps moved him strangely; but then, 'I suppose you know,' he added, as if he suddenly remembered Augusta's deep and wide ignorance, 'that she was a famous beauty & famous for the use she made of it; & that she was the love of this same Cardinal Bembo (besides a story about her papa Pope Alexander & her brother Caesar Borgia – which some people don't believe – & others do), and that after all she ended with being Duchess of Ferrara, and an excellent mother & wife also; so good as to be quite an example. All this may or may not be, but the hair & the letters are so beautiful that I have done nothing but pore over them, & have made the librarian promise me a copy of some of them; and I mean to get some of the hair if I can;' there was nothing living in Milan which could compare with this experience, and he contrived to get one single hair as a relic.

In another mood, at another time, Milan might have charmed him more. Stendhal thought it the most delightful city in Italy, and therefore in Europe. Nowhere else, he considered, were Italian gaiety and Italian good sense more certainly to be found. But then Stendhal had a reason of the sort which Byron himself would have understood to be in love with Milan. 'It was here,' he had told his sister Pauline, in 1811, 'that I spent the sweet years of my youth. It was here I fell most deeply in love. It is here too that my character was formed.' In short, Milan was to Stendhal as Greece to Byron. 'I daily perceive that at heart I am Italian . . . the mad love of gaiety, music and the freest conduct, the art of tranquilly enjoying life etc . . . all these constitute the Milanese character.'

They met at La Scala where the whole social life of the city was centred. (Stendhal doted on opera, while Byron liked only simple melodies.) It was an unequal encounter. 'I have dined,' Stendhal raved, 'with a handsome and charming young man – a face of eighteen years, though his age is twenty-eight, the profile of an angel, the gentlest of manners. 'Tis the original of Lovelace [the demonic seducer of Richardson's *Clarissa Harlowe*, Napoleon's favourite novel] – or rather, a thousand times better than that babbler. When this young man enters an English drawing room, all the women immediately depart. He is the greatest poet living, Lord Byron. The *Edinburgh Review*, his chief enemy, against which he has written an atrocious satire, says that not since Shakespeare has England had anyone so great at depicting the passions. . . .' In contrast Stendhal himself was merely a stout and loquacious Frenchman with no sort of reputation at all. Yet he discovered, to his surprise and gratification, that he had a charm for Byron, for he had served under Napoleon and taken part on the Russian campaign, and he discovered in the poet an eager audience for his reminiscences, though at first he had suspected that, as an Englishman, Byron would be hostile to Napoleon.

Byron's stay in the city was interrupted by an unpleasant incident. On the first part of his European journey he had been accompanied by a personal physician, a young man called Polidori. He had proved difficult, almost impossible, and they had parted company in Geneva. Now he surfaced again. At La Scala he embroiled himself in an argument with an Austrian officer which ended in blows. Byron was summoned by the poet Silvio Pellico (who would himself fall foul of the Austrian authorities a few years later and spend nine years in prison as a consequence), and drawn into the altercation. Eventually, with the help of other Milanese acquaintances, who included the city's most famous contemporary poet Vincenzo Monti, Byron managed to secure Polidori's release, on condition that the young doctor left the city within twenty-four hours. All this was tiresome, if stimulating.

Byron's intervention attracted the attention of the Austrian police, already perhaps suspicious of his reputation. They were naturally reluctant to take action; Byron was not only a celebrity but a British subject. Nevertheless, for the rest of his time in Italy he was kept under observation by the Austrian police and the agents of their puppet states. The decade after Waterloo was a time of considerable tension throughout Italy (though at the end of that time Stendhal considered that the Revolution would not come till the 1840s – a prescient judgment). All the restored post-Napoleonic states lived in apprehension of a liberal revolt, and Byron, with his charisma and known sympathies, was a natural object of suspicion; though he was not in fact to engage in any political activity for several years. Yet the suspicion was justified; the whole tenor of Byron's work was subversive, and the knowledge that he was regarded in this way did not displease him.

There was nothing to tempt him to stay longer in Milan, and besides, Hobhouse, whose stay in Italy could only be limited, was anxious to be off. Byron had 'seen nothing in Milan to make me forget others – or forgive myself,' and was happy enough to leave. By 6 November they had reached Verona, heading for Venice where he proposed to winter. At Lake Garda he recalled – at least for Tom Moore's benefit – Virgil's line 'fluctibus et fremitu assurgens, Benace, marino' ('rising up with waves and violent motion, like a little sea'); and was happy to tell Moore that there was a tradition there of a city buried by an earthquake beneath the lake, just like the story which Moore had preserved of Lough Neagh, which could be seen when the water was calm. Byron and Hobhouse, however, found the lake disturbed by autumn rains and wind, which also discouraged them from turning aside to visit Catullus's Sirmio, and so saw no buried city.

Verona was fine enough, though his first thought was that Catullus, Claudian and Shakespeare had done more for the place than it ever did for itself. But the Roman amphitheatre pleased him mightily – 'beats even Greece' – and he was pleased to discover that the Veronesi were 'very tenacious of the truth' of the story of Romeo and Juliet. He visited what was reputed to be her tomb: 'an open sarcophagus in a most desolate convent garden – which looks quite wild & withered,' and abstracted a few fragments for Augusta and her children and Ada, whose name, he suddenly told Augusta, 'which I found in our pedigree under King John's reign was the same as that of one of Charlemagne's sisters'. He admired the Gothic tombs of the della Scala dukes, but Juliet's tomb appealed 'more than all the antiquities'. The wife of the Austrian Governor told him later that the castle of

the Montecchi (Montagus) could still be seen between Verona and
Vicenza, and Byron was happy to allow himself to be convinced of the
fundamental truth of the story. But it was just as important to tell
Augusta that his dog – 'Mutz by name & Swiss by nation' – could shut
a door when he was told to, which was more, he added, than her Tip
could do.

IV

Byron arrived in Venice on 10 November 1816, and four days later
took up residence in 'the house of a Merchant of Venice who is a good
deal occupied with business, and has a wife in her twenty-second year.
Marianna (that is her name) is in appearance altogether like an
antelope. She has the large, black, oriental eyes, with that peculiar
expression in them which is seen rarely among *Europeans* – even the
Italians – and which many of the Turkish women give themselves by
tinging the eyelid – an art not known out of that country, I believe.
This expression she has naturally, and something more than this. In
short, I cannot describe the effect of this kind of eye – at least upon me
. . . her natural voice (in conversation I mean) is very sweet; and the
naivety of the Venetian dialect is always pleasing in the mouth of a
woman.'

He had made up his mind with his usual rapidity and was already in
love. He had, as it were, turned the corner and found himself in a new
world. He was embarking on a new emotional voyage, and the years
in Venice were to be glittering and hectic. He shrugged on a new
persona; the worldly and world-weary debauchee supplanted Childe
Harold and the Giaour to the puzzled consternation of many admirers;
they came to see the *poète maudit*, and they found a man of pleasure. He
was still avid for sensation, but the sensations he now sought were of a
more mundane, an inferior order. Yet, for all the ardour with which
he would throw himself into Venetian life, he also displayed a new
caution. His Venetian loves might delight, even intoxicate, him; but
they didn't disturb him. They weren't his equals; they were 'splendid
animals' whom he could observe with amusement, even while he was
invigorated by their presence. He had been horribly embarrassed and
discomposed by Caroline Lamb with whom he had had a turbulent
affair in his years of London glory; his wife had inflicted wounds from
which he believed he would never recover; he was not ready to risk
pain again.

Marianna's husband, a draper called Segati, was complaisant in the
Venetian manner. He was quite prepared for his wife to take a rich
milord as her lover as long as she remained respectably under his roof.

The fact that Byron was his lodger too didn't distress him; indeed it helped to maintain appearances. As for Byron, he was content with the arrangement. The house was convenient, in the Frezzeria, just off the Piazza San Marco, though it would not be long till his establishment grew to a point when he would find the accommodation disagreeably cramped.

Even without Marianna, he would have found Venice suited to his mood. 'It has always been,' he told Moore, '(next to the East) the greenest island of my imagination. It has not disappointed me; though its evident decay would, perhaps, have that effect on others. But I have been too familiar with ruins too long to dislike desolation.' After all, wasn't it an image of his own life, at least as satisfying as that Alpine forest with its withered pines? Moreover, Byron was – despite his protestations to the contrary – sufficiently a Romantic to feel the Gothic charm of transience and decay.

The decline of Venice was indeed only too evident. 'Once she did hold the gorgeous East in fee,' Wordsworth had sighed in 1799, lamenting the extinction of the Republic; but in fact the decline and fall which had preceded that extinction had been as stately and inexorable as Gibbon's most solemn and melancholy periods. In the middle of the eighteenth century the city had been reduced to a mere shadow of its old mercantile splendour. The oligarchy had dwindled to some fifty families – the so-called Barnabotti – and the port through which all the commerce of the East had passed now existed on a wretched coastal trade. The long-neglected and despised inland provinces were still ignored. Few roads – and those mean ones – ran through the territories of the Republic; internal and outdated customs duties still divided one Venetian dependency from another; the state seemed moribund, gripped, as one foreign observer put it, by a terror of the future which was only too well justified.

Yet it is to this period, paradoxically, that we owe our clearest impressions of what Venice was and what it had been. The paintings of Guardi and Canaletto record the love which the Venetians felt for their declining city, while the comedies of Goldoni testify to the sweetness of life preserved there as the candles of the Republic burned low. William Beckford, in 1780, had caught the nervous gaiety of the *fin de siècle*, a gaiety that couldn't altogether conceal a melancholy and hopeless note: 'However solemn a magistrate may appear in the day,' he had written, 'he lays up wig and robe and gravity to sleep together, runs intriguing about in his gondola, takes the reigning sultana under

Gondolas: 'just like a coffin clapt in a canoe'

his arm, and so rambles half over the town, which grows gayer and gayer as the day declines.'

By 1816 the situation of the Venetians had grown still more unhappy. The Republic had been consigned to the Austrians by the Treaty of Campo Formio in 1797. In 1806, after Austerlitz, Napoleon incorporated it into his Kingdom of Italy, which at least brought it the reforming modernism of the Napoleonic Code; but, on his downfall, though the Golden Horses of St Mark's, which had once decorated the triumphal arch of Trajan in Rome, and which the Doge Dandolo had carried from Byzantium to Venice, had been restored in 1815 by the Emperor Francis, the old Republic, despite its unrivalled claim to historical legitimacy, was disdained by the new champions of legitimate monarchy and contemptuously embodied in the new Lombard–Venetian kingdom, ruled by a viceroy appointed from Vienna and wholly absorbed in the international conglomeration that was the Habsburg Empire. A symbol of its fate might be found in the Bucentaur, the double-decked galley which had been used every year in the ceremony in which the marriage of the Republic to the Adriatic had been enacted; stripped of its gold and jewels by the Austrians, it had been used as a coastal battery and a prison-hulk, and now lay derelict, awaiting its destruction which took place in 1824.

Venice had lost its independence as it had long ago lost its reason for existence. But its absorption in the Empire brought no benefits. A customs barrier still divided the territories of the Republic from Lombardy, and so prevented a landward trade from replacing the lost maritime one. The Austrians' indifference to their new province was only equalled by their ignorance. When the new Patriarch of Venice was installed in 1817, Vienna decreed that 'he should proceed to St Mark's in a "Coach & Four" . . . the Venetians grinned,' Byron told Hobhouse, 'as you may suppose, at the knowledge of topography displayed in this Caesarean decree – which was truly "german to the matter"'.

Still Byron was happy simply to be in a place where he felt at ease. 'I like the gloomy gaiety of their gondolas,' he told Murray, 'and the silence of their canals. The Carnival too is coming – St Mark's and indeed Venice – is most alive at night – the theatres are not open till nine – and the society is proportionably late – all this is to my taste.' Other Englishmen might miss 'the rattle of hackney coaches – without which they can't sleep'; but not Byron.

The society might not amount to much, but at least it received him and made him welcome as a famous poet and English milord. He had little taste now for formality and the exchange of empty commonplaces – he had never had much – but he was pleased enough to attend

[98]

The Bridge of Sighs, Venice: 'a Palace and a Prison on each hand'

the conversazione held by Contessa Albrizzi. This lady, now in her fifties, was called by some the Italian Madame de Staël (Hobhouse was to remark that she was a poor copy of the original, though a good-natured one). Yet her appeal for Byron was more subtle. She was Greek by birth, born indeed in Corfu, though of an Athenian family, and many Greeks attended her evenings. They offered Byron a faint emanation of the magic of Greece, wafted on the Adriatic breezes across the lagoon. She was a friend of the sculptor Canova, on whom she had written, for she had literary ambitions, and whose bust of Helen was in her house; Byron thought it 'without exception the most perfectly beautiful of human conceptions – and far beyond my ideas of human execution'.

The Armenian Convent, Venice, where Byron studied

He soon fell, as he liked to do, into a routine. To occupy his mind, since he had temporarily laid *Childe Harold* aside – though he had begun work on *Manfred* – he took to the study of the Armenian language. There was an Armenian monastery on the island of San Lazzaro near the Lido – 'a church & convent of seventy monks', whom he called indifferently 'friars' – and he had himself ferried there every morning. He told Moore that his 'mind had wanted something craggy to break upon' and Murray that he had 'found it necessary to twist my mind round some severer study – and this – being the hardest I could devise here – will be a file for the serpent'. He had a taste for languages and this – 'which is twin, the literal [or as we would say 'literary'] and the vulgar' – was agreeably 'difficult, but not invincible'. It was, in the modern phrase, good therapy. Besides, there was the charm of the situation, and he could read in the library and escape the stares which followed him everywhere in Venice itself. He liked the monks (or friars) and he admired the resolution with which they worked for the enlightenment of their oppressed people. They had a printing press and Byron, from gratitude, undertook to pay for the publication of an Armenian–English grammar. He contributed a preface himself in which he paid tribute to 'the neatness, the comfort, the gentleness, the unaffected devotion, the accomplishments, and the virtues of the brethren of the order' which were 'well fitted to strike the man of the world with the conviction that "there is another and a better" even in this life'.

'These men,' he wrote, 'are the priesthood of an oppressed and noble nation, which has partaken of the proscription and bondage of the Jews and of the Greeks, without the sullenness of the former or the servility of the latter. . . . If the Scriptures are rightly understood, it was in Armenia that Paradise was placed – Armenia which has paid as dearly as the descendants of Adam for that fleeting participation of its soil in the happiness of him who was created from its dust. It was in Armenia that the flood first abated, and the dove alighted. But with the disappearance of Paradise itself may be dated almost the unhappiness of the country; for though long a powerful kingdom, it was scarcely ever an independent one, and the satraps of Persia and the pachas of Turkey have alike desolated the region where God created man in his own image.' Nor has the condition of the Armenians improved since. Though the sentiments of Byron's preface were doubtless agreeable to the Armenian fathers, the attack on the Turks seemed injudicious to them, and it was not in fact used. I have quoted it extensively, however, because it offers such a clear example of Byron's liberal sentiments; there is nothing here which Gladstone would not have endorsed half a century later.

Meanwhile in the afternoons and evenings there was Marianna. 'She does not plague me,' he told Augusta, '(which is a wonder) and I verily believe we are one of the happiest – unlawful – couples on this side of the Alps.' A calmer mood had succeeded the frenzy of the terrible year he had endured: reviled in England, half-mad, as he confessed, in Switzerland, 'between metaphysics, mountains, lakes, love inextinguishable, thoughts unutterable, and the nightmare of my own delinquencies'. It was relief and solace to find himself now in a society like that of Venice, to be able to relax in the maturity and scepticism of Italy, where it seemed to him – it was indeed a foreigner's judgment, which many Italians would have found startling – that 'a woman is virtous (according to the code) who limits herself to her husband and one lover; those who have two, three or more are a little wild'. He would find things were not quite as easy as that; he would know passion again, he would experience a true and dependent love, but he would never again be wholly disordered by sexual desire or by the incompatibility of lovers. In Venice Byron emerged from immaturity, and became a whole man. Marianna Segati and her principal successor, the baker's wife Margarita Cogni, were the agents who made this development easy and pleasurable.

[101]

In the spring, after Carnival, he intended to join Hobhouse in Rome. He had meanwhile finished *Manfred*, the gamey fruit of his Alpine experiences; and, in the intellectual isolation of the Venetian winter, in the long nights when he sat reading or scribbling, with a glass of gin and water – or brandy and water – to hand, he had taken stock of his position. He was unsure of his direction, indeed of his whole way of life. 'If I live ten years more,' he wrote to Moore, 'you will see that it is not over with me – I don't mean in literature, for that is nothing; and it may seem odd enough to say, I do not think it is my vocation. But you will see that I will do something or other.' His dissatisfaction was sharpened by his reading of Pope; he felt his inferiority to the 'little Queen Anne man', and later in the year would give it as his opinion that he and his contemporaries were all on the wrong track; Pope beat them hands down. He was reading Voltaire too, and, though irritated by his inaccuracies, delighted in the lucid irony of the Enlightenment.

But, when he resumed his travels, things were different. Then, he could not help responding as a man of his own day, with a sensibility that had been formed by the events and literature of the last twenty years. He thought as a Classicist; he felt as a Romantic. It was this division which supplied his poetry with so much of its nervous energy.

His departure was continually postponed. First, Marianna was loth to see him leave, and her demands had not yet become burdensome. (Besides, for all his frequently expressed impatience with woman-hood, he always found it difficult not to give in to their demands.) Second, he had heard that Rome was 'pestilent with English – a parcel of staring boobies' – in Switzerland they had even trained telescopes on the Villa Diodati – 'who go about gaping and wishing to be at once cheap and magnificent. A man is a fool,' he reflected, 'who travels now in France and Italy, till this tribe of wretches is swept home again. In two or three years this first rush [of tourists taking advantage of Napoleon's defeat] will be over, and the Continent will be roomy and agreeable.' Fortunately Venice was fairly free of them.

Of course, he was eager to see Rome, and even suspected that the city might inspire a fourth canto of *Childe Harold*. Moreover, Hobhouse was growing impatient. Byron apologized for his delayed departure, pleading a touch of malaria, and then apologized for the apology: 'In verity, the malaria was a pretext as I knew it was a Summer and not a Spring production – but the English crowd of the Holy Week was as sincere an excuse as need to be.' Still, it was true that he had had a fever, not, Hobhouse was to understand, 'the low vulgar typhus which is at present decimating Venice – but a sharp gentlemanly fever' – like the one he had suffered from the Marshes of Elis in Greece. Still, he would soon set off, and if by chance Hobhouse had given him up and left Rome, perhaps he would leave word at the Customs House where Byron was to lodge.

And then the proofs of *Manfred* arrived to delay him further, and it was disconcerting to discover that the last act was 'd—d bad'. He stuffed it into his travelling case to revise in Rome, and at last was off, pausing only to tell Moore that he had 'not the least curiosity about Florence' where, however, he arrived on 22 April. Forgetfulness on Fletcher's part had delayed him a day at Bologna, 'celebrated for the production of Popes – Cardinals – painters – and Sausages'. He employed the time pleasantly seeing 'bottled children and parts of shame' done in waxwork by a female Professor of Anatomy at the University of Bologna; the town itself being one of the few prosperous cities in the Papal States was one of the oldest and most famous in Italy. He travelled by Ferrara, where he was struck by a display of the poet Tasso's correspondence about his laundry, and by Arqua to see Petrarch's tomb. The dog Mutz accompanied him, and Byron was pleased that he had been mistaken for a bear by the Bolognese, though admitting that he had also been put to flight by 'a moderate-sized pig on the top of the Pennine Alps'. (In the same letter, he confessed to an inability, shared by many of us, to remember whether the 'Appennines' (*sic*) should have one 'p' or two.) He paused to visit the galleries in Florence, and remarked that they contained sculptures and paintings 'which for the first time gave me an idea of what people mean by their cant about these two most artificial of the arts'. He admired a Raphael, three Titians and a Michelangelo. On the other hand, the Medici chapel contained 'fine frippery in great slabs of various expensive stone – to commemorate fifty rotten and forgotten carcasses'. The Santa Croce was 'the Westminster Abbey of Italy – I did not admire any of the tombs – beyond their contents . . . all your Allegory and Eulogy is infernal'.

So, by way of Perugia, 'as being the longest and most picturesque-e-e,' and the Falls of Terni he made his way to Rome. 'I have taken a flight down here,' he told Augusta; 'see the map,' he added aware of her uncertain grasp of geography.

He arrived there on 29 April, and would be back in Venice within the month. It was a strangely brief visit, accounted for to Murray by the excuse that he was missing Marianna. No doubt he was, but there was more to it than that.

It was not that he was disappointed. Quite the reverse, in fact: 'As a whole – ancient & modern – it beats Greece – Constantinople – everything – at least that I have ever seen – But I can't describe because

my first impressions are always strong & confused – & my Memory
selects & reduces them to order – like distance in the landscape – &
blends them better.'

Therein lay the key. He had already hinted that Rome might set
Childe Harold in motion again, and, with the artist's sense of self-
protection, or at least of what is necessary for the protection of his
work, he knew that it was from the operation of memory on violent
first impressions that he would distil the fourth canto. The more he
accustomed himself to Rome, the more likely he was to stale his
response. There is a Roman proverb which says that a lifetime is not
enough for the city ('Roma: una vita non è basta'); yet Byron extracted
so much from his few weeks in the city and its surroundings that his
Rome has become part of the Rome we experience. It is hard to see
the Colosseum, for instance, without picturing his gladiator who
'consents to death, but conquers agony'.

> A Ruin – yet what Ruin! from its mass
> Walls, palaces, half-cities, have been rear'd;
> Yet oft the enormous skeleton ye pass,
> And marvel where the spoil could have appear'd.
> Hath it indeed been plunder'd, or but clear'd?
> Alas! developed, opens the decay,
> When the colossal fabric's form is near'd;
> It will not bear the brightness of the day,
> Which streams too much on all – years – man – have reft away.
>
> But when the rising moon begins to climb
> Its topmost arch, and gently pauses there;
> When the stars twinkle through the loops of time,
> And the low night-breeze waves along the air
> The garland-forest, which the gray walls wear,
> Like laurels on the bald first Caesar's head;
> When the light shines serene, but doth not glare,
> Then in this magic circle raise the dead:
> Heroes have trod this spot – 'tis on their dust ye tread.

The thoughts are commonplace; the expression often clumsy; the
total effect majestic. Byron has struggled to find the words which
every tourist of any sensibility would wish to say; and he has not
risked losing the sense of wonder which a first acquaintance with the
amphitheatre must arouse.

He stayed in a *pensione* or boarding-house at 66 Piazza di Spagna;
Keats would die four years later in a house on the other side of the
square. Hobhouse, who had been studying the monuments and
churches for some months, was eager to be his guide, and Byron

Byron by the Colosseum

obediently allowed him to act as such. But, for his own part, he was
happy to refer his correspondents to a guidebook if they wanted a
description, though he told Moore that the Apollo Belvedere was just
like Lady Adelaide Forbes, whom Moore had once wished him to
marry: 'I think I never saw such a likeness.'

He had brought his riding horses, and was happy to canter or trot
over the Campagna, then, with its ruins, broken aqueducts, ivy-
covered walls, pines, view of the Alban hills through the golden light,
a tenderly beautiful (if still malarial) landscape, where shepherds
played their pipes as in classical times. He visited Frascati – of which
the last Stuart had been Cardinal–Bishop, commemorated still by the
Via Duca di York – Albano, Aricia and Nemi, where a plaque on the
castle wall records that he stayed, though he does not mention doing
so in any letter. He looked for the Spring of Egeria, of which his
admired Juvenal had written. Egeria was a goddess of springs and
running water, who had befriended the Italian Muses (the 'Camenae'
or Ladies of Song), and had been the lover of the second King of
Rome, Numa Pompilius. This probably lies on the north-west slope
of the Caelian hill, above the Appian Way, but Byron was directed to

the so-called Grotto di Egeria, actually a nymphaeum belonging to the Triopus of Herodes Atticus. No matter; he was pleased to find it surrounded by flowers. 'Egeria', he wrote,

> The mosses of thy fountain still are sprinkled
> With thine Elysian water-drops; the face
> Of thy cave-guarded spring, with years unwrinkled,
> Reflects the meek-eyed Genius of the place,
> Whose green, wild margin now no more erase
> Art's works; nor must the delicate waters sleep,
> Prison'd in marble – bubbling from the base
> Of the cleft statue, with a gentle leap
> The rill runs o'er – and, round – fern, flowers, and ivy creep,
>
> Fantastically tangled: the green hills
> Are clothed with early blossoms, through the grass
> The quick-eyed lizard rustles, and the bills
> Of summer-birds sing welcome as ye pass;
> Flowers fresh in hue, and many in their class,
> Implore the pausing step, and with their dyes,
> Dance in the soft breeze in a fairy mass;
> The sweetness of the Violet's deep blue eyes,
> Kiss'd by the breath of heaven, seems colour'd by its skies.

The tenderness of the emotion communicates itself, but it leads him into one of his most wild and gloomy passages, as he broods on the delusory nature of Love, 'which dies as it was born', and the conclusion that:

> Our life is a false nature: 'tis not in
> The harmony of things, – this hard decree,
> This uneradicable taint of sin,
> This boundless upas, this all-blasting tree,
> Whose root is earth – whose leaves and branches be
> The skies which rain their plagues on me like dew –
> Disease, death, bondage – all the woes we see,
> And worse, the woes we see not – which throb through
> The immedicable soul, with heart-aches ever new.

Back in the city there was the sight of 'a live Pope & a dead Cardinal – Pius 7th has been burying Cardinal Bracchi – whose body I saw in State in the Chiesa Nuova . . . both of them looked very well indeed.' Rome was infested with criminals, partly doubtless because of severe laws, which could, for example, see a butcher consigned to the galleys for having sold meat on a Friday, partly because there was, as there has always been, a constant coming and going of visitors to the city. The death penalty was frequently imposed, though doubtless no more often than in England, and Byron went to see three robbers guillotined. The ceremony, with 'the masqued priests – the half-naked executioners – the bandaged criminals – the black Christ & his banner – the scaffold – the soldiery – the slow procession – & the quick rattle and heavy fall of the axe – the splash of the blood – the ghastliness of the exposed heads,' seemed to him 'altogether more impressive than the vulgar and ungentlemanly "new drop" and dog-like agony of infliction upon the sufferers of the English sentence'. But though the death of the first victim turned him 'quite hot & thirsty – & made me shake so that I could hardly hold the operas-glass (I was close – but was determined to see – as one should see everything once – with attention),' he was distressed and ashamed to confess that the subsequent ones did not horrify him – 'though I would have saved them if I could.'

The happiness of these weeks in Rome was disturbed not only by such horrors, and by the prying English – Lady Liddell, a friend of Lady Byron's family, coming across him by chance at St Peter's forbade her daughter to look at the wicked poet – but, more seriously, by letters from England which revived the miseries of his marriage and separation. There were disputes over his daughter Ada, and Byron wrote to Augusta saying that all he required was an assurance that the girl would not be taken out of England without his consent; and he told Augusta also that the separation had 'literally made me as much an object of proscription – as any political plot could have done – & exactly the same as if I had been condemned for some capital offence . . . To suppose that this has no effect upon a character like mine – would be absurd.'

The Rome that Byron then knew so briefly may be thought to have been at the height of its beauty and interest. It was a small city, with fewer than 150,000 inhabitants, and the broken Aurelian Wall enclosed green fields and open spaces. Except for scattered churches, monasteries, convents and their gardens, there was little to the west of the Colosseum, the Teatro Marcello and the ghetto; a piazza and a few streets surrounded San Giovanni Laterano. Likewise a warren of little streets surrounded the other Basilicas of Santa Maria Maggiore and San Paolo Fuori i Muri, which would otherwise have stood in open country. The Via dei Serpenti wound through the Suburra towards the Colosseum as it had done since Ancient times, but great streets like the Via Nazionale and the Via Cavour had not yet been built. The Napoleonic regime had encouraged the excavation of the ancient city; Trajan's column and the basilica at its base, had been excavated in 1811. The gardens of the Villa Ludovisi, the Villa Medici and the Villa Borghese stretched over the hillside above Trinita dei Monti and the

The charm of nineteenth-century Rome, captured by Edward Lear

Palazzo Barberini, where, fifty years later, Henry James would visit the American painter W. W. Storey, who had an apartment of forty rooms. Nothing had been built beyond the Piazza del Popolo, and the Tiber had not yet been embanked, so that the gardens of the Palazzi in the Via Giulia ran down to the waterside. Across the river, Trastevere and the Borgo around St Peter's were much as they are now, except, of course, that you came on St Peter's suddenly, the wide boulevard, the Via della Conciliazione, not yet having been cut through the medieval maze of little streets.

No city – at any time – could appeal more powerfully and tenderly to the imagination. Stendhal, whose *Promenades Dans Rome* was written in 1827–8, the fruit of some half-dozen visits to the city spread over a quarter of a century, knew the city thoroughly as Byron did not; yet their response shows a curious and satisfying identity.

You have to see the Colosseum alone, Stendhal considered; an impossible ambition now, difficult even then. 'How many happy mornings I have spent,' he wrote, 'lost in some corner of the immense ruins. From the upper tiers you look down on the Pope's workmen [who were engaged in patching up the fabric] who sing as they work. The noise of their chains mingles with the song of the birds, tranquil inhabitants of the Colosseum. These fly off by the hundred when you approach the scrub which covers the upper tiers where, once upon a time, the sovereign people sat. The peaceful warbling of the birds, echoing faintly through the vast building, and then, from time to time, the deep silence which follows, easily transport the imagination back to the Ancient World. In this way you attain the most vibrant delight of which memory is capable. This reverie may seem ridiculous to some, but, as La Fontaine put it: "C'est le sombre plaisir d'un coeur mélancolique". In truth it is the only great pleasure which may be found in Rome. It is impossible for those in their first youth, who are mad with hope.' Byron, though not yet thirty, had long passed that stage; he could distil the bitter-sweet honey of Roman delight. 'Since my first childhood dreams,' Stendhal continued, 'I have found only one comparable sensation which triumphs over other memories by reason of its depth and its ability to seize on the mind: this is the poetry of Lord Byron. When I told him this one day at Venice, quoting *The Giaour*, he replied:

'"As soon as the experience of the age of reason invades one of my images, I abandon it. I don't want my reader to find in my work the same sensations as in the Stock Exchange. But you, as a Frenchman, are light; you have a disposition – the cause of both your virtues and your defects – which lets you recapture something of the easy happiness of childhood. In England the frightful necessity of work is everywhere apparent. As soon as he grows up, the young man, instead of reading poetry or listening to Mozart, listens instead to the sad voice of experience which cries: 'work eighteen hours a day or you will go hungry.' The images of *The Giaour* must therefore contradict experience and the reader's memories of the reality of life. While he reads, he inhabits a different world; that's the happiness of unhappy people. But I'm astonished that you, as a Frenchman with a child's gaiety, can be sensible to this sort of merit. Can you really find something fashionable to be beautiful? My verses are fashionable now, but in twenty years you will find them ridiculous."'

'I don't claim,' Stendhal assures us with ingenuous charm, 'that these were the exact words the great poet spoke to me while his gondola took us from the Piazzetta to the Lido. . . .'

Just as well: if only because there is no evidence that Stendhal ever met Byron in Venice, and because the reference to Mozart is obviously Stendhalian rather than Byronic. When he wrote his essay, *Lord Byron in Italy*, which appeared in the *Revue de Paris* in March 1830, he made no mention of any encounters except in Milan. But, if these were not Byron's words, they were words which Stendhal reasonably thought he might have spoken; and, significantly, they arose from his own attempt to account for the charm of Rome, which aroused in him the same sentiments as Byron's poetry. It helps us to understand why the Roman stanzas in *Childe Harold* are among the best things written about the city; they catch its quintessence.

Byron left Rome on 20 May, the day after witnessing the execution. Hobhouse went on to Naples, but Byron was deterred by 'the quantity of English whom I heard of there – I prefer hating them at a distance – unless an Earthquake or a good real eruption of Vesuvius were insured to reconcile me to their vicinity'. There had been blessedly few in Rome 'except that old Blue-bore Southey – who will give a fine account of Italy in which he will be greatly assisted by his total ignorance of Italian'. Byron's letters are full of such complaints, and yet one may receive them with some scepticism. He was generally well enough pleased – for a time at least – by the company of individual compatriots, and one suspects that the vituperation was prompted by the mischievous knowledge of how it would be received when his letters were read aloud in Murray's office. All the same it was a pity he

Villa Foscarini, La Mira: Byron's summer residence outside Venice

did not visit Naples, which would have suited him, and Calabria which, in Stendhal's view, was 'as Greek as Greece itself'.

So he returned to Venice, and to Marianna, who had been sick of a fever but was now recovered. He paused on the journey to visit the Springs of Clitumnus, beloved of Propertius, which he described to Murray as 'the prettiest little stream in all poesy'; what was more he caught some 'famous' trout in it. Poussin had painted the Springs, Byron wrote of them in *Childe Harold*; later the Italian poet Carducci would devote a long meditative lyric to their beauties and significance; even now, they are one of the magic places of Italy. The best prose description – too long to quote here – is in Gilbert Highet's delightful book, *Poets in a Landscape*.

Venice was no place to inhabit in summer; it was the custom, as it still is, for all who could afford to do so to leave it – and the other principal Italian cities – during the hot weather. Byron, therefore, leased the Villa Foscarini on the left bank of the Brenta, at La Mira, a village about seven miles from the mouth of the river. It was a large Palladian building, formerly a convent, on the road to Padua. There was, he told Hobhouse, 'more space than splendour to it – & not much of that – & like all the Venetian ex-marine habitations too near the road – they seem to think they can never have enough dust to compensate for their long immersion'. It was probably chosen because Marianna had friends in La Mira with whom, to preserve proprieties, she pretended she was staying. But the life suited Byron. He swam in the Adriatic in the afternoon, rode along the river bank towards sunset, and wrote late into the night. By the beginning of July he had some thirty stanzas of the Childe's last canto written. It began – famously – with the lines:

> I stood in Venice, on the Bridge of Sighs;
> A Palace and a Prison on each hand.

'The Bridge of Sighs,' he explained to Murray, 'is that which divides, or rather joins, the palace of the Doge to the prison of the State – it has two passages – the criminal went by the one to judgment & returned by the other to death – being strangled in a chamber – where there was a mechanical process for the purpose.' Byron never allowed himself to be lulled into the comfortable delusion of so many foreign residents that Italian life and history were all sweetness and ease.

'Monk' Lewis arrived to stay in July, and Hobhouse at the end of the month. They helped put Byron into his happiest mood. He could recall London days, always a pleasure in his exile; he was working well, and in a new vein too; for besides the Childe, he had embarked on a new poem, *Beppo*.

It had its origin in a story told him by Marianna's husband. A Venetian woman, believing that her husband had been drowned, took a lover (or *cavaliere servente*). Some years passed, and then one day a man, appearing to be a Turk, presented himself before her and claimed to be her long-lost husband. He proposed that she could either leave her lover and return to him, or stay with her lover, or accept a pension and live alone. 'The lady has not yet given an answer,' Hobhouse noted, 'but Madame Segati said "I'm sure I would not leave my *amoroso* for any husband" – looking at B. This is too gross even for me.'

But not for Byron. The anecdote offered him material he could use; it was, in its acceptance of the reality of the facts of sentiment, so very Venetian. And Venice, together with his reading over the previous winter, had effected a change in him. He was certainly pleased enough with the fourth canto of *Childe Harold*, and he had re-worked the last act of *Manfred* to his satisfaction; yet he was increasingly out of sympathy with his old style, increasingly sceptical of Romantic attitudes, and correspondingly eager to dispense with fine language and fine sentiments, and try something more in keeping with his everyday mood. In short, he was tired of using one language in poetry and another in life. He wanted to bring the two sides of his personality together, and sought the means of doing so.

As long ago as the last autumn, in Milan, the poet Silvio Pellico (who would eventually die in an Austrian prison) had told him that the most delightful of the dozen Italian languages, 'whose existence is unsuspected north of the Alps,' was Venetian. Byron asked if they had any comic poet, and was told that there was one, Buratti, and 'every six months the Governor of Venice sends him to prison'. Pellico and his Milanese friends obtained a copy of a manuscript for him, having explained that 'if Buratti wanted to spend the rest of his life in prison, there was one infallible means of doing so; that was, to publish'. Byron found Buratti impossible to understand at first, but having worked his way with some help through some comedies by Goldoni, managed to do so.

This at least is Stendhal's version, and he goes on to say that 'it is my own opinion that Lord Byron only wrote *Beppo* and reached the full height of his poetic genius in *Don Juan* as a result of having read Buratti and seen the delicious pleasure which they gave in Venetian society. Venice is a world apart, whose existence is unsuspected by the rest of sad Europe. . . .'

No doubt this is an exaggeration. Byron certainly knew of the Venetian dialect and Venetian literature before he was ever in Milan. He had read the *Animali Parlanti* of Casti, which Lockhart Gordon had given him in Brussels. Moreover, for the stanza which he used in *Beppo* and *Don Juan*, he had a nearer – indeed English – model in the mock-heroic poem *Whistlecraft*, written in the manner of the fifteenth-century Italian poet Luigi Pulci, by John Hookham Frere, a diplomat and friend of George Canning. Nevertheless, the claim that it was Venice and his experience of Venetian life that made Byron's change of manner, tone and material possible cannot be denied. Moreover, it is worth observing that Stendhal, who knew Venetian literature, realized that *Don Juan* was indeed Byron's masterpiece, as his English friends did not.

Henri Beyle (Stendhal)

He had meanwhile acquired a new, and more remarkable, mistress. 'Byron's letters', Peter Quennell has remarked, 'are his biographers' despair. No one could tell the story of his relationship with Marianna Segati or with the baker's wife Margarita Cogni, more vividly than Byron has told it himself.' This can't be denied, though curiously the fullest and liveliest account he gave of his first encounters with this

Margarita Cogni, Byron's second Venetian mistress.
The portrait hardly suggests her fiery temperament

new mistress was delayed till 1819 when he had already parted from her and was living in Ravenna with Teresa Guiccioli. Then he told Murray of how he and Hobhouse had been 'sauntering' – a word which evokes the desultory character of their rides – 'on horseback along the Brenta one evening – when amongst a group of peasants we remarked two girls as the prettiest we had seen for some time'. There had been great distress in the country, he said, and by attempting to relieve it, he had won an easy reputation for generosity. So: 'One of them called to me in Venetian, "Why do you not relieve others – think of us also?" – I turned round and answered her – "Cara – tu sei troppo bella e troppo giovane per aver' bisogno del' soccorso mio" – she answered – "If you saw my hut and my food – you would not say so . . .".' Well, one thing led to another, and an appointment was made for a few evenings later. They came chaperoned, and Hobhouse's girl began to panic since she was unmarried and 'here no woman will do anything under adultery' – but Margarita was a different matter. 'In short – in a few evenings we arranged our affairs – and for two years in the course of which I had more women than I can count or recount – she was the only one who preserved over me an ascendancy – which was often disputed – and never impaired.'

Margarita – La Fornarina, or the Baker's Wife – was indeed remarkable with 'the strength of an Amazon and the temper of Medea'. She could neither read nor write – so 'could not plague me with letters'. She was passionate and scornful of Marianna's pretensions to regard Byron as her exclusive property: 'You are not his wife; I am not his wife – you are his *Donna* and I am his *Donna* – your husband is a cuckold and mine is another; for the rest, what have you to reproach me for? If he prefers what is mine to what is yours – is it my fault?' she charged her rival with splendid and ferocious logic. Nevertheless, she was possessive enough herself. At the masked ball on the last night of Carnival she 'snatched off the mask of Madame Contarini – a lady noble by birth – and decent in conduct – for no other reason but because she happened to be leaning on my arm.' In the end Byron wearied of her tantrums and demands, and paid her off, but while the affair lasted, it was the most passionate and stimulating of his life. The mere fact that they could not be equals – that they were so utterly different in background, outlook and tastes – that he regarded her as a 'splendid animal' – intensified her attraction for him.

He returned to Venice in November, still with Hobhouse, and had his horses brought in from La Mira so that they could take an evening gallop on the sands. In December he received news that Newstead had at last been sold. The buyer was Major Wildman, who had been at Harrow with him, and the price paid was £94,500. Byron had been in debt all his life – the total of his indebtedness was now almost £30,000 – and the prospect of being free of such an anxious and debilitating encumbrance, and of having a fixed income, was invigorating.

But in selling Newstead Byron was doing more than restore his financial position. The act marked the end of his youth. The possession of Newstead had been the delight of his early life; he had furiously resisted Hanson's first suggestions that he should sell the house and estate. It had belonged to his image of himself as an English nobleman. He had enjoyed happy weeks there with his Cambridge friends. His mother was buried there. Though he never fully committed himself to perpetual exile from England and never ceased to talk of possible occasions for which he might return, this sale did something to reconcile him to living abroad. It was in the year after its sale that he became an established figure in Venetian life; that one of his personae – that of the negligent and debauched *gran' signor* – crystallized.

Hobhouse returned to England in the spring with the manuscript of the last canto of *Childe Harold*, and Byron began to look for new

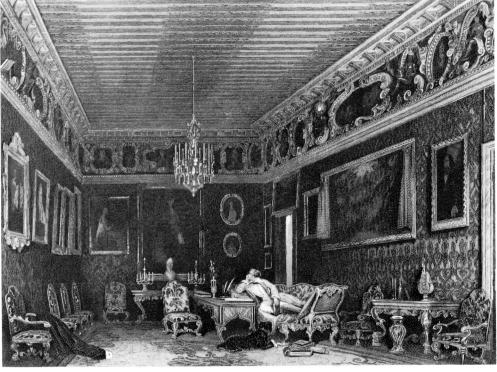

quarters. The apartment in the Frezzeria had been adequate while Marianna was his chief mistress; now its deficiencies were obvious. He tried to lease the Palazzo Gritti (now better known as the hotel where Ernest Hemingway once broke a glass door while demonstrating baseball to a young Italian) but negotiations foundered, and instead he took the Palazzo Mocenigo on a three years' lease; it cost him only £190 a year. A large grey building, more imposing than beautiful, it stood just beyond the first turn of the Grand Canal (travelling from the Accademia), near Piazza San Marco and the Rialto. It was thus in the historic heart of the city, and indeed the family from whom he leased it were among the greatest of the patriciate. One Mocenigo, Tomaso, had been Doge at the beginning of the fifteenth century and had drawn up an inventory of the city's wealth and population for the benefit of his fellow citizens; another, Giovanni had, in 1591, invited the scientist and philosopher Giordano Bruno, back to Italy, before, having fallen out with him, he betrayed or surrendered him to the Inquisition; Bruno was taken to Rome, and, after a dramatic trial, burned as a heretic in Campo dei Fiori, where his statue now stands, though it wasn't, of course, there in Byron's time.

The ground floor of the Palazzo was vast, damp, cold and uninhabitable, but there were three upper floors, with a great drawing room on the second of them. There was ample space for guests, servants, hangers-on and the menagerie that Byron habitually collected. In addition to the Swiss mongrel Mutz and the bulldog Moretto, the Palazzo soon accommodated numerous birds, including crows and at one point an eagle, many other dogs, cats, monkeys, a fox and a wolf. Many were transients, but they contributed to the atmosphere of negligent and disorganized splendour that Byron radiated.

But it was the human complement which astounded, and often dismayed, visitors. Byron, with casual tolerance and an enjoyment of the vagaries of human nature, collected an extraordinary and motley household. Shelley, who visited him in August 1818 – partly to reassure his wife and Claire about the well-being of little Allegra (the child born to Claire and Byron) who was now living with her father on condition that her mother kept out of sight – was horrified as only a high-minded freethinker could be. 'The Italian women,' he told the novelist Thomas Love Peacock, 'with whom he associates, are perhaps the most contemptible of all who exist under the moon.' Worse still, Byron consorted with 'wretches who seem almost to have

Opposite: Palazzo Mocenigo, Byron's home, 1818–19, with a view of the interior

lost the gait and physiognomy of men'. The only comfort seemed to be that Byron was, in Shelley's view, 'heartily and deeply discontented with himself'. Shelley, who was brave enough to defy any code of morality on principle, could not understand Byron's indifference to both principle and conventional morality.

Other visitors formed a similar impression of the poet's state. Newton Hanson, his lawyer's son, came from England with papers relating to the sale of Newstead and was shocked by his appearance: 'Lord Byron could not have been more than 30, but he looked quite 40. His face had become pale, bloated and sallow. He had grown very fat, his shoulders round and broad, and the knuckles in his hands were lost in fat.' Moreover, his hair was turning grey.

He might seem more like a debauched dandy than a great poet, but he had lost neither his physical nor intellectual vigour. He gave proof of the first in two swims against an Italian friend the Cavaliere Angelo Mengaldo. Mengaldo had served under Napoleon, whom he still revered; he was a republican, a patriot and a poet. He boasted that he had swum across the Danube, and across the Beresina, through drifting cakes of ice in the terrible battle of 28 November 1812. In their first race from the Lido to 'the Riva where the Gun-brig lies – that is near the Piazzetta', neither Mengaldo nor Hoppner, the English Consul, nor another resident in Venice Alexander Scott, reached the half-way mark. Ten days later Byron won a race from the Lido to the Grand Canal by more than a quarter of a mile, and told Hobhouse that 'I was in the sea from half-past four till a quarter-past eight without touching or resting – I could not be much fatigued having had a *piece* in the forenoon – & taking another in the evening at ten of the Clock.' Thus was his reputation as an all-rounder of physical pleasure substantiated.

Much more important, however, was the evidence of his intellectual vivacity. His life might seem deplorable and disorganized. His correspondence was often testy as he complained of the neglect shown by his London friends and men of business. His associates might shock and disgust the high-minded; but he was working better than he had ever done. The circumstances that enable a writer to produce his best work are not susceptible to generalization. Some require the ivory tower; others the bar room and the brothel. For some, dissipation is an alternative to creative work; for others a necessary condition, even a stimulus. Byron had arrived in Venice in a desperate and dismayed mood. He had, wilfully and carelessly, destroyed himself, his hopes of happiness, and his reputation. He felt himself to be an outcast. He was discontented with the work which he had done and despised the reputation it had won him, even while he relished his fame. Yet even his relish could not be wholly savoured, for he resented the fame also. He was aware that he had not put the best of himself into his poetry, and consequently felt that the poet whom the world admired was less than he was capable of being. He had, as he had told Moore, doubts as to whether literature was his true *métier*; but he also knew that he had given it less than he could.

All his earlier poetry had been written at a distance from much that concerned him. He sensed the element of charade. He was the only human character in *Childe Harold*; everything else was landscape, history and idealism. But the hero of the poem was not Byron. He was only a part of Byron, with none of his wit, humour and humanity. The mask of the Romantic Poet was never allowed to slip in the early work.

Venice released him. His new poem was called *Don Juan*, he told Moore, and was 'meant to be a little quietly facetious upon everything. But I doubt whether it is not free for these very modest days.' It was, he warned Hobhouse, 'as free as La Fontaine; and bitter in politics too; the damned cant and Toryism of the day may make Murray pause'. Yet all he was claiming was 'that freedom which Ariosto, Boiardo, and Voltaire – Pulci, Berni, all the best Italian and French – as well as Pope and Prior amongst the English – permitted themselves; but no improper words, nor phrases; merely some situations which are taken from life.' He was at once claiming no more than was the truth, and seeking to deceive his friends, even if he was not quite aware of the extent or depth of his deception. For the fact was that *Don Juan* was revolutionary in more ways than one.

Politically, it was subversive. The restored monarchies of Europe, which were trying to impose their so-called Holy Alliance upon the Continent, were, as Byron saw, riddled with cant and dependent on cant. They were pretending that the convulsion of the Revolution signified nothing; that it had been a mere aberration in the long unchanging history of Europe. Their actions contradicted their words, for the repression which they imposed in Italy, in France and throughout their Empires, a repression which Stendhal was to analyse with such scorn in *Le Rouge et Le Noir* and *Lucien Leuwen* and *La Chartreuse de Parme*, was proof that they feared the principles of the Revolution which they sought to deny. So, in Byron's view, every generous impulse was stifled by the powers; and almost worse than that, the whole fabric was built on a lie. The Revolution had swept aside the old cobwebby notions of a divinely appointed hierarchy; it had breathed life into subject nations, and had promised to respect the intellectual and moral liberty of the individual. That promise might not have been kept – indeed was not kept – but it was absurd to pretend that it had not been made. That promise was clear in the principles of the Revolution; it was because of that promise that Fox had welcomed the fall of the Bastille, as representing the end of an obscurantist tyranny; and it could not be willed into oblivion. The pretence that the cobwebs were a veil that screened the divine mystery of monarchy seemed derisory to Byron.

It was also an angry poem. Byron directed his scorn principally at the English oligarchy, to which he belonged by birth, but which had rejected him. He found its pretensions intolerable. England claimed to be on the side of liberty, but everywhere abetted its suppression. Castlereagh, the architect of Britain's foreign policy, was 'a tinkering slave-maker, who mends old chains', and 'cobbling at manacles for all mankind':

> Where shall I turn me not to *view* its bonds,
> For I will never *feel* them; – Italy!
> Thy late reviving Roman soul desponds
>   Beneath the lie this State-thing breathed o'er thee –
> Thy clanking chain, and Erin's yet green wounds,
>   Have voices – tongues to cry aloud for me.
> Europe has slaves, allies, kings, armies still,
> And Southey lives to sing them very ill.

All the passion of *Childe Harold* is still here, but now directed beyond Byron himself, at this 'State-thing'; yet the last line introduces the reader to a note absent from Byron's poetry until *Beppo* and then the rollicking opening to this introduction to the first canto of his new poem: 'Bob Southey! You're a poet – Poet-laureate.' And it is this new maturity, his ability to move with the ease of his letters or conversation from one topic to another, and one mood to another, that makes *Don Juan* a revolutionary poem in a literary sense also. The poem not only preaches freedom; it practises it. Byron defies the conventional restraints not only in his message, but in his manner. Wordsworth, whom he did not admire, had sought to bring the language of poetry closer to the language of common speech; and he had done so not only by excluding the poetic – which was increasingly Byron's aim too – but by simplifying both language and feeling. In doing so, Wordsworth distorted life, in a different direction certainly, yet in the same way, as the poets against whom he was rebelling. He realized this himself, and in *The Prelude*, his greatest work, he moved away again from the naïvety of the *Lyrical Ballads*. But in *Don Juan* Byron sought to capture all the complexity of life. He refused to admit that any mood, any experience, was unsuitable for poetry. He found a mode which could allow him to display his powers of narrative, characterization, reflection and criticism; which could let him be gay and melancholy, harsh and tender, playful and serious, without pretending that one mood was necessarily more to be valued than the other. *Don Juan* is a wholly adult poem, and a perennially modern one. The poem mirrors his shifting moods; it is as inconstant and enduring as the sea.

> What is the end of fame? 'tis but to fill
>   A certain portion of uncertain paper:
> Some liken it to climbing up a hill,
>   Whose summit, like all hills, is lost in vapour;
> For this men write, speak, preach, and heroes kill,
>   And bards burn what they call their 'midnight taper',
> To have, when the original is dust,
> A name, a wretched picture, and worse bust.
>
> What are the hopes of man? Old Egypt's King
>   Cheops erected the first pyramid
> And largest, thinking it was just the thing
>   To keep his memory whole, and mummy hid:
> But somebody or other rummaging,
>   Burglariously broke his coffin's lid:
> Let not a monument give you or me hopes,
> Since not a pinch of dust remains of Cheops.

Hoping for little, believing in little, expecting that things would turn out badly, Byron still asserted his will to order a disordered world. No one was less stoical in the common sense of the world than Byron, but in his philosophy experience made him a Stoic without the self-admiration that makes most Stoics repellent.

Don Juan alarmed and offended his English friends. 'It will be impossible to publish this,' squawked Hobhouse, thinking – to be fair to him – of the poet's reputation. It was indecent and dangerous and libertine, and it was too close to the events of Byron's own life. Donna Inez, Juan's mother, was clearly a portrait of Lady Byron and so on. Byron was both angry and amused: 'Don Juan shall be an entire horse or none.' Besides, he said, avoiding the issue of his own life with a manoeuvre in which he clearly took some pleasure, Juan's adventure with Donna Julia was 'none of mine, but one of an acquaintance of mine (Parolini by name), which happened some years ago at Bassano, with the Prefect's wife when he was a boy – and was the Subject of a long cause ending in a divorce or the separation of the parties during the Italian Vice-Royalty.'

But it was not surprising that Byron's friends were puzzled and alarmed. They had good reason for feeling both emotions. First, they could hardly be blamed for not immediately perceiving *Don Juan*'s surpassing merits. They had all deeply admired Byron's earlier work, and were taken aback by his change of tone and direction. Of course, they told him, they recognized that it was, in its way, a work of genius, but it was not the way to which they were accustomed. In short they received it with the suspicion that novelty so often provokes in men of judgment. Moreover, they had not lived in Venice, and so they could hardly be blamed for their inability fully to appreciate the changes which residence there had effected in their friend.

A somewhat Victorian representation of Juan and Haidée

As for their alarm, that was still more understandable. 'It will be impossible to publish this,' they cried. They were all – Hobhouse, Kinnaird (his banker as well as his friend), Murray – sensible and ultimately conventional men of business. They had stood very honourably by Byron when his reputation was at its nadir. They were all fond of him and hoped to see him able to live in London again. They had done what they could indeed to turn public opinion in his favour. And now he produced this outrageous work, which mocked and railed at all conventions and decencies, at all the hypocritical conventions in which society clothes itself. There is an Italian proverb – 'Inglese Italianizzato – Diavolo Incarnato' (The Italianized Englishman becomes an incarnate devil); and it seemed that Byron was fulfilling it. It was so clearly the work of a man who had taken on the colours of an alien and less reputable culture.

From our standpoint their views may appear ridiculous, narrow, prim. We can see the generosity and humanity of *Don Juan* far more clearly than they could. We can wonder at the lyricism of the second canto, at the tenderness with which he treats the love affair of Juan and the Greek girl Haidée, without finding a discordance between that and his generally sceptical and mocking treatment of sexual love. We can see, in fact, that the most extraordinary feature of the poem is Byron's ability to keep opposites in play: to grant the reality of passion and the simultaneous certainty that it will end. It is Byron's double vision, similar to that employed by Scott in the Waverley novels (on which Byron doted), which seems to us evidence of the maturity he had attained. But to Hobhouse and his friends it looked more like cynicism and they were afraid that the poem would be held to justify the public view of Byron as a heartless libertine.

Of course they were touched, when the second canto arrived, by verses like this:

> They were alone, but not alone as they
> Who shut in chambers think it loneliness;
> The silent ocean, and the starlight bay,
> The twilight glow, which momently grew less,
> The voiceless sands, and dropping caves, that lay
> Around them, made them to each other press,
> As if there were no life beneath the sky
> Save theirs, and that their life could never die.

That had a tender lyricism to which they could all respond, Hobhouse especially, with the memories of youthful days in Greece which he shared with Byron. But what of this?

. . . for man, to man so oft unjust,
   Is always so to women; one sole bond
Awaits them, treachery is all their trust;
   Taught to conceal, their bursting hearts despond
Over their idol, till some wealthier lust
   Buys them in marriage – and what rests beyond?
A thankless husband, next a faithless lover,
Then dressing, nursing, praying, and all's over.

Some take a lover, some take drams or prayers,
   Some mind their household, others dissipation,
Some run away, and but exchange their cares,
   Losing the advantage of a virtuous station;
Few changes e'er can better their affairs,
   Theirs being an unnatural situation,
From the dull palace to the dirty hovel:
   Some play the devil, and then write a novel.

What were they to make of this worldly weariness, in which no attitudes were struck, and only the truth was told? What would be the response of the public to Byron's observations on Christian marriage, especially in view of his own record? And didn't that last line rather too evidently refer to Lady Caroline Lamb, whose *Glenarvon* had given such a lurid view of Byron and her affair with him?

Peter Quennell has written that '*Don Juan* is the product of a completely adult mind.' And that was the problem. His friends had fallen in love with the works of an adolescent one, and that was why they found it so difficult to judge it fairly. It was no wonder on the other hand that Stendhal should see that it was Byron's masterpiece, for *Don Juan* offered the same mixture of bitter-sweet Romanticism and Realism that was to be found in his own novels.

As I have said, the relation of a writer's life to his work is always complex, not only because of the truth which Proust saw, that there is 'a gulf which separates the writer from the man of the world' (that is, the writer when he is not creating) – a gulf which remains peculiarly mysterious in the case of a poet such as Byron whose best work does actually seem to have been written by the man of the world, but in a less metaphysical sense also, since we simply cannot tell at what point influences are brought to bear and at what point they may be exhausted. Furthermore it is impossible to know to what extent the needs, possibly the unconscious needs, of the work that is to be done influence the way of life which the writer adopts, and to what extent that way of life itself helps, despite the gulf between the two selves, to influence the work's form. So, for instance, knowing that Proust wrote his great novel *A la Recherche du Temps Perdu* only when he had cut himself off from the society in which he had delighted, and had retired behind the cork lining of his room in the Boulevard Haussmann, and then to the Rue Hamelin, it is possible to believe that this was a necessary condition for the work, and that his isolation helped to give the work its peculiar character. But we cannot know this. It is only speculation, and eventually all we can say is that things are as they are, and not otherwise.

Therefore, one can observe that Byron's residence in Venice and his way of life there anaesthetized, if they did not heal, the wound inflicted on him by the failure of his marriage. No doubt dissipation would not work like that for everybody, but that seems to have been its effect on him. Careless, selfish, luxurious and immoral as his life appeared to even well-disposed observers like Shelley, it restored the mental balance which had been destroyed in London; the frenzy of which he had been aware in Switzerland in the autumn of 1816 did not return. Dissipation might damage others, but it was therapy for him; it brought him to the point at which he could embark on his master-piece.

And then he found that he had had enough of it. He was weary and ready for another change of direction. He had supped full of horrors in London and of pleasures in Venice. It was in this frame of mind that he met Teresa Guiccioli.

V

Teresa Guiccioli was only nineteen. She was very pretty, with big melting eyes, a lovely complexion and a mass of auburn curls. Everyone says – mostly with some pleasure – that her legs were too short, but her shoulders and bust were generally admired. She was also well-educated and intelligent – on the occasion of their first meeting she and Byron talked 'with enthusiasm and assurance' about Dante and Petrarch. She was also good, though impetuous and high-spirited, and after a convent education and an arranged marriage, she was ready to fall in love.

Her husband, the Count Guiccioli, was an interesting and slightly sinister figure. He was forty years older than Teresa, fifty-eight at the time of their marriage, and she was his third wife. A report, written ten years later, by the vice-legate of his home town of Ravenna to the Head of the Austrian Police gives an illuminating official view of his character and history. The existence of such a report also incidentally casts light on the Austrian methods of government, and makes it clear that the tyranny of which the Italian Liberals complained, against which they were ready to rebel, an enterprise which Byron was prepared to aid, was malignant, suspicious and degrading; apologists for the Habsburg Empire who think Italian complaints unjustified have a case to answer. Those who think Byron's involvement in the Liberal movement comic-opera playacting are wide of the mark.

'The Cavaliere Guiccioli,' the report begins, 'belongs to one of the patrician families of this city. Possessed of uncommon talents and a subtle intelligence, he was given an education suitable to his rank. . . .'

He was, in fact, a highly cultivated man, a friend of the poet Alfieri (himself the lover of Princess Louise de Stahlberg, the wife of Charles Edward Stuart). He had restored the theatre at Ravenna at his own expense, and the Austrian agent's view of his intelligence was shared by most people, including his wife, even after all the unpleasantness and difficulties of their married life.

'While still young,' the report continued, 'he lost his Father, who left him only a moderate fortune, and that in poor condition. He then married the Contessa Placidia Zinanni, who made up for the disparity of her age – much greater than that of the Cavaliere – and for her imperfections by a very large dowry.'

Rich now, the Count treated his wife abominably. He seduced her maids, by one of whom he had six children. When his wife protested at this infidelity, he shut her up in a remote country house; she returned to Ravenna only once, to make a will, leaving everything to her husband. Having done this, she died with a rapidity which led some to suspect poison. The Count then married the maid, Angelica, and managed to persuade the religious authorities to allow him to legitimize their children. Considering that the Archbishop had told him that he 'had covered himself in infamy in the eyes of all the citizens of Ravenna', this indicates that he possessed rare powers of persuasion.

Meanwhile, however, during his first marriage, the Napoleonic army had invaded the Romagna, which was part of the Papal States. Some of the nobility, including Count Ruggero Gamba, Teresa's father, were enthusiastic: they set up a Tree of Liberty in the main piazza and burned their titles of nobility at its base. Others retired to their country houses; one of these was Monaldo Leopardi, the poet's father, who, according to Iris Origo, author of *Byron: The Last Attachment*, gave it as his opinion that 'it was too great an honour for such a blackguard as Napoleon that a gentleman should rise to see him pass'. Count Guiccioli apparently felt neither enthusiasm nor repugnance. 'The only alternative now left to a gentleman,' he said, 'is either to have his head cut off by the *canaille*, or to put himself at their head; I prefer the second.'

This was the sinister realist to whom Teresa was married. There was something about him which might recall the villain of a Gothic novel. Dark rumours floated round him. He had served Napoleon, and indeed attended his coronation in Milan; but when the Pope was restored in 1814, he was soon on good terms with the Cardinal Legate of Ravenna. And he was charged with worse than political time-serving. A dispute with a certain Manzoni, a landowner in Forlí, led to a law case and the temporary imprisonment of Guiccioli in the Castel Sant' Angelo in Rome. Soon after his release Manzoni was stabbed and killed on his way to the theatre.

Teresa, Iris Origo judges, 'was tied to her husband by a bond in which there was fascination as well as fear. I think that this rigid, eccentric, ironic old man, with suave formal manners, made use of his experience to gain, by a mixture of sensuality and violence, an evil and strange hold over his young bride.' She points out that when Teresa returned to him after Byron's death, and then left him again, one of her expressed reasons was the impossibility of being 'as vilely complaisant' as he required. The reasons she had for asking for a second separation 'were "of so vile a nature" that she could not bring herself to speak of them except to her lawyer, or in confession'. The implication is that he practised some sexual perversion, and that when Byron first met her, Teresa was a girl who had already experienced much more than might have been expected of one of her youth and apparent naïvety. Indeed, the whole subject of Count Guiccioli sheds light on the nature of the society in which Byron was to live for the next few years.

Byron: The Last Attachment, the story of Byron's life with Teresa, by the Marchesa Iris Origo, from which I have just quoted, is one of the best books about him. It is so good, not only because it is written with a sympathetic understanding of both Byron and Teresa, but because, unlike so many of his English biographers, the Marchesa appreciates the importance of Italian politics to him, and gives full weight to his involvement. She realizes that this was no mere whim, no pastime undertaken to alleviate the constitutional boredom with which he was always threatened. Yet even she describes him as a dilettante in politics, which is only true to the extent that politics was never his single interest. Even stranger, she quotes with apparent approval Bertrand Russell's observation that 'the freedom he praised was that of a German prince or Cherokee chief, not the inferior sort that might conceivably be enjoyed by ordinary mortals'. This judgment seems to me absurd, and contradicted by Byron's work and life.

The more one considers his career, the truer seems his own understanding of himself. Because he was a great and famous poet (even if one in whose poetry critics have found insincerity), people have been too ready to dismiss the doubts which he continually expressed about his own poetry, and his commitment to the art, as a pose. Yet when he told Moore that he wasn't at all sure that poetry was his true *métier*, it is worth considering whether he may have meant exactly what he said. Certainly he said it often and clearly enough. In the first place his recurrent expressions of discontent with a life given to versifying can't reasonably be dismissed as affectation. They were part of his complicated nature; and they were also incidentally characteristically Scottish. Sir Walter Scott, for instance, felt his inferiority as a mere writer to the Duke of Wellington: 'What would the Duke of Wellington think of a few bits of novels, which perhaps he had never read, and for which the strong probability is that he would not care a sixpense if he did?' He regretted not having been a soldier, and, like Robert Louis Stevenson later, wondered whether scribbling verse and fiction could be considered activity worthy of a man's life. Byron had something of the same doubt. It is easy to reproach all three for not taking a sufficiently respectful view of their art, but one may also argue that the respect they showed for the reality of life beyond their art in fact enriched their work. Those artists who have elevated art into a substitute for religion have often produced thinner and less human art than those who take a humbler view of their calling.

Second, Byron belonged, however insecurely, to the English political class. His earliest ambitions had been parliamentary rather than poetic. He had laboured more intensely over his maiden speech in the House of Lords than over any poem. (He had learned it by heart so that he might deliver it more effectively.) That speech had made a profound impression; it had alarmed the ministers, and, had it not been followed abruptly by the publication of *Childe Harold* and its wild and unexpected success, establishing Byron's reputation as a poet with an ease and speed – and to an extent – which he could hardly have equalled in politics, it is likely that he would have followed up its success. As it was, close friends like Hobhouse and Kinnaird had serious political ambitions; his Harrow contemporary, Sir Robert Peel, whose superior he had proved himself in school debates, was in the Cabinet in Byron's lifetime. As a peer, he was moreover assured of a position as a legislator at a time when, as I have said, the great majority of Cabinet posts were still held by members of the House of Lords. If the scandal surrounding the failure of his marriage had cost him domestic happiness, deprived him of his daughter, and debarred him from society, it had also, for the time being, destroyed his hopes of a career in politics. One of the consequences of his affair with Teresa was to open before him a new route of political activity; and he came to hope that a reputation won first in Italy, and then in Greece, might rehabilitate him in England and English life. He was quite consistent in his political ambitions. 'A man,' he told Teresa, 'ought to do more for society than write verses.' When, in Ravenna on the morning of his thirty-third birthday, he wrote that he did not regret the years 'for what I have done, but for what I might have done', it was of politics rather than poetry that he was thinking. Of course, he was, as it happened, a poet first, and it was through his poetry rather than his actions that his influence was chiefly exerted; but he was never satisfied with this.

He had lived in Venice as a foreigner; that is, as foreigners have always lived in Italy, delightedly taking much and giving nothing but money in return. His Italian companions might not deserve the reproaches that Shelley cast at them – we can't tell, they are mostly silent and anonymous – but they were people who lived only private lives, however publicly, and took no part in political activity. His closest associates belonged to the lower classes – they taught him to respect their vitality and endurance; but, for the most part, in Italy then, such people counted for nothing. Italy would revive as its patriots hoped – and the revival indeed began, falteringly, while Byron was there, and affected him – but it would be almost entirely the work of the nobility, the bourgeoisie and the intellectuals. The peasants and proletariat were generally indifferent to the movement which came to be known as the Risorgimento. In some parts of the country – Naples for example – they were indeed openly hostile to it, and adhered with some passion to the old regime. Naples differed from other Italian states of course in that it was not ruled by foreigners. The Bourbon kings had made themselves into Neapolitans – Ferdinand IV, known as 'Nasone' ('Big Nose') so completely shared the anthropomorphic outlook of his subjects that on one occasion, hearing a servant whose backside he had kicked cry out to the Madonna, he agitatedly offered him a sum of money if he promised not to inform on him to the Mother of God; moreover, the Neapolitans looked on northern Italians as foreigners, with good enough reason, as the unhappy history of the Mezzogiorno after the unification of Italy was to reveal. All that was in the future however when Teresa Guiccioli introduced Byron into a new society, and, in doing so, made him part of Italy and of the movement that sought to revive Italian national consciousness.

First though there was the love affair. It began almost at once, for Teresa, at the instant of their meeting at a conversazione given by the Contessa Benzoni, was struck by a 'celestial apparition'. The young girl, alarmed and perturbed by the attentions of her elderly husband,

W. Brockedon.   H.T. Ryall.

Teresa Guiccioli: 'the last attachment'

toppled headlong into love. 'This Venice,' she wrote later, 'without flowers, without trees, without scents, without birds, which had pleased her so little before, with its lugubrious gondolas instead of her team of horses, now seemed to her the abode of the very light of life, an earthly paradise.' For Teresa, meeting Byron was the true Romantic *coup de foudre*. Her sentiments never altered; she adored Byron and continued to do so for the rest of her long life. She survived him by almost fifty years – she didn't die until 1873, and her second husband, the Marquis de Boissy, used to be proud to introduce her as the 'ancienne maîtresse de Lord Byron'. 'She said,' Iris Origo tells us, 'that all her papers, "whatever the effect upon my reputation" were to be published, for the sake of showing "Lord Byron's good and kind heart". Is not this,' she asks, 'after all, fidelity?' Indeed it is; and it does credit to both Teresa and Byron. No doubt Byron's fame contributed to the original attraction, but it was not the chief thing. She loved him for himself, and may have been the only woman except Augusta to do so; and her love was always generous and selfless. She would not take presents of any value from him; when, immediately before his departure for Greece, he proposed to provide for her in his will, she would have none of it. 'She declined,' Byron wrote, 'in the most positive, and indeed displeased terms, declaring that she should consider such a bequest as not only an injustice to my daughter by Lady B, and to my sister's children, but as a posthumous insult to herself. It is true that madama G. has a separate allowance by the Pope's decree from her husband, and will have a considerable jointure at his demise, but it is not an unhandsome conduct nevertheless.' The fact is that Teresa really was what Iris Origo calls her: 'A woman who was completely disinterested.' All she wanted from Byron was that he should love her and live with her; it was as if she existed to affirm that he was right in calling love 'a woman's whole existence'.

As for Byron he was soon surprised by the warmth of his feelings. It began for him as a casual affair, but he was soon in love himself. It was not surprising. He had exhausted the delights of Venetian life. He had always had a warm domestic side to his nature, which hitherto only Augusta had been able to satisfy. But he had by now put aside the hope that he and Augusta might sometime be able to settle down together, even if he did not perhaps fully realize how her spirit had been subdued and her independence curtailed by Lady Byron, who insisted on supervising Augusta's correspondence with her brother, threatening to destroy her reputation if she rebelled.

Teresa had, in fact, come on the scene at just the right moment. He was bored. Though dissipation pleased him, it also disgusted him. 'Every rake is a Puritan at heart', and Byron had enough of the Scots

Calvinist in him to have seen his Venetian life as a defiant gesture: if the English public had decided that he was a scandalous debauchee, then that is what they should have; hence the note of bravado in those letters in which he recounted his dissipations. But he was also by nature inconstant, never satisfied for long with living only through one side of his complex being. He was now offered what he had hardly believed could come his way: the unquestioning love and full devotion of a virtuous and beautiful girl. In a curious manner, familiar to many writers, life was repeating art. Byron had been dwelling in his imagination on the tender and innocent rapture of Juan and Haidée:

> She loved, and was beloved – she adored,
>   And she was worshipp'd; after Nature's fashion,
> Their intense souls, into each other pour'd,
>   If souls could die, had perish'd in that passion, –
> But, by degrees their senses were restored,
>   Again to be o'ercome, again to dash on;
> And beating 'gainst his bosom, Haidée's heart
> Felt as if never more to beat apart. . . .
>
> Haidée was Nature's bride, and knew not this:
>   Haidée was Passion's child, born where the sun
> Showers triple light, and scorches even the kiss
>   Of his gazelle-eyed daughters; she was one
> Made but to love, to feel that she was his
>   Who was her chosen: what was said or done
> Elsewhere was nothing. She had nought to fear,
> Hope, care, nor love beyond, – her heart was *here*.

Of course Teresa, being a real woman, was more complicated than Haidée. Nevertheless, in these lines he prefigured her. As for his own case, that was more complicated still. Over the next years he would from time to time rebel at the role imposed on him by the conventions of Italian society; he would feel that it made him look absurd in the eyes of his English friends, to be seen in attendance on his mistress with the other fan-carrying *cavalieri serventi*; he would break out in language of disgusted protest in his letters and he would contemplate emigration to Venezuela, the United States, even a return to England. But none of this was serious enough or went deep enough to impel action. The truest expression of his feelings is to be found in a letter which he wrote in 1819 on the index page of Teresa's copy of Madame de Staël's novel *Corinne*, which he had found in her sitting room in the Palazzo Savioli in Bologna.

My dearest Teresa

I have read this book in your garden; – my love, you were absent, or else I could not have read it. It is a favourite book of yours, and the writer was a friend of mine. You will not understand these English words, and others will not understand them, which is the reason I have not scrawled them in Italian. But you will recognize the handwriting of him who passionately loved you, and you will divine that, over a book that was yours, he could only think of love. In that word – beautiful in all languages, but most so in yours – *Amor mio* – is comprised my existence here and hereafter. I feel I exist here, and I fear that I shall exist hereafter – to what purpose you will decide; my destiny rests with you, and you a woman, eighteen years of age, and two out of a convent. I wish that you had staid there, with all my heart, – or, at least, that I had never met you in your married state.

But all this is too late. I love you, and you love me, – at least you *say so* and act as if you *did*, which last is a great consolation in all events. But I more than love you, and cannot cease to love you.

Think of me sometimes, when the Alps and the ocean divide us, but they never will unless you *wish* it.

Byron

And, in a footnote scribbled on page 92 of the novel, he said: 'I knew Madame de Staël well – better than she knew Italy, but I little thought that one day, I should *think with her thoughts*. She is sometimes right, and often wrong, about Italy and England; but almost always true in delineating the heart.'

The love affair began in Venice. Count Guccioli then took his wife back to the Romagna, inviting Byron to visit them in Ravenna later in the year. Byron was long to be puzzled by the Count's attitude. He couldn't decide if he was really as indifferent to the affair as he pretended – he couldn't of course be ignorant of it – or whether he was biding his time; whether Byron mightn't expect a dagger-thrust between the shoulder blades one dark night.

The Count took Teresa first to an estate he had recently bought called Cà Zen. It lay at the mouth of the Po, in a deserted and melancholy marsh. Teresa complained of being 'with no one to speak to, without music, almost without books,' but the mood of the lagoon – flat, lonely, decayed – suited hers; she felt in sympathy with the landscape. And then her husband took her back to Ravenna, and all the time she and Byron exchanged letters through an intermediary, and she wondered when he would come, and he hesitated to commit himself to a love affair that held a dangerous threat of sentiment.

But then Teresa fell ill – it was, in fact, a miscarriage though the baby could not possibly have been Byron's: 'I can't tell whether I was the involuntary Cause of the miscarriage,' he noted, 'but certes I was

[133]

not the father of the foetus, for she was three months advanced before our first passade . . . ;' and though Byron was made anxious by the news, he was also troubled by the vehemence of Teresa's letters. He still didn't know her properly, and he feared he might have landed himself with another Caroline Lamb. Besides, there was another girl, also eighteen, a Venetian called Angelina, who had declared herself in love with him and even proposed to arrange for the disposal of his wife. Her father had locked her up, and called the police, and Byron fell into the Grand Canal one night as he made his way to a rendezvous.

So he hesitated, and, as he did so, his thoughts turned back to Augusta: 'I have never ceased nor can cease to feel for a moment that perfect and boundless attachment which bound & binds me to you – which renders me incapable of *real love* for any other human being – what could they be to me after you. . . . I repent of nothing except that cursed marriage – & your refusing to continue to love me as you had loved me – I can neither quite forget nor *quite forgive* you for that precious piece of reformation – but I can never be other than I have been – and whenever I love anything it is because it reminds me in some way or other of yourself.'

And this – it seems likely – was one reason why Teresa pleased him. So it is not perhaps surprising that, when the uncertainties of the early months of his relationship with her had been dispelled, and they had settled, on however detached a basis, as a couple, he wrote to Augusta far less frequently than before, and then chiefly on matters of business.

But the early months were difficult. Byron could not decide how far to commit himself. He did not really understand either his feelings or his situation. That indeed was quite new to him; he had never formed an enduring relationship with an Italian woman of his own class, and he wasn't sure what was expected of him. When he did realize, he acquiesced. Despite his complaints, he was often surprisingly ready to play the part others had assigned to him.

VI

Byron visited Ravenna for the first time in June. A little provincial town of perhaps no more than 15,000 inhabitants, divided from the Adriatic by several miles of marshland, and with a deep pine forest coming to its outskirts, it was nevertheless redolent of history, with that melancholy weight that suited Byron's temperament. He had read Gibbon's description of the site, and knew that Augustus had constructed a harbour there for 250 ships. He had learned that: 'The gradual retreat of the sea has left the modern city at a distance of four miles from the Hadriatic, and as early as the fifth or sixth century of the Christian era the port of Augustus was converted into pleasant orchards, and a lonely grove of pines covered the ground where the Roman fleet once rode at anchor. Even this alteration contributed to increase the natural strength of the place, and the shallowness of the water was a sufficient barrier against the large ships of the enemy. This advantageous situation was fortified by art and labour, and in the twentieth year of his age the Emperor of the West, anxious only for his personal safety, retired to the perpetual confinement of the walls and morasses of Ravenna. The example of Honorius was imitated by his feeble successors, the Gothic kings, and afterwards the Exarchs, who occupied the throne and place of the emperors; and till the middle of the eighth century Ravenna was considered as the seat of government and the capital of Italy.' It was there indeed that the last Emperor of the West, the boy Romulus, called in mockery 'Augustulus' had been installed in 476. Such associations gave Ravenna all the charm of

Ravenna: the Byzantine church of S. Vitale

[135]

decayed greatness. Dante had died there, and his tomb was one of the sights of the city. Though Gibbon says that in classical times its air was considered 'uncommonly pure and salubrious', this was no longer so. The marshes were malarial, and the sixteenth-century geographer Giovanni Botero joined it with Brindisi, Aquileia and Rome as one of the most unhealthy towns in Italy. It had, however, one other attraction for Byron besides the presence of Teresa and its historical associations; there were few English there, it was off their beaten track and the great Byzantine mosaics in S. Appollinare in Classe had little appeal to the taste of the time.

Byron took up residence first in the Albergo Imperiale; meaner than its name suggested, it was yet the best hotel in the town, situated in the Via di Porta Sisi, near Dante's tomb. He was uncertain how to proceed, but had brought a letter of introduction to Count Alborghetti, Secretary to the Papal Legate, Cardinal Malvasia, who ruled the province under the watchful and suspicious eye of the Austrians. Alborghetti at once invited him to join him in his box at the theatre. Byron did so and was asked whether he had any acquaintance in the town. (It seems likely that his answer was already known.)

'"Yes," replied Byron, "I am very friendly with Count and Countess Guiccioli." "But alas," replied Alborghetti, "you will not be able to see the young lady, as they say she is at death's door." At this sudden and unexpected news, given so abruptly, Byron lost his head and, unable to control his emotion, replied, that, if the lady should die, he hoped he would not survive her . . . Whereupon, "Alborghetti, who had believed that Byron was attracted to Ravenna by literary interests – by Dante's tomb, the Byzantine monuments, and memories of Dryden, Boccaccio and Gaston de Foix – gaped round-eyed at the emotion of the young Lord. . . . Fortunately, Count Guiccioli who had caught sight of Lord Byron, then called on him in the box and calmed him by giving him better news."'

This account given by Teresa must have been highly gratifying to her. Her hesitant lover had arrived and had at once given proof of his passion. No wonder that very soon a Ravenna gossip was writing to a Venetian friend that 'the common opinion is that the Palazzo Guiccioli has impressed him more than the Rotonda and the ruins of Theodoric'. Wherever he went Byron attracted attention, and he had made an enormous stir in the little provincial town.

Teresa's fever abated – it may have been caused partly by her anxiety about her lover's arrival. On the evening of 16 June, a week after he

Opposite: Dante's tomb, Ravenna. Byron lodged nearby

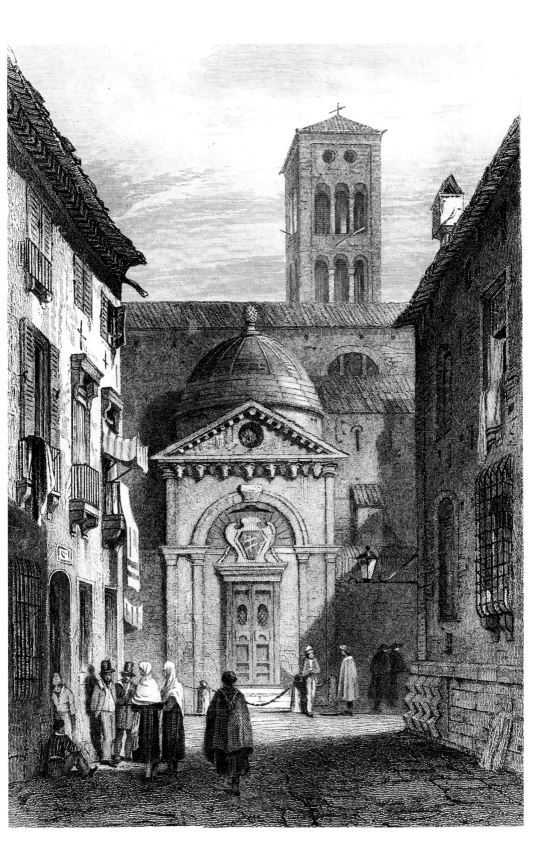

had come, she was well enough to drive out with him. 'The whole world,' she noted, 'was fresh and green; the nightingales were singing, the crickets were chirping. Lord Byron was charmed by the landscape; he seemed at once happy and melancholy.' Driving through the pine wood, Teresa asked him to write something about Dante; he promised he would and dedicated the resulting poem, *The Prophecy of Dante*, to her. They read together Dante's verses about the lovers Paolo and Francesca, and when she asked him if they had ever been translated into English, he answered with a standard Italian pun: 'non tradotto, ma tradito' ('not translated, but betrayed').

They were in the first flush of their love, and Teresa's health still caused concern. It was, he told Murray, 'very precarious. In losing her, I would lose a being who has run great risks on my account, and whom I have every reason to love – but I must not think this possible. I do not know what I should do if she died, but I ought to blow my brains out – and I hope that I should.'

Byron urged the Count to let him send to Venice for his own doctor, Professor Aglietti. Aglietti was himself a poet and scholar, and a man of great charm. Byron considered him the best doctor in Europe – he was of course always ready to apply superlatives, to doctors or scoundrels as to views and landscapes. But Aglietti came, and, prescribing leeches and Peruvian bark, restored Teresa's health; she and her family thought that Byron's intervention had saved her life. Before the doctor left, he and Byron placed a volume of Byron's own poems on Dante's tomb; the Ravennese noted approvingly that whenever Byron passed the monument he removed his hat from his head in tribute.

Meanwhile, however, he was puzzled by the attitude of the Count, who seemed overflowing with friendship for his wife's lover. It even apparently survived a lampoon sent him by an anonymous well-wisher:

> Di Lord è innamorata, ognun lo sa,
> La moglie del Falcon fatto Cucù,
> Ne ancor s'avvede il vecchio babala
> Che ormai conviengli andar' col capo in giu.
>
> Ridono i sassi ancor della città
> Del Becco e di Madonna, e molto piu
> Dei rimedi che Lord venir' le fa
> Da Venezia, da Londra e dal Peru.

Palazzo Guiccioli, Ravenna. Byron continued to live here even after Teresa and her husband had separated

[139]

(Everyone knows that, in love with the lord, the wife has made her falcon into a cuckoo, and that the old bird sees nothing, though he should now be hanging his head. The stones of the city laugh at the cuckold and his lady, and all the more at the cures which the Lord fetches from London, Venice and Peru.)

The Count actually read this to Teresa, and Byron was much puzzled by his apparent equanimity; it was not how he expected husbands to behave. There were other problems too. Teresa's brother, Pietro Gamba, a student in Rome, had heard rumours of his sister's adventure, and wrote a stiff letter warning her off. Didn't she realize, poor innocent that she was, that 'this man, whom you described to me in your last letter as an angel upon earth, is the husband of a young woman full of innocence and affection like yourself; and not satisfied with having abandoned her to give himself up to a life full of disorder, he keeps her shut up in a Castle, of which many dark mysterious tales are told. It is even said, that, in spite of his rank, he has been a Pirate during his journeys in the East.'

Pietro Gamba was later to become Byron's friend and loyal and wholehearted admirer. The letter, which had no effect on Teresa, is chiefly interesting for the evidence it offers of the Gothic reputation Byron had.

But there were pleasanter sides to life in Ravenna. Their lovemaking was difficult, even dangerous: 'the local is inconvenient (no bolts and be d—d to them) and we run great risks (were it not at sleeping hours after dinner) and no place but the great saloon at his own palace,' but it was possible, and no doubt the danger of discovery added to the pleasure. Then there were the hours of quiet enjoyment of their evening drives and rides in the pine forest:

> Sweet Hour of Twilight! – in the solitude
>   Of the pine forest, and the silent shore
> Which bounds Ravenna's immemorial wood,
>   Rooted where once the Adrian wave flow'd o'er,
> To where the last Caesarean fortress stood,
>   Evergreen forest! which Boccaccio's lore
> And Dryden's lay made haunted ground to me,
>   How have I loved the twilight hour and thee!

And though he might, in self-protective mockery, tell Augusta that in fact Teresa rode extremely badly, being unable to control her horse which would keep trying to bite his in the neck, and though he might try to cast the whole experience in ridiculous colours, in the depths of his nature he did not deceive himself:

Ave Maria! blessed be the hour!
   The time, the clime, the spot, where I so oft
Have felt that moment in its fullest power
   Sink o'er the earth so beautiful and soft,
While swung the deep bell in the distant tower,
   Or the faint dying day-hymn stole aloft,
And not a breath crept through the rosy air,
And yet the forest leaves seem'd stirr'd with prayer.

Ave Maria! 'tis the hour of prayer!
   Ave Maria! 'tis the hour of love! . . .

Count Guiccioli suddenly decided that he had business in Bologna, and, since Teresa was now well again, required her to accompany him. She urged Byron to follow them, and then, to his surprise, the invitation was reinforced by the Count himself. They had stopped at one of his estates, near Forlì, and he besought Byron to visit 'this poetic place of ours'. Byron was puzzled. Was this an example of the Count's good manners? Of his indifference? Or, was it the prelude – Byron, like most Englishmen could never quite rid himself of the Elizabethan–Jacobean view of Italian craft and duplicity – the prelude to an act of revenge? Nevertheless he followed.

Byron had already visited Bologna twice. On the boundary of the Papal States, known indeed as their land-port, it was as prosperous as it was beautiful. Its geographical situation, however, also made it a centre of espionage. And Byron was an object of grave suspicion: 'I do not conceal from Your Excellency', an agent reported to the Director General of Police in Rome, 'that this news [of his arrival] both perplexes and embarrasses me. Byron is a man of letters, and his literary merits will attract to him the most distinguished men of learning in Bologna. This class of men has no love for the Government. Your Excellency sees therefore how difficult it becomes for me to exercise the necessary supervision over my lord's private affairs.'

Bologna had become in 1818 the centre for subversive and Republican activity. A Congress of the Carboneria, the association of Liberal patriots, had approved a constitution there, and had sworn to 'give all their strength and even their lives to achieve the independence of Italy'. Hadn't Byron arrived to promote such activities rather than to engage in a love affair? The police spy Giuseppe Valtancoli of Montepulciano certainly thought so. He discovered that Byron wore the badge of a secret society on his watch-chain; he had therefore come to promote the interests of the *Romantici*, a name which despite appearances has nothing to do with Romanticism, but is derived from the republican ideal of *Roma Antica*. These men, Valtancoli informed his superiors, 'form a band that aims at the destruction of our literature, our politics, our country. Lord Byron is certainly its champion, and you deceive yourselves if you believe that he is only occupied in making a cuckold of Guiccioli. He is libidinous and immoral to excess; but he soon tires of the object of his worship, and offers it as a sacrifice on the altar of his contemptuous pride. But, at the same time, in politics he is not so inconstant. Here he is an Englishman in the fullest meaning of the term. He is like a madman in his desire to ruin everything that does not belong to him, to paralyse every tendency that our society displays towards natural independence, to involve us in ruin and bloodshed, in order that at last the deserted and still smouldering States may be divided between his greedy and demoralized conspirators.' He would soon be joined in Bologna by 'Lord Kinnaird, who shot at the Duke of Wellington'.

And so on. Spies and agents, of course, require conspirators; if these did not exist, they would themselves become redundant. Most of what they reported of Byron was nonsense, gossip gathered from the ignorant and inventive. This is common enough, and Byron suffered little inconvenience from their activities, which indeed tell us far more about the state of mind of those who ruled Italy than they do of Byron.

It was a different matter, of course, for Italians themselves. Count Guiccioli had always walked warily in the sight of authority. In 1819 he was nervous; it wasn't at all clear how things would turn out, and therefore which side he would be wise to back. He saw Byron as a sort of insurance policy. Mightn't his distinguished English friend procure for him the appointment as British Vice-Consul in Ravenna, 'without salary or emolument' of course? The Count seems to have been on poor terms with the Papal Government – as the events of the next year were to show; he wasn't at all sure how he was regarded by the Liberals; this post would be a sort of security for him.

Byron did what he could, which wasn't much. He asked Murray to see what could be done, and pointed out that he knew of cases when a British consul would have been useful. He had himself seen to the repatriation of a British seaman who had been stranded in Ravenna for some years 'from the want of any accredited agent able or willing to help him homewards'. He even suggested that perhaps he should be made British Consul at Ravenna himself, with the Count as his Vice-Consul. But he must have known that his influence was slight. Castlereagh had responsibility for consular appointments and was hardly likely to act in such a way as to gratify the author of *Don Juan*.

Then, Guiccioli returned to Ravenna, while Teresa, 'in view of her delicate health, shaken by so many emotions,' set off for Venice, to consult Professor Aglietti, Byron of course accompanying her. This was a strange development, hard to understand. According to an account which Teresa gave to her lawyers later, there was a quarrel over money. The Count had approached Byron for a loan, which he was at first ready to give; then, on the advice of his banker, refused. But, in her account of Byron's life, she said only that Byron had, in fact, lent the Count 'a few thousand francs, a sum insignificant to both of them'. The quarrel between her and the Count, occasioned by Byron's refusal of the loan, had therefore never taken place. The Austrian spy, however, thought that the Count had perhaps sold his wife to Byron.

The following months hardly cleared the confusion. For a time, Byron and Teresa lived together at La Mira. That was, of course, scandalous. It was one thing to have a lover, quite another to set up house with him. Still they were happy; for a brief spell perhaps Byron could escape the self-consciousness that plagued him in society; he was confident of Teresa's affection as he had been of Augusta's. He was able to joke and chatter, and also to work; the third canto of *Don Juan* galloped along in these weeks.

It could not last. The Count might be complaisant, though his attitude to Byron perhaps changed when the Vice-Consulship showed no signs of materializing, and Byron then declined to lend him a further thousand pounds. All the same the Count appeared ready to give Teresa permission to accompany Byron on a tour of the Lakes. Then her father intervened. He couldn't feel happy at his daughter's association with the English milord whose reputation – if not everything young Pietro had alleged – was still decidedly murky; and he told Count Guiccioli that he 'did not approve of allowing an inexperienced young woman to go off alone, and still less accompanied by a young man like Lord Byron'. Guiccioli shrugged it off; he was indifferent to the world's opinion. All the same he soon arrived in Venice himself, and took up residence in the Palazzo Mocenigo. He promptly quarrelled with Teresa and offered her the choice between himself and her lover. She, of course, was all for staying with Byron, quite prepared to make the grand Romantic gesture and sacrifice her social position, the support of her own family, and everything for the sake of her lover.

His position was more difficult. He knew too much of the world and of his own nature. Even during the happy weeks at La Mira, in benign autumn suns, he had found himself remembering 'what Curran said to Moore – "so I hear you have married a pretty woman – and a very good creature too – an excellent creature – pray – um – how do *you pass your evenings?*" it is a devil of a question. . . .' He could not believe in eternal constancy – either his own or anyone else's – and he wondered whether a woman who cast off all for love would not come to regret it. He shrank for making himself responsible for the destruction of her marriage; he would be 'saddled with her for ever'. An unpleasant phrase, and yet a revealing one; there was, as his admiration for Pope reminds us, and as *Don Juan* exemplifies, a fund of anti-Romantic good sense in Byron.

The Count, angry and perplexed, came to Byron 'crying about it and I told him, "If you abandon your wife I will take her undoubtedly; it is my duty – it is also my inclination – in case of such extremity; but if, as you say, you are really disposed to live with, and like her as before, I will not only not carry further disturbance into your family, but even repass the Alps; for I have no hesitation in saying that Italy will now be to me insupportable."'

Teresa herself was hardly consulted – though she had, of course, made her inclinations clear; but this was in a sense fair enough. In that society, at that time, she would require to have a man responsible for her; otherwise, the Pope might command her into a convent.

Byron knew he had not played the part of a Byronic hero. 'What could I do? On the one hand to sacrifice a woman whom I loved, for life; leaving her destitute and divided from all ties in case of my death; on the other hand to give up an *amicizia* which had been my pleasure, my pride and my passion. At twenty, I should have taken her away, at thirty, with the experience of ten such years! – I sacrificed myself only; and counselled and persuaded her to return with her husband to Ravenna. . . .'

He seems, however, to have promised her that he would follow, though according to the secret information received by the Austrian police, 'Byron, in order to calm the amorous agitation of Signora Guiccioli, who refused to leave him, promised to return to see her in Ravenna, but his only real intention is to return to England.'

It would be interesting to know how they ascertained that: from the gossip of servants? Or the opening of correspondence? It does seem to have been his intention. He told Teresa he was leaving a country which 'without you, has become insupportable'. But he did not go. There were excuses: his little daughter Allegra fell ill; a vile attack on *Don Juan* and his own character in *Blackwood's Magazine*, revived his dislike of his home country; Augusta did not reply to his suggestion that they might meet at one of the Channel Ports; and so on. But the truth was: he did not wish to go. He was at odds with himself: 'Your Blackwood,' he told Murray, 'accuses me of treating women harshly – it may be so – but I have been their martyr – My whole life has been sacrificed to them & by them.' He was, he said, 'indecisive because few things interest me . . . – I have got such a cold and headache that I can

John Murray, Byron's friend and publisher

hardly see what I scrawl – the winters here are sharp as needles . . .'
but he would not, could not, move.

And then the matter was resolved. Teresa fell ill again – her life even
was despaired of. No doubt her state of mind contributed to her
condition, but many of her family had a tendency to consumption,
and it was natural that her parents should be alarmed. Even her father,
hitherto suspicious of Byron, was persuaded that his recall was
necessary. As for the enigmatic Count, who, only a few weeks before,
had drawn up a stringent code of conduct that his returning wife was
to observe, who can tell what he thought? He is the most mysterious
figure in the story.

On 4 December Byron was still telling Murray that his journey
depended on the snows in the Tyrol. On the 10th he wrote to
Kinnaird: 'I shall go again to Ravenna – anything better than England –

it is better to be with a woman whom I love at the risk of assassination than in a country where I neither like nor am liked – and where my first duty & intention is to cut the throat of a scoundrel;' and, laying down his pen, he turned his thoughts back to Teresa: 'You have decided that I am to return to Ravenna. I shall return – and do – and be – what you wish. I cannot say more. . . . I kiss you 10000+ times from my heart. . . .'

Of course, since his letters to Kinnaird, and another to Murray, and this one to Teresa are all dated the 10th, it is quite possible that he wrote to her first. But it rounds off the story better to make Teresa's the third written.

On 23 December, he was at Bologna, scribbling a short and scrappy note to Augusta. On Christmas Eve, he arrived in Ravenna. On the last day of the year he wrote to Lady Byron, from 'this city of Italy [which] is out of the track of armies and travellers, and is more of the old time'. He asked for a picture of their daughter. He reminded her that it was just five years since he had been on his way to their 'funeral marriage', and he had little thought that 'Lady and Lord Byron would become bye words of division.' And he told her that he had given Moore his memoirs and 'could wish you to see, read and mark any part or parts that do not seem to coincide with the truth – the truth I have always stated – but there are two ways of looking at it – and your way may not be my way. . . .' Then he wrote to Richard Hoppner, the English consul at Venice, who disliked Teresa and whose Swiss wife had looked after Allegra for a time, to say that 'The G's object seemed to be to parade her foreign lover as much as possible – and faith – if she seemed to glory in the Scandal, it was not for me to be ashamed of it . . . everybody are very kind to her – and not discourteous to me – Fathers – and all relations quite agreeable.'

There were storms still ahead, but he and Teresa would now be together till he left on his expedition to Greece.

VII

Byron spent the whole of the year 1820 in and around Ravenna. That was a sign of how his life had been changed by the affair with Teresa. He lodged at first in the Albergo Imperiale again, but within a few weeks had moved into the upper floor of the Palazzo Guiccioli; with the help of an African page boy who acted as their scout, they were able to carry on their affair more comfortably, being under the same roof. All the same it was not long before the Count's resentment became marked. Teresa told Byron that he had broken open her writing-desk doubtless in the hope of finding some incriminating material. Since the Count cannot at any time have been ignorant of how matters stood between his wife and Byron, it seems likely that he was being urged by the government to find some evidence which could justify them in demanding Byron's expulsion from the Papal States. The equivocal nature of his own political position would have made it easy for the authorities to apply pressure on him. It may also be, however, that, disappointed in the hope that Byron's friendship could obtain him some advantages, he now let a natural resentment surface. The fact is that it is impossible to know just what promoted this secretive and devious man, first to tolerate his wife's infidelity, and then to seek to destroy her. Later in the year, Byron even suspected that there was a plan to shut Teresa up in a convent.

Before then, however, Teresa and Guiccioli had formally separated. The Count had surprised them 'quasi in the fact', as Byron put it to Murray, and broken out in anger. He asked Byron to stop his visits. Teresa would have none of this, and was ready to run away with Byron. He declined to do so, and declared that he was instead ready to withdraw from the scene. That was not a mark of indifference; he was still in love with Teresa and he would continue to love her for the rest of his days. But he was aware that he was a dozen years older, he had never believed he would live to any age, and he was very conscious, that, being already married himself, he could offer Teresa no security at all. If they ran off and lived together for a couple of years, and he then died, her situation would be extremely disagreeable. She would have lost all respectability, all social position, and have nothing but memories in return. It was not to be thought of. The fact that Byron could think in such prudential terms would seem a mark of his affection for Teresa; he wasn't prepared to see her ruin herself for love of him.

So, instead, he advised her to consult her father. Count Ruggero Gamba was now well-disposed to Byron. He much preferred him to Guiccioli. They shared the same political ideas and he had, now that he knew him better, succumbed to Byron's charm. Moreover, he was genuinely fond of his daughter, and saw that she would be miserable without Byron. Accordingly he applied to the Pope for a decree of separation for Teresa. He also wrote a very curious letter to Cardinal Rusconi, the new Papal Legate in Ravenna: in it he said that if Guiccioli 'had believed what he now attempts to make others suspect, why did he then invite the Lord to Ravenna, and in his own house too?' And then, in a very odd passage, which Teresa later tried to erase from the copy of the letter in the Gamba archives, he said, 'If I wished, by words, deeds, or writings, to prove how Count Guiccioli attempted, for vile financial considerations, to prostitute, sell and disgrace my daughter, and make her unhappy, I could show it with the greatest clearness; but the extremely delicate nature of the subject obliges me to keep silent.'

It is impossible to say just what he means by this accusation, but his sincerity cannot be doubted: he even challenged Guiccioli to a duel. Iris Origo asks whether this is 'not overwhelming evidence that what Teresa at last told him about her husband's behaviour, shocked him so deeply as to place him – against all his principles and preconceptions – wholly on her side?'

Moreover, it convinced the clerical authorities. That is even odder. After all, nobody could have had any real doubt that Teresa had committed adultery with Byron. Byron was distrusted by the Government, even though Alborghetti, the Legate's secretary, was a friend of his and probably pled his cause. But Gamba was in poor standing too, as a known Liberal. And yet they decided in Teresa's favour. On 6 July the papal decree granted her her separation on the grounds that it 'was no longer possible for her to live in peace and safety with her husband'. She was to be paid alimony, but it was also stipulated that she must live in her father's house.

In the months before the decree was made, Byron had his moments of anxiety: 'They say here that he will have me taken off, it is the custom. They pop at you from behind trees, and put a knife into your back in company, or in turning a corner, while you are blowing your nose.' Guiccioli's grandson, also called Alessandro, who wrote a history of his family, mocked these fears as 'a dream of a foreigner who . . . imagined the Italy of 1819 to be unchanged from that of the Borgias and the Farnese'. On the other hand, Stendhal who followed the story with interest, remarked that 'the husband has an income of 50,000 pounds; he is quite capable of assassinating the noble lord'.

As for Byron, as events moved to their climax, he made his commitment to Teresa evident. He told her that he had hesitated because he had not wished to put her in a position 'where the greatest reciprocal sacrifices would be needed'. A woman needed character, friendship, and 'the profoundest – and untiring love – proved often and for long – to decide on a course so disadvantageous in every way'. But 'now I can hesitate no longer. – He may abandon you – but I *never*. – I have *years* more than you in age – and as many *centuries* in sad experience; I foresee troubles and sacrifices for you, but they will be *shared*; my love – my duty – my honour – all these and everything should make me what I am *now*, your lover, friend and (when circumstances permit) your *husband*.'

On this letter Teresa scribbled: '*Promesse!!!! d'être mon Epoux!!*'

These private affairs occupied Byron's attention for the first half of the year. They did not, however, keep him from work. He had sent Murray the third and fourth cantos of *Don Juan* in February, undeterred by the poor reception given to their predecessors. His post-bag even included – a nice stroke of irony – a letter of reproof from the celebrated tart Harriet Wilson: 'Dear *adorable* Lord Byron, *don't* make a mere *coarse* old libertine of yourself . . .' She suggested that when he didn't feel up to writing in a more elevated strain, he should take 'a little calomel'. He had also written translations of Pulci and the story of Francesca da Rimini from Dante, and had begun a tragedy *Marino Faliero*. He was concerned with the education of his daughter Allegra, who he refused to return to the care of her mother ('Madame Claire is a damned bitch') or the Shelleys: 'I so totally disapprove of the mode of Children's treatment in their family, that I should look upon the Child as going into a Hospital. Is it not so? Have they *reared* one? . . . the Child shall not quit me again to perish of starvation and green fruit, or be taught to believe that there is no Deity. Whenever there is convenience of vicinity and access, her Mother can always have her with her; otherwise no.' It was another example of the way in which Byron's distrust and disapproval of Shelley always burgeoned in his absence.

Meanwhile Byron and Teresa were necessarily separated for a couple of months. She had gone to her father's country house, the Villa Gamba at Filetto some fifteen miles south-west of Ravenna. It was thought unwise that he should immediately present himself there. So he remained in his apartments in the Palazzo Guiccioli, even though the Count had naturally enough given him notice to leave. He was, however, negotiating the lease of a villa near Filetto.

The Gambas' country house was delightful. It was set on the edge of the forest, with marshes and lagoons, rich in water-fowl, spreading beyond. The house itself – destroyed by the Germans in 1944 – was a pleasant eighteenth-century building, which, like most Italian country houses combined a certain magnificence with a good deal of discomfort. There were fine hangings, furniture and pictures, but few fireplaces, rugs or carpets. It was really intended for use only in the summer, for with the approach of autumn, the Gambas, like most of the Italian nobility, would return to their town palazzo. But the summer months were charming: game was plentiful and the men and boys spent hours outdoors with their pointers shooting duck, snipe, partridge and woodcock. An English nobleman Lord Fitzharris, later the Earl of Malmesbury, who became a friend of Teresa after Byron's death and visited the house in 1828, compared it to Osbaldistone Hall in Scott's *Rob Roy*; but the comparison was inept. The Gambas were

Villa Gamba at Filetto outside Ravenna,
the summer home of Teresa's family

very much more gentle, cultured and agreeable than the boorish Northumbrian squires whom Scott depicted.

Pietro Gamba, Teresa's younger brother, had returned from Rome, and Byron enjoyed his company in Ravenna. They liked each other at once; all the doubts which Pietro had expressed in his letter of the previous year were swept away when he actually met Byron. And Byron found his enthusiasm delightful, his charm irresistible: 'I like your little brother very much.' Pietro was to be Byron's closest and most loyal male friend; with him he recaptured, in milder form, something of the mood of his Harrow days.

The Gambas were ardent Liberals and through them Byron was introduced to the society of the revolutionaries with which he had long been in sympathy, and of which the police spies had long considered him a member. It was a particularly opportune moment.

In March 1820 the King of Spain was forced by his subjects to accept a constitution. The news delighted Italian Liberals, for Ferdinand VII was an unpopular Bourbon whose restoration had only been welcomed in Spain because the French had been even more unpopular. The sequel showed how events in one country could have repercussions in another. This connectedness was indeed a feature of the nineteenth century: an international revulsion from autocratic rule was again to be apparent in 1830 and 1848. Revolution in one country always threatened the stability of regimes elsewhere. It is a short-sighted and ignorant error of our own times to assume that this sort of imitative political action is a consequence of the global village identified by Marcuse.

The first repercussions were felt in Naples. Liberal elements, assisted by army officers who had owed their commissions and allegiance to Napoleon's brother-in-law, King Joachim Murat, compelled Ferdinand IV to follow the example of his Spanish cousin. To save time, the constitution chosen was the original Spanish one of 1812, even though, according to the British Minister, 'of all the grave counsellors who advised the prince to accept the Spanish Constitution . . . there was not one who had ever read it'. That hardly mattered: 'In the balmy garden of Italy bondage is no more,' wrote a Neapolitan poet. The Austrians, who were inclined to regard Naples as a client state, if not quite a puppet, were taken aback. Prince Janoblowski, the Habsburg ambassador, remarked that a revolution might have been expected in the moon rather than in Naples. Metternich, the Austrian Chancellor, generally regarded as the subtle master of Europe, told the German Courts at the end of July that Austria could not tolerate this revolution, and would be quite ready to send an army to suppress it: 'The Revolution at Naples is the work of a subversive sect,' he declared. 'The first duty and the first interest of foreign Powers is to smother it in its cradle.'

Naturally, however, very different feelings were aroused in Italy itself, and especially among the Liberals with whom Byron consorted. Some time in the summer he became formally a member of the revolutionary Carbonari, belonging to the popular section of the Ravenna body which took the name *Cacciatori Americani*: 'They were originally a society of hunters in the forest, who took the name of Americans, but at present comprise some thousands.' The Romagna was apparently in a ferment. He had high hopes. Napoleon, he reminded Murray, had thought 'the troops from the Romagna the best of his Italic corps, and I believe it'. The Romagnuoli were 'the bravest and most original of the present Italians, though still half savage'. His own group included a blacksmith, innkeeper, merchants, lawyers, as well as young aristocrats like Pietro; there were also, of course, some spies and informers, who kept the anxious Government alert to his actions. Cardinal Rusconi, the new Papal Legate in

Ravenna, told his colleague in Bologna that 'also suspected of complicity in this bold plot is the well-known Lord Byron'. He regretted that 'the superior government has taken no measure against him', and so hesitated to do so himself.

Ravenna had become a dangerous place. There were three assassinations in one summer week, the victims being an anti-Liberal priest, an estate factor and a soldier; the inclusion of the factor suggests that the opportunity was taken, as in all such affairs, to pay off old scores and settle agrarian disputes.

Everything, however, seemed to depend on the success of the Neapolitan revolution, and the omens were not good. Not only did Byron judge that the Neapolitans were 'not worth a curse', but it was soon clear that they were themselves extremely confused. Sicily seemed to wish independence, and on the mainland, only in Calabria did the Carbonari seem to have much popular support, doubtless because of the violence with which the anti-Muratist Cardinal-brigand Ruffo had conducted his irregular war in that province in the time of the French.

Moreover, in October Metternich had summoned a Council of the Powers to Troppau, though Castlereagh declined to attend. From this emerged the Protocol of Troppau, which gives the flavour of reactionary Europe and thus a measure of all that Byron opposed: 'States which have undergone a change of government due to revolution which threatens other states, *ipso facto* cease to be members of the European Alliance, and remain excluded from it until their situation gives guarantee for legal order and stability. If owing to such alterations, immediate danger threatens other states, the Powers bind themselves by peaceful means, or, if need be, by arms, to bring the guilty state back into the bosom of the Great Alliance.' Castlereagh responded with a compromise that seemed characteristically English and therefore hypocritical; he refused to recognize the general principle, but admitted that in this case Austria was quite entitled to interfere in Naples. It came to the same thing.

Byron knew that he was in a dangerous and exposed position. His friendship with the Cardinal's secretary Alborghetti offered some protection, and Alborghetti, who liked Byron and was not averse from attempting the dangerous balancing feat of riding two horses heading in different directions, also supplied him with information about the plans the governing party was considering. They again threatened, for instance, to shut Teresa up in a convent: 'Of course I would accede to a retreat on my part rather than a prison on hers, for the former is what they really want.' They tried to involve his servants in quarrels, and in the following spring his gondolier Tita, whom he

The sage deliberations of the Holy Alliance at Troppau, a Liberal view

had brought from Venice and who would serve him till his death, was actually arrested after a knife-brawl.

The first opportunity for a rising had already been lost. It had been planned for early September. The Government were aware of their intentions: it would come, Cardinal Rusconi told his colleague at Bologna, after the fourth instalment of taxes had been paid when the Carbonari might hope to seize the Government banks. It is not quite clear why it was postponed. The Bolognese were the first to withdraw, and though Pietro Gamba urged that they should nevertheless proceed with the rising, if only because the Government already had enough information to arrest most of them, he found little support. If Bologna was unwilling, it seems to have been thought there was no chance of success. 'Our puir hill folk' – Byron wrote to Murray, seeing himself for the moment as a character in one of Scott's novels, and forgetting, as Iris Origo points out, that 'his *Americani* came from the flattest of plains' – 'offered to strike and raise the first banner. But Bologna paused, and now 'tis Autumn and the season half over.'

Nevertheless – this was before Troppau – there was still hope in the position at Naples. He even wrote a letter to the Neapolitan people offering money and his own services: 'As a member of the English House of Peers, Lord Byron would be a traitor to the principles which placed the reigning family of England on the throne if he were not grateful for the noble lesson so lately given both to peoples and to kings.' He offered to 'repair to whatever place the Neapolitan Government might point out, there to obey the orders and participate in the dangers of his commanding officer, without any other motive than that of sharing the destiny of a brave nation defending itself against the self-called Holy Alliance, which but combines the vice of hypocrisy with despotism.'

There was a touch of rhetoric to this, but what other tone would satisfy the opera-loving Neapolitans? And of its sincerity there can be no doubt. Teresa was profoundly moved: 'What generosity, what modesty, what greatness of soul!' she exclaimed. Unfortunately the letter did not reach Naples; the man to whom it was entrusted, himself a Neapolitan called Giuseppe Gigante, may have been an Austrian spy. He was, the story went, arrested by the Austrian police at Pesaro; but there are times when it is convenient for spies to be arrested. Teresa, who did not think him a spy, believed that he had swallowed Byron's letter. The copy we have is probably a first draft.

His expectation of a rising became so acute in October – despite the earlier disappointment – that he wrote to Douglas Kinnaird to tell him to sell the Government Stock which he held: it would drop in value since 'in the impending event of the passage of the Po by the barbarians now in great force on that river – your Tory scoundrels will right or wrong take part in any foreign war'. As evidence of the state of Italy, he told Kinnaird that the Liberals had recently blown up a house belonging to 'a Brigand (so they call here the Satellites of the tyrants)', and had threatened the Cardinal with defenestration – and the windows were 'rather lofty'.

So the autumn wore on, in a mood of alternating hope and disillusion. But there were, of course, other activities. Teresa and her father had returned to the city from their country house, and so Byron was able to call on her every evening. He rode most afternoons, into the forest, generally with Pietro; and they practised with their pistols. He worked hard: the fifth canto of *Don Juan* was ready for despatch by the end of the year. He read voraciously, sent his love to Walter Scott, who had just received a baronetcy – 'I shall think better of knighthood ever after for his being dubbed' – and demanded that he should write two novels a year. He tossed reflections and information to his correspondents with his old fecundity: 'A deathbed is a matter of nerves & constitution – & not of religion – Voltaire was frightened –

Frederick of Prussia not – Christians the same according to their strength rather than their creed.' His mind reverted to his Cambridge days and he wrote Murray a long letter about Matthews, and he wrote to Augusta discussing Scott's observation in *The Abbot* that 'every five years we find ourselves another and yet the same with a change of views and no less of the light in which we regard them; a change of motives as well as of actions.' He himself, he reflected, must have gone through two such changes in the same period; but what of her? Had she simply made her house 'a Lying-in Hospital? – there never was such a creature except a rabbit – for increase and multiplication'. Lady Byron, he supposed, retained 'her old starch obstinacy'. People accused him of using her as the model for Don Juan's mother; but he couldn't see more than a superficial resemblance – Donna Inez 'was only a silly woman – and the other is a cut and dry made up character.' Meanwhile he had 'got a flourishing family (besides my daughter Allegra) – here are two Cats – six dogs – a badger – a falcon, a tame Crow – and a Monkey. – The fox died – and a first Cat ran away.' And

Byron's illegitimate daughter, Allegra

on the whole they all got on very well together and didn't make more noise than 'a well-behaved Nursery'.

So life was by no means all politics and waiting for the revolution. Yet that still dominated his thoughts. It would be, in a sense, his justification: to do something for Italy. The police, he told Kinnaird in November, open all letters, but he had 'no objection so that they can see how I hate and utterly despise and detest those *Hun brutes* & all they can do in their temporary wickedness – for Time and Opinion & the vengeance of the roused up people will at length manure Italy with their carcasses – it may not be for one year – or two – or ten – but it *will be* – and *so* that it *could be* sooner – I know not what a man ought *not* to do. . . .'

Byron's violence was, however, only verbal. His humanity recoiled from the fact of revolutionary enthusiasm. An incident on 8 December showed this very clearly. As he was putting on his overcoat in order to make his nightly visit to Teresa – she was in her father's house, while he remained incongruously in the Palazzo Guiccioli – he heard a shot. His servants were scared to go to find out what had happened, so Byron, followed by Tita, ran into the street where he found a wounded man. An adjutant of the Cardinal's Guard was standing over the body, which Byron recognized as being that of Captain Luigi Dal Pinto, the commandant of the Papal troops at Ravenna. He had been wounded in five places – there must have been other shots which he had not heard. Byron at once ordered him to be carried into his house, where he died. He was then left there – so great was the authorities' state of alarm – for sixteen hours. He had been an unpopular, but brave man; Byron had met him at evening parties, and though he disliked his politics, had felt a respect for him. The murder upset him – the man had left a widow and children 'quite destitute' – and he was more than a little shocked to hear 'a very pretty young woman of high rank' defend the deed. Byron reflected, inaccurately, that Bacon had called assassination 'a sort of wild justice' – Bacon had in fact said 'revenge' – but it didn't satisfy him. It was, of course, 'the consequence of a negligent administration of the laws, or of a despotic government', and he approved of the cause . . . nevertheless he couldn't like murder. He would doubtless have been offended to be told that he lacked the temperament of a freedom-fighter, but it was true; he couldn't view the deaths of others, even political enemies, with the equanimity terrorism demands.

VIII

The New Year of 1821 came in vilely, with rain and mist. It was impossible to ride out for a fortnight. The roads were blocked with mud, and even the post did not arrive. Byron lounged through the days in his apartments till it was 8 o'clock and time to call on Teresa. He read – Mitford's *History of Greece* and Scott's novels (all of which he claimed to have read fifty times) – dipped into poetry, read Grillparzer's *Sappho* in an Italian translation, and Frederick Schlegel who irritated him because he seemed always on the verge of making sense. And all the time he waited, now hopefully, no doubtfully, on the turn of politics. News was brought that the King of Naples had gone to meet the Allied Sovereigns at Leibach also known as Leybach (the modern Llubljana in Yugoslavia); ostensibly he had done so in order to protect the Constitution that he had granted, but since he had told Lord Burghersh, the British Minister at Naples, that the Constitution had been extracted from him by force, and that he therefore did not consider it binding, it was perhaps naïve of his Neapolitan ministers to trust him. Byron noted that 'the interests of millions are in the hands of about twenty coxcombs, at a place called Leibach (sic)'.

The rising planned for the autumn was again fixed for the end of the month. Byron alternated between optimism and scepticism. He collected weapons and let his apartments be used as an arsenal. He admired the spirit of his confederates, but doubted their judgment and ability to work together. He wished they had the support of the peasants who were 'a fine savage race of two-legged leopards'. As for the leaders of his party, he was not impressed to learn that they had left the city for a shooting party. 'If it were like a "highland hunting", a pretext of the chase for a grand re-union of counsellors and chiefs, it would be all very well.' But it was no such thing. To say that Byron, in the midst of these events, could not help seeing himself as a character in one of Scott's novels is not to impugn his sincerity. Subsequent revolutionaries were often to model themselves on the heroes of his own poems.

There were other diversions in these weeks of ever more impatient waiting. He met an old peasant woman on one of his rides, asked her her age, and was puzzled when she said 'tre croci'. His groom explained that her three crosses meant she was ninety, but that in fact she 'had five more years to boot'. He asked her to call on him, which she did, and he was pleased to find that her head resembled drawings of Pope's mother. He gave her money, ordered a new set of clothes for her and awarded her a weekly pension. She had supported herself by gathering pine nuts and wood in the forest – 'pretty work at ninety-five'. But he was vexed to have forgotten to ask her if she remembered Cardinal Alberoni, the Spanish Minister who had been Papal Legate at Ravenna in the 1730s. That would have been another Jacobite link, for Alberoni had instigated the abortive Jacobite Rising in 1719. Byron's treatment of this old woman was typical of his benevolence and the generosity which had made him a popular figure among the Ravennese – the police reports, of course, suggested that his charitable gifts were merely intended to build up support for him among the People, and that his motive was political.

22 January was his birthday, always a melancholy occasion for him. 'I go to my bed,' he scrawled, 'with a heaviness of heart at having lived so long, and to so little purpose.' He had been puzzled during the wet weather which confined him to the house by the cause of his habitual low spirits. Why had he been, 'all my lifetime, more or less *ennuyé*?' There was no answer; it must be constitutional. The strange thing was that he seemed better able to bear it now than in his youth. Then he had had recourse to violent exercise; now he could 'mope in quietness'. He might go mad – like Swift; but the prospect didn't alarm him. Some quieter stages of 'idiotism or madness . . . must be preferable to much of what men think the possession of their senses'.

Such moods of introspection were habitual to him. They alternated throughout his life with others when he seemed at the mercy of his passions. In this respect, indeed, he bears a curious resemblance to James Boswell. Neither found anything more consistently engrossing than the scrutiny of his own nature; neither, despite continual self-examination, could direct his conduct by the exercise of mind or conscious will. Both alternated between melancholy and enthusiasm.

The weather had changed on 15 January. There were days of fine frosty weather in which he could ride out in the forest, which helped to raise his spirits. The prospect of action was like a glass of champagne – or a dose of salts – which, he said, had the same effect on him. On the 23rd came news that the Barbarians – as he now regularly called the Austrians – were building a bridge of boats over the Po. Byron wondered what he would do if Teresa and her father were forced into exile. The question of Allegra troubled him too – he could hardly take her to 'the seat of war'. The outbreak of hostilities would spoil the Carnival – 'the blackguards might as well have waited till Lent'.

But the next day he found that the Ravennese would have their Carnival whatever the political situation. He met 'masques in the Corso – "Vive la Bagatelle"'. And why not? Nothing is more vivid as a representation of Byron's character and daily life than this snatch of journal kept as he waited for the outbreak of war – which he both desired and dreaded, the first because of his detestation of the dull brutishness of the authoritarian governments which deadened Italy, the second because of the natural humanity which he had displayed in the affair of the Commandant. His mind caught at every rumour. He brooded on the immortality of the soul: 'a *grand peut-être* – but still it is a *grand* one. Everybody clings to it.' A letter from an old friend, Lord Sidney Godolphin Osborne, who was the stepson of Augusta's mother and State Secretary of the Septinsular Republic, suggesting that he should visit Corfu the following spring tempted him for a moment. He wondered if he might write something about the Emperor Tiberius: he might 'soften the details' and exhibit 'the despair which must have led to those very vicious pleasures. For none but a powerful and gloomy mind overthrown would have had recourse to such solitary horrors' – Byron knew from his own experience that dissipation could be the consequence, as well as the cause, of misery. And then he reverted to more immediate perplexities. Something might be happening in Piedmont – all the letters and papers had been stopped. Meanwhile 'of the decision at Leybach nothing is known'.

They edged into February. He heard an organ playing in the street: a waltz tune 'which I have heard ten thousand times at balls in London between 1812 and 1815. Music is a strange thing.' But so was life, so was poetry – 'the feeling of a Former world and a future'. It was all, everything, a mystery; where we had come from, why we were here, where we were going; not only immortality, but life itself, might be described as *un grand peut-être*.

And then, at last, the date of the rising was fixed. It was to be 11 February. The Carboneria had gathered that the Austrians would cross the Po on the 15th; instead of being able to march towards the Neapolitan frontier, they would find the whole of central Italy in insurrection. Unfortunately the Austrian spies were at least as well-informed as the Carbonari ones, and so, the Austrians, learning of this intention, advanced their plans and crossed the river on the 7th. The Carbonari were surprised and dismayed. Their headquarters in Bologna ordered that the Austrians were to be 'allowed to pass and only to be attacked on all sides on their return.' The decision was a blunder. It threw the success of the whole movement upon the Neapolitans, and, though their army was large, it was also ill-trained and disunited. Moreover, it made it seem to the Neapolitans that other Italians were unwilling to do anything for the cause of Liberty until they had borne the brunt of the battle. Finally, the Neapolitans had performed so poorly even under the Napoleonic marshal Murat that the only chance they had of offering a successful resistance to the Austrians depended on the Austrian army being harassed on the march and in the rear.

There was a week of gathering apprehension, though Byron doggedly pursued his usual occupations, even to the extent of finishing the first act of his tragedy *Sardanapalus*. The Papal Government, emboldened by the successful passage of the Austrian army, now began to suppress dissidents: houses were searched, arrests made, and on the 15th the Cardinal issued a proclamation which declared that anyone found in possession of arms was liable to arrest; Alborghetti obligingly sent Byron advance notice of this. He paid no attention. Indeed, his alarmed associates made it difficult for him to do so, for Pietro Gamba had decided that the only place where the weapons and ammunition which they had collected might be safely concealed was Byron's cellar; he had accordingly had them brought there, without warning Byron who happened to be out at the time.

The next week the Pope himself intervened, warning all Catholics to take no part in the rebellion, on pain of excommunication. Again, Alborghetti, carefully playing both sides, sent him a copy of the order in confidence. Two days later Byron received an anonymous letter warning him that the Barbarians were 'ill-disposed towards me'. It was hardly news, and he thought that its author was probably a spy hoping to entice him into some rash rejoinder. He kept that for his Journal: 'They cannot bestow their hostility on one who loathes and execrates them more than I do, or who will oppose their views with more zeal, when the opportunity arises.'

That was his true, his constant position. Byron was no theoretical revolutionary like Shelley. He had little capacity for abstract thought, and his imagination and humanity combined to make him distrustful of schemes and enterprises which were careless of the suffering of others. But, as a result of circumstance – his friendship with the Gamba family – he had been thrown into the company of men who were devoted to the idea of a Free Italy, and had done what he could to help them. Shelley, who had little acquaintance with Italians, remained a man of theory; Byron, doubtfully, with much hesitation, committed himself to action.

The next day their hopes were finally destroyed. The Neapolitan army had disintegrated. In Naples itself most of the Deputies promptly deserted the Revolution they had been part of, and declared their loyalty to the king. Instead of drama it had all turned into Comic Opera. Byron was disgusted: 'The Neapolitans have betrayed themselves and all the World, and those who would have given their blood for Italy can now only give their tears.' Teresa herself wept: 'Alas! the Italians must now return to making operas.' 'I fear,' Byron muttered, 'that that and maccaroni (sic) are their forte.'

It had all fizzled out. Yet the effort – Byron might have reflected –

had not been in vain. Early in January, ruminating in his journal on the chances of success, with some pessimism, Byron had nevertheless written: 'It is not one man, nor a million, but the *spirit* of liberty which must be spread. The waves which dash upon the shore are, one by one, broken, but yet the *ocean* conquers, nevertheless. It overwhelms the Armada, it wears the rock, and, if the Neptunians are to be believed, it has not only destroyed, but made a world.'

He was quite right. The rising of 1821 was a fiasco. But a few years later, Stendhal, observer rather than actor, concluded that revolution would break out in Italy in the 1840s. And it did, though that was suppressed too, and they had to wait till 1859 for success.

The governments of Italy had received a shock. All over the peninsula they reacted severely. Dissidents were imprisoned or exiled, houses searched. Byron's position was anomalous, for they dared not act directly against him. It was now that a quarrel was fixed on his servant Tita, who was arrested; it was hoped that Byron would take the hint and move from Ravenna. Instead he used his enduring friendship with Alborghetti to have Tita released, and even extracted an apology. Then they decided to strike through the Gamba family. Count Ruggero and Pietro were both sentenced to exile. It was assumed Byron would follow Teresa. Instead, at first Teresa remained in Ravenna, while Byron used what influence he thought he had at Rome to try to have her father's sentence rescinded. He didn't succeed, and Teresa, with many tears, followed her father to Pisa, having extracted a promise from Byron that he would follow. He did not hurry to do so. There were various reasons. He was settled in Ravenna, and liked the place despite its dismal winter climate. He was expecting Shelley who wanted to discuss Allegra's future with him, as Claire's representative. He hoped that Count Ruggero at least might be permitted to return when the first alarm that had provoked the repression was stilled. He had a temperamental dislike of removing from any place where he had put down roots, and the thought of transporting his swollen household and his menagerie was daunting. Finally, he may have been a little bored, even displeased, with Teresa. She had come to represent now a finality which was not entirely welcome. He told Augusta in October that the affair had not been his fault: she would have it and 'you know all my loves go crazy'. Nevertheless, 'this is a finisher – for you know that when a woman is separated from her husband for her Amant – he is bound both by honour (and inclination at least I am) to live with her all his days. . . . It is nearly three years that this liaison has lasted – I was dreadfully in love – and she blindly so – for she has sacrificed everything to this headlong passion – That comes of being Romantic – I can say that without being so furiously in love as at first – I am more attached to her – than I had thought it possible to be to any woman after three years (except one & who was she you can guess) and have not the least wish – nor prospect of separation from her.' Indeed, he added, if Count Guiccioli and Lady Byron were both to die, they would probably marry, though he would rather not 'thinking it the way to hate each other'.

This was a firm enough declaration. All the same he may have been glad of some respite from her affection, all the more perhaps since she had extracted a promise from him that he would abandon *Don Juan*, just at the moment when he had three cantos ready for publication, and thought it rightly the best thing he had done. He was confirmed in this opinion by an anonymous pamphlet – in fact written by Scott's son-in-law John Gibson Lockhart – which advised him to stick to *Don Juan*: 'It is the only sincere thing you have written . . . by far the most straightforward, the most interesting and the most poetical.' Shelley, when he arrived, agreed: 'Every word of it is pregnant with immortality.' Byron would later persuade Teresa to withdraw her interdict; meanwhile he was engaged on another work which could hardly please her: *The Vision of Judgement*, in which he pictured George III's arrival at the Gates of Heaven, and burlesqued his old enemy Southey's laudatory ode on the late king.

Shelley found him 'totally recovered in health' and was pleased to report that he 'lives a life totally the reverse of that which he led at Venice . . . in every respect an altered man.' This was not quite true, for he also reported to Mary that he had met on the staircase of the Palazzo 'five peacocks, two guinea hens, and an Egyptian crane'. The household, he said, contained 'eight enormous dogs, three monkeys, five cats, an eagle, a crow and a falcon; and all these walk about the house, which now and then resounds with their unarbitrated quarrels, as if they were the masters of it.'

Byron was pleased to see Shelley – the first English friend, except his faithful valet Fletcher, he had seen since he left Venice. The Gambas were considering removal to Switzerland, and Byron, who had at first been attracted by the idea, changed his mind, for Switzerland held too many unhappy memories of 1816, and got Shelley to write to Teresa explaining why; he also used him to find a house for him in Pisa.

At last, reluctantly – 'it is awful work, this love, and prevents all a man's projects of good or glory', he told Moore – the caravan of coaches and wagons lumbered out of Ravenna at the end of October. Some of the less satisfactory animals were left in the charge of his banker Pellegrino Ghigi – what did he do with them?, one wonders –

and little Allegra remained in her convent school at Bagnacavallo. The Ravenna sojourn was over.

It marked the passage of an intense period of his life, and appropriately, on the road between Imola and Bologna, a chance encounter brought another stage in his history vividly and poignantly to life again. A few weeks before he had noted in the journal which he called 'Detached Thoughts', and which he kept intermittently from October 1821 to May 1822 that: 'My School friendships were with me passions . . . that with Lord Clare began one of the earliest and lasted longest – being only interrupted by distance that I know of. – I never hear the word "Clare" without a beating of the heart – even now, & I write it – with the feelings of 1803–4–5 – ad infinitum.' And now, a carriage coming the other way halted, and Clare emerged. The meeting 'annihilated for a moment all the years between the present time and the days of Harrow – It was a new and inexplicable feeling like rising from the grave to me.' Clare was, Byron thought, affected in like manner. Viewed objectively, there was something almost absurd in this recrudescence of a boyish intensity of feeling experienced by two men on the verge of middle-age; but of course all emotion can seem absurd from such a standpoint. They were together only for five minutes – probably neither could find words adequate for the expression of what they felt – but Byron could hardly 'recollect an hour of my existence which could be weighed against them'. Clare was on his way to Rome. They arranged to meet again when he returned north in the spring, and indeed did so. Then Byron noted his own incapacity for friendship: 'I do not know any male being, except Lord Clare, for whom I feel anything that deserves the name. All my others are man-of-the-world friendships.' When Clare left him after his spring visit Byron turned to Teresa and said, 'I have a presentiment that I shall not see him again.' And, she notes 'his eyes filled with tears'.

IX

Byron would spend another twenty months in Italy. He was in Pisa from November 1821 to September 1822, and in Genoa from then till July 1823 when he set out on the Greek expedition. It could not be called a placid time – Byron never really experienced tranquillity – but it was so in comparison with his stay in Venice and Ravenna. The reasons are obvious. He was living in something approximating to domesticity; Teresa and he maintained separate apartments in each of the houses in which they lived, they met little during the day and then by appointment, spending only their evenings together unless there

Pisa, where Byron lived 1821–22

was visiting English company in which case Teresa often kept to her own rooms; throughout the day they communicated by scribbled notes. She was wise enough to respect his desire for privacy, and of course her reverence for his writing was such that she would not interrupt him at work. His passion had died, though hers had not, and they had settled into a species of loving and familiar friendship, which suited Byron; it was what Augusta had given him, without the guilt, and it was what he really wanted from a woman and from marriage.

So there was no dissipation such as had characterized his life in Venice; and there were no Italian politics either. The Liberal movement had not been snuffed out, but it was temporarily eclipsed. The Pope had published an Encyclical against the Carbonari in which he threatened all who remained members of the Society with excommunication. In the short run, this was effective. Many good Catholics who had thought they could combine patriotism with the practice of their faith were horrified to discover this was impossible, and defected from the Carboneria. But in the long run, it was a mistake and weakened the appeal of the Church to Liberals and Nationalists. Meanwhile, even those who remained committed to the cause, like Pietro Gamba, were momentarily disillusioned.

There was another change in Byron's life. In Ravenna he had lived in an entirely Italian society. Now, though the Gambas had become in effect his family this was all changed. He was still an object of suspicion to the Austrian spies; the government of the Grand Duke of Tuscany had given the Gambas only a limited permit to stay there, and when Byron arrived letters began to fly to Vienna: 'We are aware,' the head of the Financial department in Pisa wrote, 'of certain rumours about the political attitude of this Englishman, who combines with high birth, literary celebrity, and a considerable fortune, a great determination to favour all political novelties.' It was feared that he might influence the students, and the writer recommended that 'most careful and secret instructions should be sent for the supervision of the aforesaid foreigner'.

Despite this, Byron was actually moving away from any direct participation in Italian affairs. His sympathies remained unchanged, but the circle that surrounded him was now English. The Shelleys were already in Pisa, and they had other English friends there: the Williamses, the Masons, old Mr Dolby and young Mr Taaffe. There was Walter Savage Landor, the poet, and young Mr Medwin, whose *Conversations with Lord Byron* were hurriedly published within months of the poet's death. Soon there was Leigh Hunt, the poet, journalist and inveterate borrower, and the absurd Edward Trelawny, whom Byron himself recognized as having walked out of one of his own

Oriental tales. 'I long to meet him,' Teresa said when he told her this. 'You won't like him,' he replied. There was even an English clergyman, Dr Nott, whose love of scandal was such that Byron said he had revised the Commandment to read: 'Thou shalt, Nott, bear false witness against thy neighbour.'

Leigh Hunt: the artist has caught his calculating charm

They were mostly middle-class – and all, it may be said, except for the Shelleys and Landor (who refused anyway to talk to other English people) – second-rate, and none of them had much interest in Italy, though all enjoyed the climate, the beauties of landscape and its cities, and the delicious sense of living free of the stuffy conventions of England. Some of them had need of this freedom for Mr Williams was not in fact married to Mrs Williams, and Mr Mason was really Mr Tighe and Mrs Mason Lady Mountcashell.

They could not quite escape Italian politics if only because Byron remained an object of suspicion. A brawl involving a sergeant-major of dragoons, by name Masi, in March 1822, alerted them to the danger of their position. It was a trivial affair, starting with some clumsy horsemanship, but it threatened to turn nasty when Masi tried to arrest the party of Byron's friends, which included Pietro Gamba, and did indeed turn so when one of Byron's servants rushed out of the Palazzo Lanfranchi, the house he had taken, and stabbed Masi in the stomach. Rumours flew round the city. It was said that Mr Taaffe, who had indeed provoked the incident, had killed the dragoon and was now hidden in Byron's house, guarded by Byron's bulldog. The chief Austrian spy, the Cavaliere Luigi Torcelli, even reported that Byron 'had mounted two small pieces of field artillery at the door of his room'. The excitement caused by the incident died away, but it led to a request from the Government that the Gamba family should leave Pisa.

There were three other things worthy of note concerning his life there. On 20 April his little daughter Allegra died in the convent school to which he had sent her. She had suffered a fever, made a partial recovery, and then, according to his banker Ghigi, who had visited her and found that 'if there is any fault, it is of too much care', had died suddenly 'of a convulsive catarrhal attack'. He had been fond of the child and believed he had done what was best for her, though, as he told Shelley, 'It is a moment when we are apt to think that, if this or that had been done, such event might have been prevented.' He had admired her spirit, but had been irritated by faults which he saw in himself, and by her occasional resemblance to her mother. Our understanding of small children has probably improved since the nineteenth century, and we are all likely to believe that, whenever possible, a child should be brought up by the mother – and indeed, in the case of his legitimate daughter Ada, Byron made that point himself; but in his view the two cases were not comparable: he admired Lady Byron and he did not admire Claire. He seems to have thought that nothing could be worse for a girl than to be brought up by such a mother. Iris Origo observes that 'it plainly never occurred either to him or to Teresa, to go to the child themselves,' when news of her illness first arrived; but if it had occurred to them, they could not have done so. They would have required passports to enter the Papal States and, even if the bureaucracy had been willing, which is unlikely, could not have received them in time.

The second was the arrival of Leigh Hunt. Hunt, four years older than Byron, had been in and out of trouble all his adult life. Byron had first met him as a visitor in the Cold Bath prison in 1813, where Hunt had been consigned for two years for a libel on the Prince Regent. He had called on him several times with gifts of books, and had himself been grateful when Hunt expressed sympathy at the time of his own troubles in 1816. Now Shelley suggested that the three of them should collaborate in a magazine, which would be published in London by Hunt's brother John. Most of Byron's friends tried to dissuade him: Hunt was politically and socially disreputable: a radical and a Cockney. Byron could only damage his own reputation if he had anything to do with him.

He wasn't daunted by this. He admired Hunt's courage and was not frightened by his politics. He offered him and his family lodging in the Palazzo Lanfranchi, and gave *The Vision of Judgement* to Hunt's brother John, who was to publish their magazine *The Liberal*. Although he soon tired of Leigh's total incapacity to help himself, and of his wife and children, whom he described as 'Yahoos', he supported the magazine with contributions for all its four numbers, and continued to let John Hunt have his manuscripts; in fact, he published the last eleven cantos of *Don Juan* on a profit-sharing basis.

The third event was the death of Shelley in a drowning accident. It was not only a sore loss to Byron, whose respect and affection for Shelley were great, but it destroyed any chance of the collaboration with Leigh Hunt proving successful. Moreover, the circumstances of

The funeral of Shelley, on the beach at Lerici: the three mourners to the fore are (from left to right) Edward Trelawny, Leigh Hunt (depicted as an old man although he was only thirty-eight) and Byron

[169]

Shelley's death and the cremation of his body on the beach at Lerici were horrible: Shelley's brains 'literally seethed, bubbled and boiled as in a cauldron for a very long time'. Driving home through the pine forests Byron and Hunt were seized with an attack of nervous hilarity.

The death made a profound impression on Byron. It sharpened his awareness of his own mortality too. He had always had a Gothic side to him – skulls were ornaments of his study from early youth. Byron had none of the Romantic absorption in death; he had never been 'half in love' with it and could never have described it as 'easeful'. Yet he was oppressed by the thought of how many of those he had known and loved had died: his mother, Edlestone, Matthews, little Allegra, now Shelley. There was soon poor Dr Polidori too, who killed himself: 'It seems that disappointment was the cause.' And he himself was now in his mid-thirties; his father had died at thirty-five.

It was time to move. The Gambas, expelled from Pisa, partly as a consequence of the Masi affair, partly because the Tuscan government was confident that their departure would hasten Byron's, had already gone to Lucca. Byron, with his usual hesitation and procrastination, after much discussion, had fixed on Genoa as his next port of call. It was growing wearisome, this constant shifting, but Mr Hill, the British Minister at Genoa, assured him he would not be disturbed there; and since hopes that the Gambas might be permitted to return to Ravenna had proved illusory, while Lucca was full of English, Genoa it must be.

Before he left, however, he had a visit from Hobhouse. They had not met since Venice in 1818, and Hobhouse found him: 'much changed – his face fatter and the expression of it injured'. He did not like Teresa either, and he disapproved both of Byron's political activities and of his association with Hunt. Despite this, Byron was delighted to see him: they had experienced so much together and Hobhouse represented to him the days of his youth, of his Greek travels and the memory of unclouded days. He didn't feel for him as for Lord Clare, but all the same: 'these glimpses of old friends for a moment are sad remembrancers'.

Byron moved into the Casa Saluzzo, in the little village of Albaro, in the hills behind Genoa at the beginning of October. It was a large square building with its own garden, and sufficiently roomy to allow for separate apartments for the Gamba family. Meanwhile the Hunts and Mary Shelley were accommodated in the Casa Negrotti, a mile down the hill. This at least diminished the irritation which the close proximity of the Hunt family had caused. The journey had been as complicated as Byron's habitually were. He insisted on bringing three geese with him, as well as the rest of the menagerie, on the grounds that it would be bad luck not to eat goose at Michaelmas. But as it turned out, he couldn't bring himself to kill them, and decided instead 'to test the theory of their longevity'. They lived in the garden and took to accompanying him wherever he went. An ironic sight: to see the wicked poet surrounded by fat waddling birds.

From the moment of his arrival in Genoa, Byron's biographers can hardly escape the awareness that he had only eighteen months to live. It is a temptation – which few have resisted – to interpret everything in this light. Accordingly they stress his boredom, his apathy, his conviction that his race was run, and his death imminent. But in fact all this had been part of Byron's complicated character since he was an adolescent. If he had survived Greece, we would read his days in Genoa differently.

His industry had not ceased. Throughout 1822 he had been working on new cantos of *Don Juan* (Teresa having rescinded her ban) with the greatest energy, even though their reception by his friends in England and even, it seemed, by the public was cooler than ever. (But the reception may have owed something to the fact that they were published by John Hunt rather than Murray.) There is nothing, however, in these later cantos to suggest that his genius was at all dimmed. On the contrary, having got Juan to England, the poem bubbled with a new zest, with wit, occasional nostalgia and outbursts of political passion:

> Alas! could she [England] but fully, truly, know
> How her great name is now throughout abhorred;
> How eager all the earth is for the blow
> Which shall lay bare her bosom to the sword;
> How all the nations deem her their worst foe,
> That worse than *worst of foes*, the once adored
> False friend, who held out freedom to mankind,
> And now would chain them, to the very *mind*; –
>
> Would she be proud, or boast herself the free,
> Who is but first of slaves? The nations are
> In prison, – but the gaoler, what is he?
> No less a victim to the bolt and bar.
> Is the poor privilege to turn the key
> Upon the captive, freedom? He's as far
> From the enjoyment of the earth and air
> Who watches o'er the chain, as they who wear.

It irked him from time to time that his life was so unremarkable. He told Pietro Gamba that he was tired of doing nothing but write, and he was sure that the public must be tired of his stuff too. On the other hand, there is no real reason to disbelieve Teresa when she wrote that: 'He loved simple pleasures – sometimes solitude – always retreat. He was never tired today of what he had enjoyed yesterday. He felt no desire for movement or activity except for great purposes – then indeed he seemed lifted above the earth by mysterious wings of glory and virtue.'

Of course, it is easy to say that Teresa required to believe Byron happy; but she had one advantage over his biographers and contemporary observers who saw him briefly: she lived with him, saw him every day and knew him well. What he hated was to be fussed, and she did not fuss him. When she says that he enjoyed strolling with her in the garden or down to the sea, playing with the animals in the menagerie, taking his ride, spending the evening chatting to her and her family, and then working late into the night, and that this life suited him, I think she has a right to be believed.

The clearest picture we have of Byron in these last days in Italy is offered by Lady Blessington, who published her *Conversations of Lord Byron* ten years after his death. It is a fascinating and unreliable work, rather like its author.

Lady Blessington had a good deal in common with Byron. She came from a great family – her mother was a Desmond, one of the old Anglo-Norman aristocracy of Ireland – but she had grown up poor and disregarded – she had been sold at the age of fifteen by her father to her first husband, a Mr Farmer, who had beaten her and from whom she had fled. She had then become the mistress of a Captain Jenkins who had passed her on to the Earl of Blessington for the sum of £10,000. Soon after this, Farmer fortunately died, and in March 1818, Lord Blessington married the young woman whom he had kept for a couple of years. She was beautiful, she was intelligent, she was, despite everything, virtuous, but she was not respectable. Her husband was immensely rich, but this could not compensate for his wife's background. Moreover, there was soon another element in their household which made respectability still more difficult to achieve: this was Count Alfred D'Orsay. D'Orsay was a very beautiful and exquisite young Frenchman, who drew nicely and was extremely decorative. Both Lord and Lady Blessington adored him, whether as lover, son or younger brother, or a combination of all three, it is impossible to say. (Later, disgracefully, a marriage was arranged between him and Blessington's daughter by his first marriage; it turned out unhappily and D'Orsay lived with Lord and Lady Blessington for the rest of their lives.)

This was the glittering trio who now arrived in Genoa with an equipage as splendid and extravagant as Byron's own. Lady Blessing-

Marguerite, Countess of Blessington, beautiful if not respectable

ton was a-gog to see the famous poet: 'And am I indeed in the same town with Byron? And to-morrow I may perhaps behold him!!!!! I never felt before the same impatient longing to see anyone known only to me by his works. I hope he may not be fat, as Moore described him in Venice; for a *fat poet* is an anomaly in my opinion.' Well, he wasn't, for he had been dieting during the winter, and she was surprised to find him very thin. She was surprised and dismayed, too, to find him sociable, nervous and eager to chatter. Her 'preconceived notion of the melancholy poet' was shattered. She concluded that this man was 'witty, sarcastic and lively enough' to be the author of *Don Juan*, but she couldn't understand how he could have written *Childe Harold*.

Lady Blessington had, in the words of her biographer Michael

[173]

Sadleir, 'a rare gift of understanding the complex characters of clever men'. She was able to 'distinguish between his genuine feelings and his self-protective readiness to sneer, to wound and to shock'. Her book is, of course, unreliable, for she lacked the self-abnegation of a Boswell; conversations are turned in such a way that she has the best of them. Moreover, she could never quite reconcile herself to the discrepancy between the Romantic poet of her imagination and the sociable and rattling talker whom she had met. Her own charm for Byron was partly personal, but it was also one of association: she brought to him that London where he had shone, where he had known fame and in which part of him still delighted.

Teresa was jealous, naturally enough; Lady Blessington belonged to a part of Byron's life which she could not share. Moreover, though his Italian was fluent he could not converse in Italian with the lively idiosyncrasy of his native tongue – Teresa's English was slight, his letters to her prove that. You would hardly take them for his. Yet this makes all the more striking Lady Blessington's judgment that Teresa was 'his last attachment'.

In the end, however, these *Conversations*, however vivid their picture of Baron's daily life, raise the central question of all biography and memoir-writing: what are we to believe? According to Lady Blessington, Byron 'said he had a conviction that he should never return from Greece. He had dreamt more than once, he assured me, of dying there.' Are we to believe this? Or is it perhaps what she thought he should have said? And if he said it, how much meaning should we attach?

Or take the story of their parting. In her version: 'Byron seemed to have a presentiment that we met for the last time, and yielding to the melancholy caused by this presentiment, made scarcely an effort to check the tears that flowed plentifully down his cheeks.' Moore accepted her account and reproduced it in his *Life*; Hobhouse scribbled in the margin of his copy: 'very unlike him'.

For him, their visit was no more than an interlude. He was all but ready to leave for Greece. The police spy Torelli had had wind of this intention the previous year: 'He has expressed his intention of not remaining in Genoa, but of going on to Athens to purchase adoration from the Greeks.'

PART III

THE HERO

I

The Greek Rising had broken out on 25 March 1821. The European Powers, still in conference at Leibach, as a result of the Neapolitan Revolution, which had just disintegrated, promptly condemned it. Even the Sultan's authority was regarded as inviolate by the Holy Alliance of Christian monarchs. Despite the disunity that made any consistent course of action impossible for the Greeks, the rising met with initial success, partly because the Turkish commander-in-chief, Kurshid Pasha (himself by birth an orthodox Christian), was campaigning in the north against Byron's old admirer Ali Pasha, whose power was at last destroyed the following February. Soon, however, the division of the Greeks into rival factions, inspired by misunderstanding and mistrust of each other and each other's intentions, made itself apparent. The Turks recovered while the Greeks prematurely occupied themselves with the making of constitutions. The Patriarch Grigorios was hanged in Constantinople, and the population of Chios massacred. It was not perhaps the first of the war's atrocities, for one Scottish Philhellene, Thomas Gordon, a connection of Byron's, had been so appalled by the conduct of the Greeks after capturing Tripolitsa, that he had defected.

However, if the rising stuttered, if the *klephte* bands distrusted the Phanariot constitutionalists, if the Church's attitude was ambivalent, if the European powers were officially hostile, there was still great goodwill for the Greeks among Western Liberals, while, in every European government, there were those who were already wondering how they might snatch some advantage for themselves from the Greek Revolution. In London and Edinburgh, Paris and Geneva, and in many Italian and German cities, Philhellenic Committees were formed to collect funds for the Greeks, while young men from all over Western Europe and even America, inspired by their classical education as well as by Liberal political principles, volunteered to fight for the Greek cause.

Hobhouse and Kinnaird were both members of the London Committee; Byron, throughout the months that followed his removal from Ravenna, had been turning over the idea of leaving Italy. Sometimes he thought of Venezuela, sometimes of the United States; the notion of returning to England even crossed his mind. But, as the months passed, his opinion hardened, these other choices were seen to be chimerical; he would go back to Greece. It was the place where he

Venice, 1823. At work on Il Liberale, *the newspaper Byron founded with Leigh Hunt. The preservation of freedom was of paramount importance to Byron*

had been happy, and he had, in a sense, even as a young man, consecrated his life to the idea of Greek freedom. There would certainly be something of desperation in this decision. The Greek venture was a resolution of his personal problems, his intermittent boredom with the life he was leading, his recurrent sense of futility and frustration. But it was also a good deal more than that. It offered him fulfilment, the life of action which, with one part of his complex nature, he had always craved; and it presented him with an opportunity which was unlikely to recur in any other form, to do something which was objectively good, which went beyond any personal satisfaction he might obtain. The Greek cause offered him the chance to escape from self-absorption.

Nevertheless, there were other reasons to make him hesitate. In the spring of 1823 he received a visit from Captain Edward Blaquière, as the representative of the London Greek Committee. He brought with him a delegate of the provisional government of Greece, Andreas Lourios: this was stimulating enough, but when Byron later learned

[177]

that he had been elected to the Committee and would be trusted with the disbursement of its funds, he had some doubts. It was one thing to go on such an adventure as an independent person; another with the responsibility of being the Committee's representative.

And then there was Teresa. Byron found himself caught between two self-imposed duties, the one of which excluded the other. He recognized that he had assumed responsibility for Teresa. He loved her, even if he was no longer in love; he also liked her, and her company irked him less than that of anybody else, except Augusta, with whom he had spent any length of time. Greece was a duty too, and yet it was also an evasion. He knew that, had always known it.

> Alas! the love of women! it is known
> To be a lovely and a fearful thing,

he had written, going on to say:

> for man, to man so oft unjust,
> Is always so to women; one sole bond
> Awaits them, treachery is all their trust;

and reflecting that: 'Men grow ashamed of being so very fond' and that:

> There's doubtless something in domestic doings
> Which forms, in fact, true love's antithesis.

He knew that Teresa would be desolated – even more than a wife would have been, for she lacked the security of marriage – by his decision to go to Greece. He was in a difficult position: he could not respect himself if he went; he could not respect himself if he stayed. He wrote to Sir John Bowring, the Secretary of the Committee, offering 'to go up into the Levant in person', but adding that 'the only objection is of a domestic nature, and I shall try to get over it; if I fail in this I must do what I can where I can, but it will always be a source of regret to me.' It is clear that he wasn't at all certain that he could bring himself to distress Teresa by leaving.

Doing what he could meant money. Byron had been comparatively rich since the sale of Newstead. In 1822, he became much richer. The death of Lady Byron's mother, Lady Noel, brought him a substantial inheritance, according to the terms of his marriage contrace. (Nevertheless, though he had frequently sighed for her death and resented the part he believed that she had played in the break-up of his marriage, he told Augusta that he 'regretted the pain which the privation must occasion to Sir Ralph Noel and Lady Byron'.)

He had always been interested in money, but as he grew richer he became more careful about how he spent it. 'I loves money,' he told Teresa to her puzzlement. 'For a good old gentlemanly vice, I think I shall take up with avarice,' he informed his public. Leigh Hunt observed that the public 'were to regard it only as a pleasantry, issuing from a generous mouth', but that Byron really meant it. In fact, it was both true and false. Hunt himself had no reason to complain that Byron was mean, except that, as an habitual borrower, he never felt that he received enough; and Byron remained notably generous towards the poor people whom he met and towards his dependents. Yet he spent hours scrutinizing his accounts, and was delighted if he found that he could save a small sum. It was partly eccentricity, partly the consequence of his transition from chronic indebtedness, which had brought him to financial disaster, and partly because he was anxious to save money to spend on the Greek cause. By the spring of 1823 he was calculating that he could devote £9–10,000 of his own money to his expedition, and to supporting the Greeks.

In the end he could not bring himself to break the news of his intention to Teresa. He had always disliked scenes, knew one was inevitable, and asked Pietro Gamba to let her know what he had decided; he could be sure that Pietro, who was himself delighted by the prospect of fighting for the Liberal cause in Greece, his hopes for Italy being dormant, would present his case in the most glowing terms. Even so, her first reaction was bitter. By her own account she wrote to Byron accusing him of sacrificing her happiness to his own reputation, and adding 'I know that we shall never see each other again.' What could he say to this? He knew that her first charge was true and could not fail to be irritated by the knowledge; and he feared that her foreboding was well-founded. Or rather he occasionally feared this; at other times he talked in a more rational manner of how he would come back to her. Then she pleaded that she be allowed to accompany them. This was impossible, of course; he had very little idea of just what might confront him in Greece, but he knew it was no place for a girl like Teresa.

It is impossible not to sympathize with Byron in his dilemma, just as it is impossible not to feel sorry for Teresa. She had lost her reputation for his sake, and she felt that she was being discarded for the sort of reason that she could never fully understand.

Then came relief for Byron. The decree which had banished Teresa's family from Ravenna was rescinded. Her father was over-joyed at the prospect of being allowed to return to his houses and

Trelawny, as seen in his memoirs, in characteristically self-dramatizing pose

Byron's Homeric helmet, procured by Pietro Gamba

estates. He had been miserable in exile. Naturally Teresa would return with him; for one thing, the decree of separation which the Pope had granted her had also enjoined her to live in his house. It seemed a solution of a sort. It didn't, however, commend itself to Teresa. Instead she proposed staying at Genoa with an elderly female friend or even going to a convent in Nice. Neither scheme was practical, and besides, her father desired her company. All the same she could not bring herself to go till Byron had departed.

Meanwhile he was assailed by all sorts of problems. There was the expedition to organize. He had obtained a boat, called the *Hercules*, though Trelawny, who was the sort of man who must always know better than the next man, didn't think much of it: 'a collier-built tub of 120 tons, round-bottomed and bluff-bowed'. There were uniforms to buy – Pietro returned with Homeric helmets which Byron liked and Trelawny thought ridiculous. There were stores to buy and a doctor to engage. There was the matter of finance – Kinnaird had sent him letters of credit for £4,000 and, with what he had put by himself, it was enough to be going on with. In all this he was greatly helped by his admirable banker in Genoa Charles Barry, who also proved adept at fending off the attentions of exiled Greeks who hoped that Byron could be induced to provide for them. And in the midst of this he had also to see to the affairs of the Hunts and Mary Shelley, who had become his complete dependents, and who now wished to return to England and looked to Byron to pay their passage.

It was no wonder he was harassed. He had lost weight since his illness at Lerici the previous year; his hair was grey and thin; he looked older than his years. Teresa was worried by his recurrent moods of depression and the difficulty he displayed in coming to decisions. She wrote to Mary Shelley that he was 'very sad'. She wasn't in this case transferring her own feelings to him. He had good reason to feel anxious and uncertain. He was embarking on a dangerous expedition of a kind for which he sometimes – and with reason – thought himself unsuited. Despite his love of travel he hated starting on journeys, and this was no ordinary one. He knew himself to be high-strung and impatient, and he was of his own accord undertaking a responsibility for others which, if it was to be successfully executed, would require calm and patience.

He had fixed the date of departure for 13 July. This appalled Teresa; she knew him to be superstitious and he had always been reluctant to do anything of importance on the 13th; she couldn't fail to regard it as ominous. She didn't see him at all on the 12th which he spent transacting business; one cannot but suspect that he avoided her because they had nothing to say which they had not said many times

before, and he knew that there could be nothing but pain and grief for both of them. On the 13th he was due to leave the villa at 5 o'clock, in order to sleep on board so that they might sail the next morning. He spent his last two hours with Teresa and arranged that Mary Shelley should come to her at 5 o'clock. Then he rode down to the shore, and she left with her father for the Romagna the following morning. A few miles out of Genoa she felt faint. Her father stopped the carriage. She got out and scribbled a note to Byron: 'I have promised more than I can perform, and you have asked of me what is beyond my strength.'

The letter was never sent, but Byron was wondering the same thing of himself. They were unable to sail that morning for there was a dead calm, and they were still becalmed on the 14th. He landed again, but hearing that Teresa had already left the villa, hadn't the heart to visit the empty house. On the 15th they got out of harbour, but a storm blew up in the night, the horses kicked down their partitions in panic, and they had to put back to port to refit.

This time he and Pietro visited the villa, and Byron was in low spirits: 'he spoke much of his past life, and the uncertainty of the future. "Where," he asked Pietro, "shall we be in a year?"' He confessed to his banker Barry that he would even now have withdrawn from the expedition but for the thought that 'Hobhouse and the others would laugh at him.' Yet these were only momentary doubts; his commitment was fundamental, though he could not hope for great success. A few weeks before sailing he had scribbled a fragment of a stanza in a notebook, which he later used as a journal in Cephalonia. They expressed his true feelings:

> The Dead have been awakened – shall I sleep?
>   The World's at war with tyrants – shall I
>   crouch?
> The harvest's ripe – and shall I pause to reap?
>   I slumber not – the thorn is in my Couch –
> Each day a trumpet soundeth in mine ear –
>   Its Echo in my heart –

'The thorn is in my couch' – the line might be taken as expressive of his whole life. 'The World's at war with tyrants'; that was precisely how he saw things, and the conviction stimulated his involvement in public affairs.

Byron, 1823. The sketch by Count D'Orsay shows him thin again, after illness and dieting

II

At last the *Hercules* was under way. It touched at Leghorn, passed within sight of Elba – what thoughts of Napoleon? – and the Lipari Isles, then through the straits of Messina, until on 3 August they anchored off Argostoli, the chief port of Cephalonia. This was one of the Ionian Isles and Byron had chosen it in place of Zante which he had originally intended to make his base, because the British Governor and Military Resident Lt-Colonel Charles James Napier, the future conqueror of Sind and author of the most famous military pun – 'Peccavi', was known to be favourable to the Greek cause. (There was a British Governor because the Ionian Isles had been consigned to the protection of Great Britain according to the terms of the Treaty of Vienna in 1815.) Argostoli would remain his base till the end of 1823.

The popular view is that Byron went to fight for Greece; and so in a sense he did. But his real role was less glorious, more doubtful and very much more difficult than that of a combatant, and one is bound to misrepresent his time in Greece, and what he achieved there, if one does not first try to establish just what that role was. This was something which caused him some perplexity himself. As he wrote to Napier on 9 September: 'It is lucky for me so far – that fail or not fail I can hardly be disappointed – for I believed myself on a fool's errand from the outset . . . I will at least linger or here on there till I see whether I *can* be of *any* service in *any* way, – and if I doubt it – it is because I do not feel confidence in my individual capacity for this kind of bear-taming, and not from a disbelief in the powers of a more active or less indifferent character to be of use to them – though I feel persuaded that that person must be a military man – But I like the Cause at least and will stick by it while it is not degraded nor discredited.'

This painfully honest and self-doubting letter is not written in the language of a crusader; and two days later, he made his doubts still more clear in a letter to Teresa: 'I shall fulfil the object of my mission from the committee – and then probably return into Italy – for it does not seem likely that as an individual I can be of use to them – At least no other foreigner has yet appeared to be so – nor does it seem likely that any will at present.' Meanwhile he explained that he was remaining in Cephalonia until he should receive what appeared to be an accurate account of the situation on the mainland.

This letter to Teresa may be dismissed as being written to console her for his absence and hold out the hope that he would be back with her before too long. Yet it also exposes his perplexity. He knew,

Argostoli, Cephalonia. Byron's base during his first months in Greece, with the Black Mountains behind. Sketch by Edward Lear

despite the play-acting, the Homeric helmets and the bodyguard of Suliotes whom he was soon supporting, that he was not a soldier. There were moments certainly when he imagined himself leading troops in the field, and he would have agreed, sometimes anyway – as Scott would have – with Johnson's judgment that 'every man thinks the worse of himself for not having been a soldier'; but he knew his own character too well to believe that he had any natural gift for commanding men in the field; he knew his own tendency to be indecisive, and he lacked the ruthlessness a general must possess. He had no experience of war, though he had come close enough to it, and had a sufficiently lively imagination to be disgusted by its cruelty and by any carelessness of human life. Tenderness of heart kept breaking in, and his most characteristic gestures in Greece were all directed to alleviating the horrors of war. Besides it was not in search of any delusive glory that he had come to Greece.

He was there, it seems, for three reasons. First, and generally, overlaying the other reasons, was his belief in the justice of the Greek cause, and his wish that the Greeks should be independent. This survived all the evidence of their shiftlessness, ingratitude, inability to combine, dishonesty and cruelty. 'Whoever goes into Greece at present,' he wrote in his journal, 'should do it as Mrs Fry went into Newgate' – Elizabeth Fry was the Quaker who had been one of the first to reveal the horrors of English prisons and to seek to reform them – 'not in the expectation of meeting with any especial indication of existing probity – but in the hope that time and better treatment will reclaim the present burglarious and larcenous tendencies which have followed this General Gaol delivery. When the limbs of the Greeks are a little less stiff from the shackles of four centuries – they will not march so much "as if they had gyves on their legs" . . . the worst of them is,' he reflected, 'that they are such d—d liars; – there never was such incapacity for veracity shown since Eve lived in Paradise.'

Second, he had gone there in the hope that he might in some degree resolve his personal problems. Many people undertake difficult and dangerous tasks for just this reason, and it was to Byron's credit that he realized it; and intermittently despised himself for it. He was seeking in action to dispel the disillusion of middle age, and, in returning to scenes where he had been happy in his youth, to recover something which in his heart he knew had been lost for ever. It was in this mood that, on their voyage, sighting the mountains of the Morea in the distance, he had turned to one of his companions and said, 'I don't know why it is, but I feel as if the eleven long years of bitterness I have passed through since I was here, were taken off my shoulders, and I was scudding through the Greek archipelago with old Bathurst in his frigate.' But, in the nature of things, this mood could not last, and he was soon indeed to receive harsh proof that he was no longer the ardent youth he had been.

Third, and most important, he was in Greece as the representative of the London Committee. It was made up of his friends, and it was, of course, gratifying that they trusted him. He undoubtedly hoped that his exertions in Greece would rehabilitate him in the eyes of the English public. But far more important was the fact that he had been entrusted by them with the responsibility of applying the money which they had collected in the best interest of the Greek cause. And just what that was proved devilish hard to determine.

The first surge of the rebellion against the Turks had spent itself. For the moment the war seemed in abeyance, except for the occasional brigand raid and Turkish reprisals. The Turks commanded the seas around the mainland so that the Greek fleet, mostly merchant vessels, was confined to the island harbours. On land the Greeks were divided. Prince Alexander Mavrocordatos had been elected President the previous year, but in the summer of 1823, he had resigned office and retired to the island of Hydra. The most effective Greek force seemed to be that commanded by the klephte leader Kolokotrones, but he was considered to be unreliable, and held no official or constitutional position. For Byron, the first question was to whom he might properly or effectively hand over the funds with which he had been entrusted. To try to obtain authentic information about what was happening he wrote, on his arrival in Cephalonia, to Marco Botsaris commanding the Greek forces in Acarnania north of Missolonghi; Mavrocordatos had recommended him to Byron as 'one of the bravest and most honest of the Greek captains' and he had also been praised by the Metropolitan Bishop Ignatius of Arta whom Byron had met at Leghorn. Botsaris was delighted to receive his letter, and replied inviting Byron to come and join him. However it was the last letter he wrote, for he was killed in a skirmish the next day, and Byron told

Marco Botsaris, the Greek commander

[187]

Hobhouse that he could not have 'the same confidence in his successor who is less well known'. So he waited 'in a very pretty village between the Mountains and the sea – waiting what Napoleon calls "the March of Events" – these events however keep their march somewhat secret'. It was perplexing, but if he was to 'endeavour to do my duty by the Committee and the Cause' he must try first 'to collect something like positive information'.

While waiting he crossed the straits to Ithaca – 'which as a pendant to the Troad – a former Greek traveller would like to see'. This excursion to an Homeric site – for Ithaca was the island of Odysseus, though scholars who disputed the existence of Troy were not disposed to credit this either – delighted and refreshed him. The journey across Cephalonia to the port of St Euphemia – nine hours, on mule-back under a blazing August sun – was as wild and strenuous as any he had experienced in Greece, and on Ithaca itself he was delighted to visit the Fountain of Arethusa and the so-called 'School of Homer'. Two other incidents of this visit are worthy of note. At the monastery where they stayed the night he was seized with a species of nervous fit in which he cried out that his head was burning, and was only quietened with great difficulty by his companions; this was at least an indication of the strain to which he had subjected himself, aggravated by his exertions and meagre diet. Then, before returning to Cephalonia, he was made aware of the unhappy condition of many Greek families who had fled to the island from the mainland. He contributed generously to a fund that had been established for their relief. Among these refugees were a mother and three daughters called Chalandritsanos, who came from Patras and who had been reduced from prosperity to near destitution. He interested himself in them, and arranged for them to be brought over to Cephalonia. There they were soon joined by the only male in the family, a boy Loukas, who had been fighting in Kolokotrones' forces. He was only fifteen, dark and good-looking. Byron made him his page.

Back in Cephalonia he settled in a little villa in Metaxata. It was idyllically positioned: he could gaze over to the mountains of the Morea, and the house stood in vineyards and olive groves half a mile from the sea, with a mountain rising behind. Letters at last arrived from London – at this stage he was experiencing both delays in correspondence and difficulty in having his bills of exchange cashed except at a ruinous discount. The Committee now requested him to 'act as their representative near the Greek Government and take charge

Previous pages: Monastery of Sami, Cephalonia. Today only the bells survive

Byron drilling his Suliotes outside Missolonghi

of the proper disposition and delivery of certain stores.' These, however, had not arrived by the end of September.

He now took over a band of forty Suliotes, paying them a dollar a month more than the Greek government would, but was soon disillusioned as they seemed more interested in further financial demands than any other form of action. Before long he was eager to be rid of them, and, on receipt of a further month's pay, many of them crossed the straits to Acarnania, being able to do so because the Turkish fleet had abandoned the blockade of the coast.

The Governor of Missolonghi, Count Metaxa, invited him to join him there, and the offer, promising a closer involvement, was tempting. Yet all the time Byron was conscious that he had 'not come here to join a faction but a nation'; and this was difficult because the nation was made up of conflicting factions. As he saw it, 'it was necessary in the present state of the parties that I should have some communication with the existing Government on the subject of their opinion *where* I might be – if not *most* useful – at any rate *least* obnoxious.' Knowing the Greeks, he had never pretended to himself that his expedition would be straightforward, but it was proving even more perplexing than he had expected.

Trelawny, being irresponsible, felt only irritation at the delay. He would later talk of Byron 'falling back into his old routine of dawdling habits, plotting – planning – shilly-shallying and doing nothing'. It wasn't for this that the bold Trelawny had come to Greece; so he took off, along with George Hamilton Browne, a young Scottish officer who had attached himself to Byron, for the mainland, where, before long, Trelawny attached himself to one of the *klephte* leaders, who had adopted the name Odysseus and who could provide 'excellent sport between Turk and woodcock-shooting'.

Byron was not so fortunate. He was besieged on all sides with invitations and requests; but he was restrained by the knowledge that to commit himself in any one direction might be detrimental to the whole enterprise. If only the provisional Greek government possessed some real authority, if only the Greeks were not so given to quarrelling among themselves; 'a foreigner,' he wrote to Mavrocordatos, 'must refrain with certain caution from every act that might sustain parties and foster discord. No one is surprised, certainly, that discords are awakened in a country that has undergone a revolution and only just escaped from so long and barbarous a tyranny; but I cannot conceal my displeasure – and also the hope that I had, encouraged by the honourable examples of the past years – that in a war in which the Greeks did not fight for Political theories, nor for Independence only, but for their very existence, they would be able to keep themselves far away from those very serious evils that always manifest themselves in all Revolutions.' He went on to speak of the consequences of this discord: how the Turks would benefit, how the Western Philhellenes might grow discouraged, how 'the natural enemies of liberty' – whom he did not identify, though they were clearly the Russian and Austrian emperors – might find in this a pretext 'to meddle in Greek affairs, with the collapse of all the noble hopes of the Greek people.' Nevertheless, his own sentiments were unchanged. He had sent Trelawny and Browne to the Government in the Morea – though they had in fact drifted off to join Odysseus in Attica – to try to find out what was happening. Meanwhile, for all his desire to work with Mavrocordatos, 'the state of things up to now seems such that I do not see how or what a foreigner might do that could be of benefit to Greece and to the honour of himself'.

This was an important letter. It reveals very clearly why Byron remained in Cephalonia. It shows how acute his political understanding was. It displays an admirable fortitude of mind. He knew that there was only one justification for his being in Greece, and he was not prepared to put the chance of success in jeopardy by committing himself, his name and resources to any single faction, aware that, by doing so, he might hinder the creation of the unity that seemed to him the necessary condition for the achievement of Greek Independence. And he was ready to speak plainly to that purpose.

Five days later, 6 October, he wrote a long letter to Hobhouse in which he analysed the situation, and said 'they want a regular force to support a regular System quite as much as to repel their enemies – in the interim every man that can pay or command from one hundred to a thousand Gillies is independent – and seems to act for himself'. To prove the truth of this assertion, he told Hobhouse that he had himself been approached from half-a-dozen quarters, to put himself 'at the head of some hundred boys of the belt and the blade' but 'it must be the *Cause* – and not individuals or *parties* that I endeavour to benefit'. Unlike Trelawny he had not come to Greece for fun.

Sometimes, indeed, he wondered why he had come: 'I was a fool to come here,' he told Teresa, 'but being here I must see what is to be done.' And Pietro Gamba, the young enthusiast, also told his sister, 'This is a veritable school of disillusion.'

So the autumn passed, tediously. For diversion, Byron rode, fired his pistols, played with his dogs – the Newfoundland Lion and the faithful bulldog Moretto, which he had now had for seven years. It

Byron with Lion. Described as a Newfoundland, he is very different from modern examples of the breed

was rather like being in Ravenna again, waiting for something to happen. There was no Teresa, of course, and indeed Pietro wrote approvingly of Byron's 'monkish existence'. He was not, however, quite without a sentimental attachment – he never had been, and could not exist happily without being at least a little in love; and he had transferred his affections to the Greek boy Loukas Chalandritsanos, whose family he was supporting. It was reminiscent of his Harrow friendships, tender, idealistic and inconclusive. They had represented an intense fraternity; now his attitude was quasi-paternal. But there was one significant difference: his feelings were not reciprocated. Loukas, though vain and ardent, seems to have looked on Byron merely as a provider, and to have felt nothing more for him. Byron's consciousness of this would oppress his last months – it seemed to him yet another sign that he was old before his time. The experience of unrequited affection was new to him, and he responded by spoiling the boy still more devotedly.

This was only one trouble among many. It added to his sense of uselessness, to his fear that he had exerted himself, destroying his tranquillity and Teresa's happiness, to no purpose. Yet to his credit, despite occasional moans, he stuck to his self-appointed task. He would do what he could for the Greeks. He agreed with Napier that it was necessary to form a disciplined body of troops from the Phil-hellenes, but was that possible when all were volunteers, some of them perhaps more eager to distinguish themselves than to serve the cause?

There were other diversions. There was Dr James Kennedy, for instance, the Scottish medical officer who was a fervent Evangelical and who welcomed the opportunity given him to 'save' the wicked poet. Byron would not be saved, but he had always had a serious attitude to religion – Scott had once told him he would end as a Roman Catholic – and he relished theological and philosophical discussion. He had argued metaphysical and ontological questions in *Don Juan*, *Cain* and *Manfred*, and to the surprise of some of his companions, he was pleased to argue them with Dr Kennedy. Kennedy, who had had little success with most of the British officers whom he had tried to convert, was flattered by Byron's attention and impressed by his knowledge of the Bible. Kennedy failed to convert him – Byron asked whether he thought there had been less misery and bloodshed in the world since the introduction of Christianity, and was unconvinced by his answer – but he won Byron's respect; Byron had always been ready to honour virtue when he encountered it, and this was indeed one of the reasons for his enduring admiration for his wife.

As Christmas approached, Greek affairs seemed to go better. He had regularized his financial transactions in November, when he found two bankers, Charles Hancock in Cephalonia and his partner Samuel Barff in Zante, who were prepared to cash his bills of exchange on reasonable terms. He was thus able to make the Greek deputies Jean Orlando and Andreas Luriottis a loan of £4,000 to equip and pay the Greek fleet. Hancock for his part was delighted by Byron; he had never met anyone like him before. As a result Byron was relieved of at least one of his anxieties.

Then a new agent of the London Committee arrived: Colonel Leicester Stanhope. Stanhope was an experienced soldier, who had served in India, but a somewhat absurd man, the prototype of the race of high-minded enthusiasts who would draw up blueprints for oppressed or backward peoples without any considerations of the particular circumstances of their life, culture and history. A philosophical Radical and disciple of Jeremy Bentham, the high priest of Utilitarianism, he was precisely the sort of theorist who irritated Byron and aroused his mockery. Byron was soon referring to him as 'the typographical Colonel', for Stanhope had brought a printing press with him and believed that Greece could be freed by pamphleteering. Nevertheless, Byron was happy enough to see him: Stanhope was ready to relieve him of routine correspondence, he could share the responsibility which weighed heavily on Byron; and early in December Byron sent him to the mainland with a letter to the Provisional Government.

In this letter he spoke even more frankly than before: 'Unless union and order are established, all hopes of a loan will be vain; and all the assistance which the Greeks could expect from abroad will be suspended and destroyed.' He warned them that the Great Powers, whom he so deeply – and with reason – distrusted, might be tempted to intervene; and that, if they did so, they might settle the affairs of Greece 'in such a way as to blast the brightest hopes of yourselves and your friends'. This repeated warnings he had given privately; he had told individual Greeks that they might achieve independence, they might fall again under the control of the Turks, or they might be 'liberated' by the Tsar, in which case their situation would be no happier; they would be merely exchanging one tyranny for another, and the Christian, even Orthodox, tyranny of Moscow might prove harsher than the Muslim tyranny of Constantinople, which was at least mitigated by gross inefficiency and frequent indifference.

Then he uttered a final warning, aware of the high hopes which the Greeks had placed in him and the confidence of his support which they felt: 'Allow me to add once for all – I desire the well-being of Greece, and nothing else; I will do all I can to secure it; but I cannot consent, I never will consent that the English public or English individuals, should be deceived as to the real state of Greek affairs.'

III

Eventually the Greek fleet had put to sea. Fourteen Greek ships met four Turkish ones in the Gulf of Patras, that scene of famous battles where both Lepanto and Actium had been fought. The Greeks were victorious, as of course they should have been at these odds, but then driving one of the Turkish ships ashore on Ithaca, massacred its crew, and, in doing so, violated the admittedly somewhat tenuous neutrality of the Ionian Isles. Byron did not learn of this till later, but one consequence was that, when Mavrocordatos, now arrived at Missolonghi, sent a ship to bring Byron to the mainland, the British authorities refused to admit it to port, as a protest at this breach of neutrality. Once again the Greeks had proved their ability to snatch disadvantage from victory.

The Greek leader Prince Alexander Mavrocordatos, spectacles removed to make him more impressive

Anecdotes of Byron — or a touch of the Marvellous.

Weather Wise — One Day on a voyage to Athens, a dark cloud appeared to windward, his Lordship regarded it steadily for some time, untill at length feeling a few drops of rain fall, he called to Fletcher to bring him Cloak, so certain he was of an approaching shower.

En voyage. Fletcher and Byron on their way to Greece

All the same Byron had concluded that he must now commit himself. If Mavrocordatos couldn't be said to represent an established Provisional Government and if unity had not yet been achieved, nevertheless he had recovered his position and was at least as much in command as it might ever be hoped he would be. Accordingly, in the middle of December, Byron made his own plans to cross over to the mainland.

The journey was eventful. They travelled in two ships. Byron with his medical man Dr Bruno, Fletcher, Tita Falcieri – now perhaps the servant on whom he most relied – Loukas and the Newfoundland Lion, were in a light speedy barque of a type known as a mistico. The baggage, military and medical supplies, the horses and Moretto the bulldog were all in a heavier and more clumsy boat – a bombard – together with Lega Zamebelli the steward, all under the care of Pietro Gamba. They touched at Zante where Byron collected about £1,600 in Maria Teresa dollars (8,000 of them) from his banker Barff. On the point of departure Dr Kennedy, coming to say goodbye, found him reading his beloved Scott. It was *Quentin Durward*, published only a few months before in June, and, apart from the delight it afforded him, Byron could hardly fail to be struck by a certain similarity between the position of the eponymous Scottish hero, an honest man in a corrupt, dangerous and devious world, and his own.

His arrival was eagerly expected in Missolonghi. Stanhope compared the mood of exaltation to that of 'the coming of a Messiah'; a Messiah, as Leslie Marchand points out, carrying 'an abundance of dollars'. But there was trouble in the town; the Greek sailors were near mutiny, and, on the very day that Byron sailed – on a journey that might be expected to take no more than twelve hours – Turkish ships were sighted in the gulf, and the Greek ones abruptly fled, leaving the approaches to the port unguarded.

Byron was ignorant of all this until, before it was light, the mistico encountered a large ship, which the captain identified as Turkish. It was a moment of extreme danger. Even the dogs, Fletcher said, fell quiet. The captain changed course and the speedy barque eluded the Turkish ship, which may not indeed have been aware of its presence. They sailed down the coast and when it was light were able to discern two enemy ships one of which was apparently pursuing the bombard, while the other was cutting off the passage to Missolonghi.

They put into an inlet and Byron sent Loukas and a sailor ashore with a message to Stanhope. In language reminiscent of that in which he had explained his decision fifteen years earlier to sent young Robert Rushton home, he expressed his anxiety for Loukas' fate if they should be taken by the Turks. Then they crept down the coast to Dragomestri, the modern Astakos, where more than a century later even such a devoted Philhellene as Patrick Leigh Fermor found himself depressed by 'the fly-blown streets, the sluggish sea, the sirocco, the blighting heat, the stricken and tormented nights'. Byron, of course, was there in winter, and he was warmly received by the citizens; nevertheless, the five days he spent there, sleeping on the deck of the ship, were anxious and depressing, though he told Henry Muir, the Health Officer at Argostoli that they were 'all very well and in good spirits'.

Meanwhile the bombard had been taken by a Turkish boat. Though ostensibly a neutral vessel with papers in order, its position was precarious. Pietro loaded a collection of Byron's letters, which might be compromising, with lead-shot and dropped them overboard. Then they were all rescued by a coincidence, which might seem rather to belong to the adventures with which Byron had credited Don Juan, than to real life. The Turkish captain was about to order the execution of the bombard's skipper, when he recognized him as a man who had saved his life after a shipwreck in the Black Sea. He therefore sailed

Byron arriving in Missolonghi, a fanciful representation. Botsaris, shown with Mavrocordatos, was already dead, and Trelawny (behind Byron) was not present

into Patras where he handed the prisoners over to Yussuf Pasha, the captain of the Turkish garrison, who, accepting their neutral status, released them. In fact, therefore, Gamba reached Missolonghi before Byron.

Mavrocordatos had now managed to send an escort to Drago-mestri. To smarten himself for his arrival – and to kill the fleas he had attracted as a result of spending several days without changing his clothes – Byron defied his doctor, who prophesied cramp or fever, and took a swim. 'My cold bath set all to rights.' He donned a smart red uniform, and disembarked at Missolonghi.

With the arrival at Missolonghi we are entering on the last act of the Byronic drama. He had a little less than four months to live. Because we know this – and because he so frequently talked about the prospect of his death – but then he had always done so – it is tempting to read these months retrospectively; and to interpret everything as leading up to his death. It is a temptation to which many of those with him there, who subsequently wrote memoirs, were to succumb. But it is of course nonsense. Byron certainly and naturally contemplated death. He was often ill; he knew that his situation was dangerous; he expected to be engaged in action – and indeed much of the spring was occupied with plans for an assault on Lepanto (Naupactos). Throughout these months, however, he was occupied with plans for the future conduct of the war, and he no more expected to die in April than he expected to be in England then or to be reconciled with his wife.

There was certainly much to lower his spirits. There was Missolonghi itself. Commanding the north shore of the Gulf of Patras, which itself leads to the narrow Isthmus of Corinth, it was of great strategic importance. It had withstood one siege by the Turks, and it was likely that this would be renewed in the summer, but before then the opportunity existed for a successful attack on Lepanto and the two forts on the south side of the gulf, which, along with Patras itself, were the only strong points still held by the Turks in that part of Greece.

Its importance was clear, even though the town itself hardly seemed to merit this distinction. Low-lying, divided from the open sea by a lagoon and mudflats, it was unhealthy and charmless. That spring the wind blew clouds constantly from the west against the mountains behind the town. It rained and rained. The unpaved streets were churned into mud. There were many days when it was impossible to ride out – Byron kept his horses stabled across the lagoon – and the whole atmosphere in the crowded town was one of nervous frustration. Byron had been there in 1809 with Hobhouse at about the same time of year, but conditions which were tolerable in his irresponsible and adventurous youth were more irksome now that he was weighed down with the responsibility of the Cause.

He was lodged in a three-storeyed house set on a promontory at the edge of the lagoon. Colonel Stanhope was established on the first floor, Byron on the second which had either four or five rooms for himself, his dogs and his servants. The ground about the house was reduced to a swamp, and there were days when it could only be approached by boat. When the weather was clear – but that was seldom – he could look across the gulf to the mountains of the Morea. There was a courtyard at the back where he could drill some of the Suliote guard whom he had taken into his personal employ. (There were 600 of these, and he had undertaken to pay for 500 himself if the Greek Government paid for the remaining 100; there is no evidence that they ever did so.) He had an affectionate admiration for the brave and picturesque Suliotes dating from his first visit to Ali Pasha, but they proved difficult, quarrelsome, greedy and unreliable; they were a sore trial to him.

He drilled them; he rode out when the weather permitted; but most of the time was spent in his sitting room: receiving Greek visitors who always asked for money; writing letters to his bankers and Kinnaird

Byron's house in Missolonghi

about money; writing letters urging the Greeks to reconcile their differences; trying to plan action, but restrained from action by circumstances; chatting, drinking, shooting pistols and playing with his dogs. Lion was his chief solace: '"You are no rogue, Lion,"' he would say, according to the firemaster Parry whom the Committee had sent out to try to organize an artillery unit for the Greeks. 'The dog's eyes sparkled, and his tail swept the floor . . . "Thou art more faithful than men, Lion, I trust thee more." Lion sprang up, and barked and bounded round his master. "Lion, I love thee, thou faithful dog!" and Lion jumped and kissed his master's hand.'

It was as well he had such pleasant distraction and company, for on 20 January the town was again blockaded by the Turkish fleet, the Greek ships having slipped away in panic on sight of the enemy. A plan was formed to make a night attack on the Turks in small boats with the intention of cutting their rigging. Byron was eager to lead it himself. Gamba thought that 'he was now intent only upon exposing himself to danger'. With others he worked to dissuade him. It was unnecessary, for nothing came of the plan, and Byron was instead diverted when Mavrocordatos commissioned him to command an attack on Lepanto.

Two days before he had celebrated his thirty-sixth birthday. He had spent two previous birthdays in Greece, both in Athens. The first in 1810 he and Hobhouse had followed with their first visit to Sounion, the second had come by while he was living in the Capuchin Convent and feeding 'upon Woodcocks & Red Mullet every day'. His present mood was far removed from that of his blithe youth.

Missolonghi: the lagoon

'Tis time this heart should be unmoved,
   Since others it hath ceased to move:
Yet though I cannot be beloved,
    Still let me love!

My days are in the yellow leaf;
   The flowers and fruits of Love are gone;
The worm, the canker, and the grief
    Are mine alone!

The fire that on my bosom preys
   Is lone as some Volcanic isle;
No torch is kindled at its blaze
    A funeral pile!

The hope, the fear, the jealous care,
   The exalted portion of the pain
And power of Love I cannot share,
    But wear the chain.

But 'tis not *thus* – and 'tis not *here* –
   Such thoughts should shake my Soul, nor *now*
Where Glory decks the hero's bier
    Or binds his brow.

The Sword, the Banner, and the Field,
   Glory and Greece around us see!
The Spartan borne upon his shield
    Was not more free!

Awake (not Greece – she *is* awake!)
   Awake, my Spirit! think through *whom*
Thy life-blood tracks its parent lake
    And then strike home!

Tread those reviving passions down
   Unworthy manhood – unto thee
Indifferent should the smile or frown
    Of Beauty be.

If thou regret'st thy youth, *why live?*
   The land of honourable death
Is here: – up to the Field, and give
    Away thy Breath.

Seek out – less often sought than found –
   A soldier's grave, for thee the best;
Then look around, and choose thy ground,
    And take thy Rest!

How does one test the sincerity of a poem in the context of a life? The question presents itself to any biographer of a poet, and it is only when one has brooded on the nature of artistic creation and its ability to endure, and, enduring, to colour judgment, that one may realize that the question is so fundamentally improper as to be ultimately insignificant. Even a poet like Byron who works unusually close to experience manifests a self in his poetry which is different from his social self. The Byron who wrote this poem in which he wrestled with his feelings for Greece and for Loukas was a Byron whom neither Greece nor Loukas knew. (Moreover it is impossible to know to what extent his feeling for Loukas was part of his feeling for Greece, even though he set them in opposition to each other here.)

Then a poem is a matter of hours. It is written from a phrase, an image or a mood; but, if it works at all it achieves a sort of permanence. The poet said this; therefore this is what he thought, now and for ever more amen.

Finally a poem is also a matter of convention. Poems fall into certain modes. The opposition of war and love, duty and inclination, is a poetic commonplace. It is unfortunate when the commonplace is made the explanation of the poet.

Of course, Byron felt a sentimental attachment to Loukas, and was hurt by the boy's indifference. But the opposition he sets out in the poem is a false one. His work for Greece was no more likely to be affected by his feelings for the boy than by his fondness for his dog. It was no more than a murmur, disturbing occasionally, perhaps distracting, in the busy, confusing and frequently disheartening bustle of his mission. The poem, as I say, expressed the mood of a particular moment: the last stanza, sincere enough, is also nevertheless a rhetorical commonplace: poet-soldiers had been demanding a hero's grave of their muse for at least two and a half millennia. A poem is something apart from the poet. Its sincerity may be real, but it is not the poet's; the poet finds no difficulty in turning from a forlorn stanza to a beefsteak.

IV

The day after his birthday Byron seized an opportunity to mitigate the cruelty of war. In recognition of Yussuf Pasha's clemency in freeing Gamba and his friends, he sent to him, under escort, a group of four Mohemmedan prisoners 'without conditions – but if the circumstances could win a place in your memory I would only beg your Highness to treat with humanity any Greeks who may fall into the hands of the Mussulmans – Since the horrors of war are sufficient in themselves without adding cold-blooded ruthlessness on either side.'

Plans for the attack on Lepanto went ahead. It was garrisoned by Albanians who, it was established, might be willing to surrender the fort, with little show of resistance – for a consideration, of course. Then on 5 February Parry at last arrived with English workmen to form the artillery force which would be necessary either to defend Missolonghi in the event of a renewed Turkish siege, or if it was necessary to bombard any Turkish stronghold. Byron at once took to Parry, whose blunt honesty seemed a refreshing change, and he soon entrusted him with the dispensation of funds to the Greeks as well. However, there was disappointment here too. Expectations had been too high. The English workmen Parry had brought were discontented and asked to be sent home. The artillery force failed to materialize.

February indeed was a dismal month, though the Turkish fleet had, for the moment at least, lifted the blockade. It continued to rain, day after day – 'the Dykes of Holland,' he said, 'when broken down are the Desarts (sic) of Arabia for dryness in comparison.' On the 14th the Suliotes infuriated him with new demands: that out of a force of some 400 about 150 should be regarded as officers and paid accordingly. He resolved that they could go to the Turks or the Devil. It is possible to have some sympathy for the Suliotes: they were essentially soldiers of fortune, the inhabitants of Missolonghi feared and resented them, and they had never in all probability found themselves so close to so much money as Byron was said to have at his command. All the same his anger and disappointment are understandable: he had invested much – emotion as well as money – in the Suliotes whom he had liked since his first visit to Greece, and with whom he had found a certain affinity. Now his anger persuaded them that they had overstepped the bounds. They agreed to form a new corps under his direct command, and, in its formation, some of the most difficult were weeded out. But all this had meant that the attack on Lepanto was postponed.

Then on the 15th Byron suffered some sort of fit. It struck onlookers as resembling epilepsy. Dr Bruno applied leeches – the only remedy, it seems, that the poor man knew. When they were removed Byron continued to bleed. They had been put, Byron told Murray, 'too near my temporal artery for my temporal safety'. The bleeding continued for several hours, and Byron fainted again. Pietro Gamba considered that the attack had been brought on by Byron's exertions – a few days earlier he had been soaked bringing in some stores which the townspeople declined to shift because it was a Saint's Day – by his miserable diet, and the habit he had formed of drinking grog and brandy with Parry. No doubt all these contributed to the attack –

Byron had never eaten wisely – but nervous strain must also have been a factor.

He recovered, but there was no relief for his nerves. On the 18th the Suliotes rioted. A Swedish officer was killed, and a little boy who was the son of Mario Botsaris was wounded. The townspeople were terrified that the wild mountaineers would sack the place. Byron ordered his few cannon to be trained on the Suliotes, and himself confronted them. Stanhope said that 'the more the Suliotes raged, the more his calm courage triumphed'. The danger was averted, but it was not the sort of convalescent activity that a doctor might recommend. And, to cap it all, two days later there was an earthquake.

Yet, though all this might seem disheartening enough to justify Byron's occasional complaints that he was wasting his time, all was not uniformly bleak. True, the Suliotes soon made off on an expedition that offered easier plunder than the siege of Lepanto, so that enterprise had to be abandoned or at least postponed yet again, even though the garrison had now lowered their price for offering only a token resistance from 40,000 dollars to 25,000. On the other hand there were some developments which offered a more optimistic prospect. There was the return of George Finlay for instance. Finlay, a young Philhellene who would later write a history of Greece from ancient times to the present day, had made Byron's acquaintance in Cephalonia, and had then travelled through the Morea and on to Athens. His return now was trebly welcome. In the first place, he was a man of Byron's own world, and one with whom he could converse freely and indulge in the reminiscences in which he delighted. Second, and more important, he could bring what Byron entirely lacked: reliable information as to the state of things in other parts of the country. And third, even more welcome, he came with firm proposals from the guerrilla leader Odysseus – urged on, perhaps, by Trelawny – for a meeting with Mavrocordatos and Byron. He proposed a congress at Salona about sixty miles from Missolonghi near the foot of Mount Parnassus, where, it was hoped, the various leaders and their parties might be reconciled in unity. Byron distrusted what he knew of Odysseus – as did Mavrocordatos – but the opportunity was too good to be lost. It represented indeed a justification of Byron's policy since his arrival in Greece. He had, he believed, stabilized the government of Western Greece, and might now restore the nation's broken unity. Hearing of his plans, the Greek Government of the Morea invited him to join them, and even offered him the office of Governor-General of Greece. But he only said that he would consider their offers after he had been to Salona, which journey was now fixed for the end of March.

While planning war, he still struggled to correct its cruelties. He obtained the release of thirty Turkish prisoners, taken when their brig ran ashore. One of them, a nine-year-old girl called Hato or Hatadje, he even proposed to adopt. Perhaps he might send her to England to be brought up with his daughter Ada – they were the same age; or perhaps he could send her to Teresa in Italy. In either case he hoped 'so to provide for her as to enable her to live with reputation either singly or in marriage, if she arrive at maturity'. Eventually, however, the child was sent with her mother to Dr Kennedy in Cephalonia, until both could be returned to the child's father in Patras.

He told Murray that his health was now better, but in fact his constitution had been seriously weakened by the fit – and by its cure – by fatigue, principally nervous, and strain. Gamba remarked how easily he lost his temper over little things, though he was calm enough when matters were serious. He was aware of the risks he was taking. He told Kennedy he knew his health was precarious and that he was not deceived on that subject. 'But it is proper that I should remain in Greece; and it were better to die doing something than nothing. My presence here has been supposed so far useful as to have prevented confusion from becoming worse confounded, at least for the present. Should I become, or be deemed useless or superfluous, I am ready to retire; but in the interim I am not to consider personal consequences; the rest is in the hands of Providence, – as indeed are all things. I shall however observe your instructions, and indeed did so, as far as regards abstinence, for some time past.'

This was an exact statement of the case.

Stanhope left for Athens with his printing press, eager to win the war by words, convert Greek brigands to Benthamite principles and establish Parliamentary government in a nation emerging from four hundred years of servitude. Byron was less optimistic. He thought some form of Federation would be best for Greece. Switzerland commended itself as a model; so did America, still in the years before the Civil War, a loose association of largely autonomous States. But, he observed to Parry, 'there is no abstract form of Government which we can call good'. It was something the Greeks would have to work out for themselves.

On 11 March he wrote to Demetrius Parucca who had sent him the invitation to come to the Morea, saying that, while he hoped to see the Greeks at peace with each other, he did not think he should leave Roumeli for the Peloponnesus: 'the more so, as this part is exposed to a greater degree to the enemy'. And indeed, an attack by the Turks on Missolonghi was expected in the spring.

Though it still rained, that was almost on them. On 17 March he told Teresa he had seen a swallow. It was the last letter he wrote to her, but in the same despatch Pietro spoke of their plans of meeting Odysseus at Salona, 'though the unfavourable weather and the impossible roads have kept us here until now . . . Arm yourself, too,' he told her, 'with patience and sacrifice your sufferings to this unhappy Greece and to Byron's glory, which is now spreading more and more to the most remote districts . . . The influence of Mylord is necessary in Greece every day, and he seems to have a great role to play there. He has already received a naturalization note from the Greek government and has been awarded the citizenship of Missolonghi.' Pietro's whole tone was as usual optimistic. It is possible to contend that it was ridiculously so. Difficulties still abounded: he boasted to Teresa of the artillery corps which had been established, and offered his brothers 'a suitable rank and fine prospects' if they should join him; but in truth it was a wretched affair. He talked to her of the *Telegrafo Greco*, the Italian version of Stanhope's paper which he was editing, in apparent ignorance of Byron's opinion that it was likely to do more harm than good. He spoke enthusiastically of the Salona meeting, though that would never take place.

Yet it is really Byron's death which punctures his optimism, and our knowledge of that death. It was, after all, that which prevented the meeting with Odysseus. And there were indeed grounds for optimism. The Greek loan had at last been raised in London. It was admittedly heavily discounted – by 41 per cent – and two years interest at 5 per cent was withheld – so that out of the nominal £800,000 the Greek government would receive only about £300,000, but this was still a substantial sum. The agreement was signed by the Greek Deputies, Jean Orlando and Andreas Luriottis on 2 February, and the first instalment arrived in Zante, to be held by Samuel Barff, in May; Byron, Stanhope and Colonel Napier were named as administrators, but of course Byron was dead before any money arrived. He was delirious before final confirmation of the Loan reached Missolonghi, but he knew it was settled in the last week of March. On the 30th he wrote to Kinnaird suggesting that the £4,000 he had advanced to the Greek government in anticipation of the loan, should now be repaid, though of course, 'I shall still spend it in the Cause, for I have some hundred men under my command, regularly paid and pretty men at that.' It was no wonder he sought this repayment; demands on his own purse by now seemed endless; Parry even said later that it was Byron's residence in Missolonghi which had procured food for the poor people of the town, and in one day at the end of March he received requests for 50,000 dollars.

Yet, as in any war, there were vexations and reasons for anxiety.

Some of the foreign volunteers were difficult. An Italian soldier was expelled for theft – his German officers wanted to flog him, but Byron would not permit this. Then a Prussian officer 'rioted' in his quarters and had to be put under arrest when his Greek landlord complained that he dared not return to his own house without a guard to protect him. Byron told the German that he ought to recollect that 'entering into the auxiliary Greek corps, now under my orders, at your own sole request and positive desire, you incurred the obligation of obeying the laws of the country, as well as those of the service'.

He was still troubled by his feeling for Loukas and by the boy's indifference, but he made sense of these at least, in the last verse he wrote:

> Thus much and more; and yet thou lov'st me not,
>   And never will! Love dwells not in our will.
> Nor can I blame thee, though it be my lot
>   To strongly, wrongly vainly love thee still.

He had always known – none better – the involuntary nature of love; never before expressed it with such bleak flatness.

V

Byron had little time to brood, however. The Turkish fleet was back apparently to blockade the gulf, though it soon sailed off again. It was rumoured that they had landed a force at a nearby village, and though the rumour was false, it was immediately followed by a report that was alarmingly true. A young Greek, who happened to be the nephew of a *klephte* chief called Karaiskakis, was wounded in a quarrel with some boatmen. One hundred and fifty of his adherents demanded revenge, seized two of the chief citizens of the town, and took over a fort at the mouth of the harbour. The rumour flew round the town that they had been betrayed to the Turks. Byron acted at once. He sent a couple of gun-boats against the fort, and himself rode out with his bodyguard to restore the confidence of the citizens. The show of force was sufficient. The dissidents surrendered the fort and their prisoners and departed for Anatolico. It was a reminder – superfluous as far as Byron was concerned – of how the innate quarrelsomeness of the Greeks threatened the success of the cause. He was at once worried that news of this dissension would jeopardize Greek credit, irritated, too, because Mavrocordatos had been so feeble in this minor crisis. Though he had been told the loan was settled, he could not be easy till the first instalment arrived. On 9 April he was writing to Barff asking if there was any further news: 'Is it really settled, and how?' But on the same day he wrote to Charles Barry, his banker in Genoa, speaking of the loan as certain, and saying that, as they had it, they might as well repay his: 'They were welcome to it in their difficulties – and also for Good and all – supposing they had not got out of them – but as it is – they can afford repayment – and I assure you – that besides *this* – they have had many "a strong and long pull" at my purse – which has been (and still is) disbursing pretty freely in their cause – besides – I shall have to re-expend the same monies – having some hundred men under orders – at my own expence for ye Greek Government and National service.'

These two letters were the last he wrote. They show his commitment to be as firm as on the day he arrived in Greece.

That morning he had had letters himself from England by way of Zante. They were the first to have arrived for some weeks. There was one from Augusta which told him that Ada had been ill but was now recovered. Byron was much struck by the coincidence of her illness and his own, possibly epileptic, fit. Hobhouse also wrote encouragingly: 'Nothing can be more serviceable to the Cause than all you have done – Everybody is more than pleased and content . . .' The final success of the great cause 'will indeed be doing something worth living for – and will make your name and character stand far above those of any contemporary'.

Buoyed up by these letters, he decided to ride out, which he had not been able to do for several days, even though it looked like rain. They galloped through the olive groves and then, three miles from town, were overtaken by a heavy storm. They rode back wet to the town walls where they were accustomed to dismount, leaving the horses to be stabled, and making the last part of the journey by boat, Pietro urged Byron, on account of the weather, to ride straight home – someone else could bring the horse back – rather than endure a still more thorough soaking in the rowing boat. But he clung to habit and remarked: 'I should be a pretty soldier, indeed, if I were to care for such a trifle.' Usually, as Byron was ferried back, he sang; they were Western songs, his boatman Costa Ghazis said later. (I find this touching: he puzzled and often irritated his English friends by singing Greek, Albanian and Suliote songs, which they found discordant and tuneless, but in Greece itself, perhaps through shyness, he sang Western melodies – one wonders what.) This day, however, he sat shivering in the stern, quite silent.

That evening he complained that he was feverish and suffering rheumatic pains. He lay on a sofa, and told Pietro: 'I suffer a great deal of pain; I do not care for death; but these agonies I cannot bear.' It was the sort of exaggerated remark he had been making all his life; it takes on a new significance now. However he wasn't so ill that he was ready to forgo his ride the next day, and seemed in good spirits to Pietro as they rode through the olive groves again. He scolded his groom for having put the wet saddle of the previous day on the horse, but he might have been thinking of the consequence for the beast as much as for himself. That evening Finlay and Dr Millingen, who was in charge of a clinic in Missolonghi and who would later be Court Physician to the Sultan in Constantinople, called on Byron, and Millingen remembered that Byron had recalled a warning to beware his thirty-seventh year given him as a boy by a famous fortune teller in Scotland. But he had no real thought of death and declined, with some reason, to consult the doctors. When he did so, both Bruno and Millingen prescribed bleeding, but Byron refused. Parry, though no medical man, was alarmed by his condition: he suggested that Byron should move to Zante, thinking he might benefit from the change of air. A wind blew up and made this impossible. Parry then suggested brandy. 'Brandy, my lord, is the only thing that will save you.'

Meanwhile, the doctors still continued to beg Byron to let them bleed him. After his last experience with leeches, his refusal is not to be wondered at. However, his resistance weakened as he grew more feverish and at times delirious. Almost all those present left differing accounts of his last days; not surprisingly, of course, for not all were in the room at the same time. Parry thought that 'there was something so serious and so firm, so resigned and composed, so different from anything I had ever seen in him, that my mind misgave me, and at times foreboded his speedy dissolution'. But, though Parry published his account, *The Last Days of Lord Byron*, the following year, when the events were fresh in his memory, he may well have credited himself with a prescience he did not feel. We have no immediate account of his last days in the form of letters or a journal; everything is recollection. Parry tells us also, for instance, that he spoke of retirement in England with his wife and daughter. He may have done so, or it may be that Parry thought, for one reason or another, that he should have spoken like this.

What we do know is that he resisted being bled as long as possible, but that the doctors were adamant. Millingen, according to his own account, clinched the argument by telling him that the disease might act on his nervous and cerebral system in such a way 'as entirely to deprive him of his reason'. This we may believe, for it is hardly the sort of story a man would invent against himself. Byron then called the doctors 'a d—d set of butchers' and submitted. On the 17th they called in two more doctors, and, at Bruno's insistence, continued to bleed him. The 18th was Easter Sunday. Though it was the custom for the citizens to fire off muskets in celebration, Mavrocordatos arranged that this should be done at some distance from the town, so that Byron might obtain some peace. That morning letters arrived. Gamba brought them in and Byron was still strong enough to read them himself. One from Luriottis confirmed that the loan was secure, and that Byron was named one of its administrators. This pleased him, but Pietro did not tell him that there was a letter from the Archbishop with the news that the Sultan had proclaimed Byron an enemy of the Sublime Porte. It is hard to see why he concealed this from him; it was surely agreeable confirmation of the impression he had made on events. But Pietro cannot be blamed; none of them was thinking clearly. Most of the time Pietro was in such floods of tears that he could not stay in the room. At one point, however, he heard Byron say to Tita and Fletcher 'che bella scena' (what a fine scene); it was the last flicker of the irony he had directed at the world.

That afternoon he thought of death and asked to be buried in Greece. He tried to ensure that his servants – Fletcher, Tita and Loukas – would be provided for. He asked Fletcher to tell Augusta and Lady Byron how he died: 'you are friends with her', he said to Fletcher,

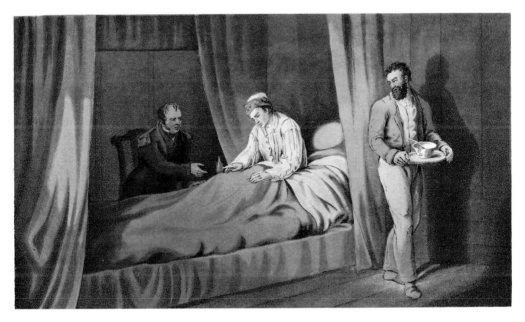

Byron's deathbed

[213]

speaking of his wife. He drifted in and out of delirium, in and out of sleep. At one point, Pietro says, he muttered: 'Io lascio qualche cosa di caro al mondo, per il resto sono contento di morire.' The meaning of these words has been much debated, since 'al mondo' can signify both 'in the world' and 'to the world'. Iris Origo thinks it might have been 'a last, veiled message to Teresa', which is possible if he realized it was to Pietro that he was speaking. But Pietro may have misheard him: he might have said 'qualche cose' (a few things); or possibly it represented a last flicker of consciousness that he had indeed achieved something for Greece, and thus left something dear to the world, an example. We cannot tell.

He died at six o'clock on the evening of 19 April, 'without', Fletcher said, 'showing any symptoms of pain, or moving hand or foot'. 'Oh, my God, I fear his Lordship has gone.'

As he died, there was a most tremendous thunderstorm. Mavrocordatos issued a proclamation calling for general mourning, and ordered a thirty-seven gun salute to be fired. The guns boomed over the grey lagoon at dawn, one for each year of his life.

It was not quite the end of his travels. Despite his request that he be buried in Greece, it was decided to embalm his body and return it to England. An autopsy was first performed. The doctors found that 'the bones of the cranium were very hard without any trace of the sutures like the bones of a person of 80 years'. Their treatment of their patient doesn't, however, encourage one to have much faith in this diagnosis.

A service was held in Missolonghi on the 22nd and this was followed, as the news spread, by memorial services in almost every town in Greece. A day of mourning was proclaimed throughout the land, and the Executive Council of Nauplia declared him 'a Father and Benefactor of the nation'.

The citizens of Missolonghi asked that some part of the body should be left with them; a jar containing his lungs was placed in the church of San Spiridione. Then the coffin, in a cask containing 180 gallons of spirits, was taken to Zante and there put on board the *Florida*, under the charge of Stanhope and in the company of Byron's servants and dogs. The voyage took five weeks. Hobhouse joined the ship in the Thames, reflecting that he had been the last man to shake Byron's hand when he left England in 1816. The body lay in state in London for several days, and was then carried to Nottinghamshire to be buried in the family vault at Hucknall Torkard Church by Newstead. Many of the forty-seven carriages which followed the funeral procession through London were empty, for there were still those who shrank from an association with Byron, even while they did not wish to offend his friends. It passed the house where Mary Shelley was staying: 'It went to my heart,' she wrote, 'when the hearse that contained his lifeless form, a form of beauty which in life I often delighted to behold, passed my window going up Highgate Hill on his last journey.'

The young Jane Welsh who had never met Byron, and who would become Mrs Thomas Carlyle, felt that 'if they had said the sun or the moon had gone out of the heavens, it could not have struck me with the idea of a more awful and dreary blank in the creation'.

That was how the young of Europe felt. His struggle for liberty had made him a hero. His poetry and his life were alike liberating. There had been no one like him before, and there has been none since.

Of course, the real Byron was more complicated than they imagined, just as the poet of *Don Juan* was a different and more perplexing being than the author of *Childe Harold*. The great Romantic was also a great anti-Romantic; the man who gave his life for Greek freedom also abused the Greeks, worried about money and cursed the rain. Even his part in the Greek war, when examined, turned out to be lacking in the conventional attributes of heroism. He was never in action; most of the time his role was something between a quarter-master and a diplomat. Yet it is precisely in his acceptance of this, it seems to me, that his greatness of character lies. A swaggering Trelawny had neither time nor taste for the business that occupied Byron in Greece, sneered at his efforts and took himself off to the mountains. That was how a Romantic should behave. But Byron stayed in his quarters by the dismal lagoon while the rain fell, and scribbled letters about loans and supplies and accommodations. When I was young, it disappointed me that Byron's role in Greece had been apparently so unheroic, that he seemed so often on the brink of abandoning hope, that it appeared even as if he did not know what he should do, having come to Greece, and was dismayed by the whole enterprise. Now it is precisely his willingness to accept the limitations of what was possible, and his acceptance of necessity that proves him a hero.

The Greeks have always recognized him as such, and, not resenting the strictures he cast on them, have accorded him honour and gratitude. In the Garden of the Heroes at Missolonghi, Byron's statue is the only full-length figure.

I have tried to show that his commitment to the Greek cause was not the result of a whimsical dissatisfaction with his way of life, but the consequence of deeply held and consistent beliefs. Almost no man is all of a piece, and Byron, selfish, self-indulgent, touchy, vain, and vulnerable, frequently showed himself petty and capricious. But, underneath his neuroticism and affectations, there was a layer of

ΒΡΕΤΤΑΝΙΗΣ ΟΜΟΤΙΜΟΝ ΑΘΡΕΙ ΣΤΑΣ ΣΕΙΝΕ ΒΥΡΩΝΑ
ΟΝ ΠΕΡΙ ΚΗΡΙ ΦΙΛΕΥΝ ΜΝΗΜΟΣΥΝΗΣ ΘΥΓΑΤΡΕΣ
ΤΩΝ Δ ΕΥΕΡΓΕΣΙΩΝ ΜΝΗΣΤΙΝ ΣΩΙΖΟΝΤΕΣ ΑΓΗΡΩ
ΕΛΛΗΝΕΣ ΣΤΗΣΑΝ ΛΑΙΝΟΝ ΕΣ ΕΡΑΝΟΥ
ΕΥΤΕ ΓΑΡ ΕΛΛΑΣ ΕΤΕΙΡΕΤ ΕΛΕΥΘΕΡΙΗΣ ΕΝ ΑΕΘΛΩΙ
ΚΛΥΘΕ ΘΑΛΠΩΡΗ ΧΑΡΜΑ ΤΕ ΜΑΡΝΑΜΕΝΟΙΣ

granite. He hated cruelty and oppression; he committed himself to the cause of liberty. Aware of the misery war caused, he was ready to engage in it when it seemed necessary, though full of doubt as to his own capacity for action. In small matters the most self-regarding of men, he was able to transcend self in a greater cause. He often wondered if he was achieving, or could ever achieve, anything substantial for the Greeks, yet stuck to the task he had imposed on himself. He did not live to see Greece free, but no man contributed more to its liberation.

His life is rich in irony. On the day before he died, a letter came from Hobhouse in which his old friend told him: 'Your monied matters, Kinnaird will tell you, are going on swimmingly; you will have – indeed you have – a very handsome fortune; and if you have health, I do not see what earthly advantage you can wish for that you have not got. Your present endeavour is certainly the most glorious ever undertaken by man. Campbell said to me yesterday that he envied what you are now doing (and you may believe him, for he is a very envious man) even more than all your laurels blooming as they are.'

Byron was unconscious when the letter arrived and never heard these words. Hobhouse later recalled: 'Of all the peculiarities of Byron, his laugh is that of which I have the most distinct recollections.' It must have rung out in the Shades at this conjunction of circumstance.

Statue of Byron in the Garden of Heroes, Missolonghi

PICTURE
ACKNOWLEDGMENTS

Illustrations have been supplied by the following sources:

BBC Hulton, 20, 40, 67, 73, 75, 77, 79, 84 (bottom), 100, 110, 113, 116 (bottom), 138, 155, 182; Bibliothèque Public et Universitaire, Geneva, 82, 83; British Library, 3, 23, 99, 153, 167, 173, 175, 177, 197; Camera Press, 96; J. Allan Cash, 10, 57, 58, 88, 90; Cruikshank, *Forty Illustrations to Lord Byron* (1825), 87; Mary Evans Picture Library, 22, 54, 64, 130, 135; Finden, *The Life and Works of Lord Byron* (1835), 34, 57, 61, 145; Heath, *Illustrations to the Works of Lord Byron* (1846), 105; John Cam Hobhouse, *Journey through Albania* (1813), 43, 50 (bottom); Thomas Hughes, *Travels in Greece and Albania* (1830), 42, 44, 46, 48; *Illustrations to the Life and Works of Lord Byron* (1846), 105; A. F. Kersting, 53; Rev. W. M. Kinsey, *Portugal Illustrated* (1829), 30; Edward Lear, *Views in the Ionian Islands*, 185; Edward Lear, *Views in Rome*, (108); Jorge Lewinski/Weidenfeld & Nicolson, 188/9, 202/3, 216; The Mansell Collection, 16, 22; National Portrait Gallery, 84 (top); Newstead Abbey/Nottingham Library, 180; Nottingham Library, 18, 89, 164/5; Iris Origo, *The Last Attachment* (1949), 150; William Parry, *The Last Days of Lord Byron* (1875), 191, 201, 213; E.G. Trelawny, *The Last Days of Shelley and Byron* (1858), 180 (top); Victoria & Albert Museum, 25, 116 (top), 137; Walker Art Gallery, 169; Weidenfeld & Nicolson, 187, 193, 196, 199; Hugh Williams, *Select Views in Greece* (1826), 36, 50 (top), 52.

ACKNOWLEDGMENTS

Everyone who writes on Byron is deeply indebted to Leslie A. Marchant for his incomparable edition of *Byron's Letters and Journals* (twelve volumes, 1973–82) and also for his detailed, rich and sympathetic biography. I also owe much to Doris Langley Moore's *The Late Lord Byron* (1961) and, for an understanding of Byron's time in Ravenna, his involvement in Italian politics and his relationship with Teresa Guiccioli to the Marchesa Iris Origo's *The Last Attachment* (1949). I have also benefited, and derived deep enjoyment, from Patrick Leigh Fermor's *Roumeli*.

All these books are published by John Murray, and no one working on Byron can fail to be aware of the devotion which the House of Murray, Byron's original publishers, has shown to his memory and reputation. The relationship between Byron and the House of Murray is without parallel in the history of publishing.

I have found C.E.M. Woodhouse's book, *A History of Modern Greece* (Penguin), invaluable as a means of understanding the Ottoman Empire and the background of the Greek Revolt, while *A History of the Italian People* by Giuliano Procacci (Pelican) has been similarly useful in relation to Byron's Italian years.

The library of books on Byron is well stocked. Peter Quennell's *Byron in Italy* still holds its own after nearly half a century, even though I do not share his apparent preference for Shelley rather than Byron. But of all those who have written at length or briefly on Byron, I owe most, apart from those mentioned in the first paragraph, to Henri Beyle (Stendhal). Frequently inaccurate, far from veracious, he yet supplies in two or three essays and in his Italian writings generally a truer understanding of what Byron meant to his contemporaries than anyone else.

I am grateful to my publishers, Sidgwick & Jackson, and especially to my editor, Carey Smith, for constant and judicious encouragement; and likewise to my agent, Giles Gordon. Finally, as ever, my chief debt is to my wife.

INDEX

INDEX